KING LEAR

The RSC Shakespeare

Edited by Jonathan Bate and Eric Rasmussen

Chief Associate Editor: Héloïse Sénéchal

Associate Editors: Trey Jansen, Eleanor Lowe, Lucy Munro,
Dee Anna Phares, Jan Sewell

King Lear

Textual editing: Eric Rasmussen and Trey Jansen

Introduction and Shakespeare's Career in the Theater: Jonathan Bate

Commentary: Penelope Freedman and Héloïse Sénéchal

Scene-by-Scene Analysis: Esme Miskimmin

In Performance: Karin Brown (RSC stagings), Jan Sewell (overview),
Jonathan Bate (captions)

The Director's Cut (interviews by Jonathan Bate and Kevin Wright):
Adrian Noble, Deborah Warner, Trevor Nunn

Editorial Advisory Board

Gregory Doran, Chief Associate Director,
Royal Shakespeare Company

Jim Davis, Professor of Theatre Studies, University of Warwick, UK

Charles Edelman, Senior Lecturer, Edith Cowan University,
Western Australia

Lukas Erne, Professor of Modern English Literature,
Université de Genève, Switzerland

Jacqui O'Hanlon, Director of Education, Royal Shakespeare Company

Akiko Kusunoki, Tokyo Woman's Christian University, Japan

Ron Rosenbaum, author and journalist, New York, USA

James Shapiro, Professor of English and Comparative Literature,
Columbia University, USA

Tiffany Stern, Professor and Tutor in English, University of Oxford, UK

The RSC Shakespeare

William Shakespeare

KING LEAR

Edited by Jonathan Bate and Eric Rasmussen

Introduction by Jonathan Bate

The Modern Library
New York

897

CONTENTS

INTRODUCTION

AN OLD MAN TOTTERING ABOUT THE STAGE?

"*King Lear*," wrote the early nineteenth-century Romantic poet Percy Bysshe Shelley in his *Defence of Poetry*, "may be judged to be the most perfect specimen of the dramatic art existing in the world." For all the Romantics, *Lear* was Shakespeare's most "sublime" and "universal" play. John Keats wrote a sonnet "On sitting down to read *King Lear* once again": having burned his way through the play, he would feel somehow purified and regenerated. For Keats' contemporary Charles Lamb, Shakespeare's anatomy of the human condition was so profound and tempestuous that the play seemed too vast for the stage. It is the centerpiece of his essay "On the tragedies of Shakspeare, considered with reference to their fitness for stage representation":

> So to see Lear acted,—to see an old man tottering about the stage with a walking-stick, turned out of doors by his daughters in a rainy night, has nothing in it but what is painful and disgusting. We want to take him into shelter and relieve him. That is all the feeling which the acting of Lear ever produced in me. But the Lear of Shakspeare cannot be acted. The contemptible machinery by which they mimic the storm which he goes out in, is not more inadequate to represent the horrors of the real elements, than any actor can be to represent Lear: they might more easily propose to personate the Satan of Milton upon a stage, or one of Michael Angelo's terrible figures. The greatness of Lear is not in corporal dimension, but in intellectual: the explosions of his passion are terrible as a volcano: they are storms turning up and disclosing to the bottom that sea his mind, with all its vast riches. It is his mind which is laid bare. This case of flesh and blood seems too insignificant to be thought on; even as he himself neglects it. On the stage we see

nothing but corporal infirmities and weakness, the impotence of rage; while we read it, we see not Lear, but we are Lear,—we are in his mind, we are sustained by a grandeur which baffles the malice of daughters and storms; in the aberrations of his reason, we discover a mighty irregular power of reasoning, immethodized from the ordinary purposes of life, but exerting its powers, as the wind blows where it listeth, at will upon the corruptions and abuses of mankind. What have looks, or tones, to do with that sublime identification of his age with that of the *Heavens themselves*, when in his reproaches to them for conniving at the injustice of his children, he reminds them that "they themselves are old." What gestures shall we appropriate to this? What has the voice or the eye to do with such things?

For Lamb, the technical necessities of the theater—the backstage machinery that creates the storm, the actor's repertoire of gestures, looks, and vocal variations—are exterior and superficial distractions from the play's inward and remorseless exploration of reason and madness, humankind and nature, the corruptions and abuses of power. Few theater lovers would agree with Lamb, but few would deny that the role of Lear presents perhaps the greatest of all challenges to the Shakespearean actor. There is a theater saying that by the time you're old enough to play it, you are too old to play it.

A generation before the Romantics, Dr. Samuel Johnson confessed that even reading the play was almost too much to bear: "I was many years ago so shocked by Cordelia's death, that I know not whether I ever endured to read again the last scenes of the play till I undertook to revise them as an editor." The shock for Johnson was both emotional and moral. The death of Cordelia—Shakespeare's boldest alteration of his sources, in all of which she survives—was an extraordinary breach of the principal that Johnson called "poetical justice," whereby "a play in which the wicked prosper, and the virtuous miscarry, may doubtless be good, because it is a just representation of the common events of human life: but since all reasonable beings naturally love justice, I cannot easily be persuaded, that the observation of justice makes a play worse; or, that if other excellencies are equal, the audience will not always rise better pleased from the final triumph of persecuted virtue." It had been in order to impose poetical justice on the play that during the 1680s Nahum Tate, author of the hymn "While Shepherds Watched Their Flocks by Night," had rewritten *King Lear* with a happy ending, in which Cordelia was married off to Edgar. Johnson had some sympathy with this alteration, which held the stage for a century and a half, whereas for Lamb it was yet one more indication that the theater was not to be trusted with Shakespeare's sublime vision of universal despair.

THE DIVISION OF THE KINGDOM

Written soon after King James united the thrones of England and Scotland, and performed in his royal presence at Whitehall, *King Lear* reveals the dire consequences of dividing a united kingdom. In principle, the aged Lear's decision to take voluntary retirement does not seem a bad thing: he is losing his grip on matters of state, his daughters and sons-in-law are "younger strengths" with more energy for government, and, most important, the division is intended to prevent a future civil war between rival claimants, which would have been a definite possibility in the absence of a son who would automatically inherit the whole kingdom. But can an anointed king abnegate his role at will? If he does, he certainly should not expect to retain the trappings of power. Goneril and Regan have a case for stripping him of his rowdy, extravagant retinue of one hundred knights.

Lear's mistake is to link the division of the kingdom to a public show of affection. The two older sisters, well versed in the "glib and oily art" of courtly flattery, tell him what he wants to hear, but Cordelia cannot. She is one of the play's truth tellers and simply lacks the capacity or the experience to dress her love in fine rhetoric. Lear knows that she loves him best, but we may assume that until this moment her love has always been expressed privately. As youngest and unmarried daughter, Cordelia has probably never spoken publicly before the court. Lear's intention for the opening scene is that it will be Cordelia's coming out: she is supposed to give public expression to her great love and in return she will be rewarded with the richest portion of the kingdom and the most prized husband. He does not bargain on her inability to play the role in which he has cast her. Kings and earls do not necessarily have to be blind to true virtue—witness the examples of Kent and France—but Lear, too long used to having his own way and hearing only the words of flatterers, has blinded himself. Only when he has been stripped of the fine clothes and fine words of the court, has heard truth in the mouths of a fool and a (supposed) Bedlam beggar, does he find out what it really means to be human.

Where *Macbeth* and *Othello* are focused tightly upon a single plotline, the action of *Lear* greatly extends the technique of parallel plotting with which Shakespeare had experimented in *Hamlet*, where Laertes and Fortinbras serve as foils to the hero. In *Lear*, the Gloucester family plot is a sustained presence. Gloucester is another father who is blind to the true nature of his children; that blindness leads, in Shakespeare's cruelest literalization of metaphor, to the plucking out of his eyes. Edmund corresponds to the wicked daughters; several of the play's many letters pass between them. It is wholly appropriate that he should end up promised to them both. Like the king's favorite daughter, Cordelia, Edgar (who is the king's godson) is unjustly exiled from home and excluded from parental care. It is fitting to the parallel structure of the twin plots that the play ends in the Folio version with him returning to take the reins of power, just as there is a certain, though very different, logic to Nahum Tate's infamous Restoration-period rewrite.

RIPENESS IS ALL?

Shakespeare never takes one side of a question. In the very opening lines of the play we discover that it is Edmund who has previously been unjustly exiled from home and excluded from parental care. Kent, the play's best judge of character, initially describes Edmund as "proper": he has the bearing of a gentleman, but his illegitimacy has deprived him of the benefits of society. His first soliloquy makes a good case for the unfairness of a social order that practices primogeniture and stigmatizes bastardy; his discovery near the moment of death that "Edmund was beloved" is curiously touching. He is not, then, an uncomplicated stage "Machiavel," an embodiment of pure, unmotivated evil.

Astrology and astronomy were synonymous in the Elizabethan age: the signs of the times were read in the signs of the skies. *King Lear* is a play about bad times. The state drifts rudderless, child turns against parent, the clouds of war gather, the king and all around him totter on the brink of the abyss. So it is that Gloucester blames it all on the stars: "These late eclipses in the sun and moon portend no good to us." Edmund, however, disputes this: "an admirable evasion of whoremaster man, to lay his goatish disposition on the charge of a star!" He argues that things often regarded as the product of the "natural order" are actually shaped by "custom"—for him, primogeniture and legitimacy would come into this category. The position articulated here is close to that of the sixteenth-century French essayist Michel de Montaigne in the closing section of his *Apology of Raymond Sebond:* any custom abhorred or outlawed by one nation is sure to be praised or practiced by another. But if you have nothing save custom, no divinely sanctioned hierarchy, then where does your value system come from? Montaigne's answer is blind faith in God, whereas Edmund, like an apologist before the letter for the political philosophy of Thomas Hobbes, commits himself to "nature" as a principle of survival and self-seeking.

Gloucester's philosophical orientation, meanwhile, turns toward the classical Stoic idea of finding the right timing for death. After his mock suicide, he says "henceforth I'll bear / Affliction till it do cry out itself / 'Enough, enough' and die." But he cannot sustain this position: when Lear and Cordelia lose the battle, he is found in "ill thoughts again," wanting to rot. Edgar responds with more Stoic advice: "Men must endure / Their going hence, even as their coming hither: / Ripeness is all." But this idea of ripe timing doesn't work out: by mistiming the revelation of his own identity to Gloucester, Edgar precipitates his father's death.

The play's pattern, then, is of Stoic comfort not working. At the beginning of the fourth act Edgar reflects on his own condition and cheers himself up with thoughts about the worst, but then his father comes on blinded and he is instantly confounded—things are worse than before. If the case of Edgar reveals the deficiency of Stoic comfort, that of Albany demonstrates the inadequacy of belief in divine justice. His credo is that the good shall taste "The wages of their virtue" and the bad drink from the poisoned "cup of their deservings." This scheme works for the bad, but not for the good. In the closing scene, Albany tries to orchestrate events, to make order out of chaos, but each of his resolutions is followed by new disaster: he greets the restored Edgar, then immediately hears the news of Gloucester's death, then the news of the two queens' deaths; then Kent comes on, dying; then in response to the news that Cordelia is to be hanged, Albany says "The gods defend her!," only for Lear to enter with her in his arms already hanged. The gods have not defended her. Then Albany tries to give power back to Lear—and he promptly dies. Then he tries to persuade Kent and Edgar to divide the kingdom, and Kent promptly goes off to die.

The final lines of the play—given to different speakers in the Quarto and Folio versions of the text—suggest that the lesson has been learned that Stoic comfort will not do, that it is better to speak what we feel than what we ought to say. The Folio's ascription of this speech to Edgar makes more dramatic sense than the Quarto's to Albany, since Edgar's stripping down in Act 3 is an exposure to feeling, occurring in conjunction with Lear's feeling with and for the poor, which makes him the character better prepared to voice this sentiment.

THIS GREAT STAGE OF FOOLS

The Stoic philosopher tries to be ruled by reason rather than passion. But for the great sixteenth-century humanist Desiderius Erasmus in his *Praise of Folly*, there is inhumanity in the notion that to be wise you must suppress the emotions. The most important thing is to "feel"—as Gloucester has to learn, to see the world not rationally but "feelingly." Erasmus' personification of Folly points out that friendship is among the highest human values, and it depends on emotion. The people who show friendship to Lear (Fool, Kent disguised as

Caius, Edgar disguised as Poor Tom and then as Peasant) and to Gloucester (Servants, Old Man) are not the wise or the rich.

We are ruled by our passions and our bodies; we go through life performing a series of different roles of which we are by no means in control. "All this life of mortal men, what is it else but a certain kind of stage play?" asks Erasmus' Folly. Lear echoes the sentiment: "When we are born, we cry that we are come / To this great stage of fools." In the great theater of the world, with the gods as audience, we are the fools on stage. Under the aspect of Folly, we see that a king is no different from any other man. The trappings of monarchy are but a costume: this is both Folly's and Lear's discovery.

Erasmus' Folly tells us that there are two kinds of madness—one is the thirst for gold, lust, and power. That is the madness of Regan, Cornwall, Edmund, and the rest. Their madness is what Lear rejects. The second madness is the desirable one, the state of folly in which "a certain pleasant raving, or error of the mind, delivereth the heart of that man whom it possesseth from all wonted carefulness, and rendreth it divers ways much recreated with new delectation" (*Praise of Folly*, in the sixteenth-century English translation of Sir Thomas Chaloner). This "error of the mind" is a special gift of the goddess Folly. Thus Lear is happy when his mind is free, when he is running around in his madness like a child on a country holiday: "Look, look, a mouse! Peace, peace, this piece of toasted cheese will do't." Lines such as that bring a smile to our faces, not least because the mouse isn't really there. Lear repeats his "look, look" at the end of his life. Cordelia is dead, but he deceives himself into the belief that she lives—that the feather moves, that her breath mists the looking-glass. His final words are spoken in the delusion that her lips are moving: "Look on her, look, her lips, / Look there, look there!" Her lips are not moving, just as there is no mouse, but it is better for Lear that he should not know this. Philosophers say that it is miserable to be deceived; Folly replies that it is most miserable "not to be deceived," for nothing could be further from the truth than the notion that man's happiness resides in things as they actually are. Lear's Fool says that he would fain "learn to lie." Lying is destructive in the mouths of Goneril, Regan, and Edmund at the beginning of the play, but Cordelia—who has a special bond with the Fool—has to learn to lie. At the beginning, she can only tell the truth (hence her banishment), but later she lies beautifully and generously when Lear says that she has cause to do him wrong, and she replies, "No cause, no cause."

The closing section of Erasmus' *Praise of Folly* undertakes a serious praise of Christian "madness." Christ says that the mystery of salvation is hidden from the wise and given to the simple. He delighted in simple people, fishermen and women. He chose to ride an ass when he could have mounted a lion. The language of his parables is steeped in simple, natural things—lilies, mustard seed, sparrows, a language analogous to that of Lear in his madness. The fundamental folly of Christianity is its demand that you throw away your possessions. Lear pretends to do this in Act 1, but actually he wants to keep "The name and all th'addition to a king." Only when he loses his knights, his clothes, and his sanity does he find happiness.

But he also becomes kind. Little things show us this: in Act 1, he's still always giving orders. Even in the storm he continues to make demands: "Come, unbutton here." But in the end he learns to say "please" and "thank you": "Pray you undo this button: thank you, sir." He has begun to learn true manners not at court, but through the love he shows for Poor Tom, the image of unaccommodated man, the image of himself: "Did'st thou give all to thy daughters? And art thou come to this?" True wisdom comes not in Gloucester's and Edgar's words of Stoic comfort or Albany's hapless faith in divine providence, but in moments of folly and love, as in this exchange:

EDGAR   Bless thy five wits!
KENT   O pity! Sir, where is the patience now
         That you so oft have boasted to retain?

Patience is the boast of the Stoic. It's a retainer like the hundred knights. To achieve true wisdom, you must let it go. You must let even the wits, the sanity, go. What you must keep are the *pity* and the *blessing*. Pity and blessing are at the very heart of *King Lear*. Pity means the performance of certain deeds, such as showing kindness to strangers. Blessing is a performative speech act, an utterance that effects an action by the very act of being spoken. Typically blessing is accompanied by a small but forceful *gesture*, a kind of action that is of vital importance on the bare boards of the Shakespearean theater.

The play ends on a note of apocalypse, millennial doom. A trumpet sounds three times to announce the final showdown. Then when Lear enters with his beloved daughter dead in his arms, loyal Kent asks, "Is this the promised end?" He is thinking of Doomsday, but the line is also a sly allusion on Shakespeare's part: in all previous versions of the Lear story, several of which would have been familiar to members of his audience, Cordelia survives and Lear is restored to the throne. The death of Cordelia is all the more painful because it is not the end "promised" by previous literary and theatrical tradition.

King Lear is a play full of questions. The big ones go unanswered. The biggest of all is Lear's "Why should a dog, a horse, a rat have life, / And thou no breath at all?" In this world, there is no rhyme or reason, no pattern of divine justice. Here again, Shakespeare departs strikingly from his source, the old anonymous play of *King Leir,* in which Christian providence prevails. Shakespeare reimagines his material in a bleak pagan world. In this, he not only looks back to the past, but also anticipates a future that is ours—a time when the old religious hierarchies and moral certainties have been stripped away.

But in a strange way an answer *is* to be found in Edgar's reply to Kent's line about the promised end. A question is answered with a question: "Or image of that horror?" It's not *really* the end of the world; it's an *image* of the end. Hamlet said that the player holds up a mirror to nature, but in *King Lear* we are again and again reminded that what you see in a mirror is an image, not the thing itself. Gloucester doesn't really jump off the cliff: it's all an elaborate game, designed by Edgar to teach him a lesson. In uncertain times, we need images, games, and experiments as ways of trying to make sense of our world. We need plays. That is why, four centuries on, we keep going back to Shakespeare and his dazzling mirror world in which everyone is a player.

Looked at in one way, the world of *King Lear,* with its images of doom, its mad king, scheming ugly sisters, its fool and its (pretend) mad Bedlam beggar, could not be further from *ordinary life*. But looked at another way, it is an image of ordinary things, but seen in *extremity*. It is a play that has more time for a language of ordinary things—garden waterpots, wrens, and toasted cheese—than for the "glib and oily art" of courtly speech.

So is the whole play, like the "Dover cliff" scene, an elaborate game designed by Shakespeare to teach us a lesson? Only if we think of it as a lesson in feeling, not in high-minded judgment. To be truly responsive to the play we must, as the final speech has it, "Speak what we feel, not what we ought to say." To be human is to *see feelingly*, not to fall back on easy moralizing, the "ought to say" that characterizes people like Albany. And seeing feelingly is to do with our sympathetic response to the images that confront us, both on the stage and in the great theater of the world. Lear becomes human when he stops caring about one kind of *image* (the glorious trappings of monarchy) and instead confronts another: the image of raw human being, of a fool and a Bedlam beggar, of poor naked wretches. Come the last trump, the play tells us, we will be judged by our fellow feeling for the dispossessed, not our status in society. In this, as in so much else, Shakespeare speaks not only for his own age, but for ours.

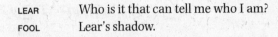

LEAR   Who is it that can tell me who I am?

FOOL   Lear's shadow.

1. Robert Armin took over as company clown after Will Kempe left the Chamberlain's Men in 1599. A playwright as well as the author of joke books, he practiced a more intellectual form of comedy than Kempe, full of witty verbal pyrotechnics: his style was given full rein in such parts as Lear's Fool, Feste in *Twelfth Night,* and the sour Lavatch in *All's Well That Ends Well*.

ABOUT THE TEXT

Shakespeare endures through history. He illuminates later times as well as his own. He helps us to understand the human condition. But he cannot do this without a good text of the plays. Without editions there would be no Shakespeare. That is why every twenty years or so throughout the last three centuries there has been a major new edition of his complete works. One aspect of editing is the process of keeping the texts up to date—modernizing the spelling, punctuation, and typography (though not, of course, the actual words), providing explanatory notes in the light of changing educational practices (a generation ago, most of Shakespeare's classical and biblical allusions could be assumed to be generally understood, but now they can't).

But because Shakespeare did not personally oversee the publication of his plays, editors also have to make decisions about the relative authority of the early printed editions. Half of the sum of his plays only appeared posthumously, in the elaborately produced First Folio text of 1623, the original "Complete Works" prepared for the press by Shakespeare's fellow actors, the people who knew the plays better than anyone else. The other half had appeared in print in his lifetime, in the more compact and cheaper form of "Quarto" editions, some of which reproduced good quality texts, others of which were to a greater or lesser degree garbled and error strewn. In the case of a few plays there are hundreds of differences between the Quarto and Folio editions, some of them far from trivial.

Who is left in charge at the end of *King Lear*? According to the conventions of Elizabethan and Jacobean tragedy, the senior remaining character speaks the final speech. That is the mark of his assumption of power. Thus Fortinbras rules Denmark at the end of *Hamlet*, Lodovico speaks for Venice at the end of *Othello*, Malcolm rules Scotland at the end of *Macbeth*, and Octavius rules the world at the end of *Antony and Cleopatra*.

So who rules Britain? The answer used to be something like this.

As the husband of the king's eldest daughter, Albany is the obvious candidate, but he seems reluctant to take on the role and, with astonishing stupidity given the chaos brought about by Lear's division of the kingdom at the beginning of the play, he proposes to divide the kingdom at the end of the play, suggesting that Kent and Edgar should share power between them. Kent, wise as ever, sees the foolishness of this and gracefully withdraws, presumably to commit suicide or will on the heart attack that he is already sensing. By implication, Edgar, who was the king's godson and is now Duke of Gloucester, is left in charge. So it is that in the Folio text, which is the most authoritative that we have, Edgar speaks the final speech:

> The weight of this sad time we must obey:
> Speak what we feel, not what we ought to say.
> The oldest hath borne most: we that are young
> Shall never see so much nor live so long.

If we were being very scrupulous, we would have added that there is some uncertainty over the matter, since in the Quarto text it is Albany who speaks the final speech, an ascription that has been followed by many editors since Alexander Pope.

Thanks to the textual scholarship of the late twentieth century, the new answer is something like this. Ah: that's a question over which Shakespeare himself seems to have had some uncertainty. In his original version of the play Albany speaks the final speech and thus rules the realm. But then Shakespeare changed his mind. In his revised version of the play Edgar speaks the final speech and thus rules the realm. We must posit two very different stagings. In the first one, Kent's words of refusal of his half-share in the kingdom would have been accompanied by some gesture of refusal, such as a turning away, on Edgar's part. In the second one, Edgar's speaking of the final speech would have been staged so as to betoken acceptance of Albany's offer. This alteration to the ending marks the climax of Shakespeare's subtle but thoroughgoing revision of the roles of Albany and Edgar in his two versions of *King Lear*. We do not know exactly when the revision took place, but it is a fair assumption that it was as a result of experience in the playhouse and with the collaboration of the company. Presumably there was dissatisfaction on the part of dramatist and/or performers with the way in which the two roles had turned out, so various adjustments were made. Shakespeare's plays were not polished for publication; they were designed as scripts to be worked upon in the theater. To be cut, added to, and altered.

Until recently, editors were remarkably reluctant to admit this. From the eighteenth century until the 1980s, editions attempted to recover an ideal unitary text, to get as close as they could to "what Shakespeare wrote." There was a curious resistance to the idea that Shakespeare wrote one thing, tested it in the theater, and then wrote another. It was assumed that there was a single *King Lear* and that the editorial task was to reconstruct it. Generations of editors adopted a "pick and mix" approach to the text, moving between Quarto and Folio readings, making choices on either aesthetic or bibliographic grounds, and creating a composite text that Shakespeare never actually wrote.

How, then, did editors deal with the following awkward fact? *King Lear* exists in two different texts, the Quarto and the Folio. The Quarto has nearly three hundred lines that are not in the Folio; the Folio has more than a hundred lines that are not in the Quarto; there are more than eight hundred verbal variants in the parts of the play that the two texts share. The standard editorial response to this difficulty was the claim that the Quarto was some kind of "Bad Quarto," that is to say a text based on memorial reconstruction by actors, not on Shakespeare's own script (his "foul papers") or the playhouse script (the "promptbook"). It was, however, a difficult position to maintain because the Quarto text of *Lear,* although corrupt in many places, does not have the usual characteristics of memorial reconstruction, the kind of features so apparent in the Bad Quarto of *Hamlet,* such as the actor remembering "The first verse of the godly ballad / Will tell you all," where Shakespeare wrote "the first row of the pious chanson will show you more" (*Hamlet,* Act 2 Scene 2). Getting the structure of a line just about right but the actual words nearly all wrong is typical of texts based on memory, but not typical of the textual anomalies in Quarto *Lear.*

In the 1970s the scholar Peter Blayney proved decisively by means of meticulous and highly technical bibliographic investigation that Quarto *King Lear* was not a bad text based on actors' memories but an authoritative one, almost certainly deriving from Shakespeare's own holograph (*The Texts of "King Lear" and their Origins: vol. 1 Nicholas Okes and the First Quarto*, published 1982). The poor quality of the text was the result of the personnel in the printing shop being unused to setting drama. Thus the fact that much of Shakespeare's verse was set as prose was due to the printer running out of the blocks that were needed to fill in the margins where text was set as verse—Okes' shop didn't have the proper equipment, so the compositors resorted to prose.

Both Quarto and Folio texts are authentically Shakespearean, yet they differ substantially. Logic suggests that Quarto was his first version of the play, Folio his second. The textual variants give us a unique opportunity to see the plays as working scripts.

In the received editorial tradition, there is a very puzzling moment in Act 3 Scene 1 where Kent reports to the Gentleman on the division between Albany and Cornwall (3.1.13–23). The syntax halfway through the speech is incomprehensible and the content is contradictory: are there merely French spies in the households of great ones or has a French army actually landed in Dover? The confusion comes from editors having conflated alternative scenarios: in Quarto the French army has landed, whereas in Folio there are only spies reporting to France (thus lines 30–42 in conflated texts are Quarto only, 22–29 are Folio only: in the RSC text, compare and contrast 3.1.13–23 and Quarto Passages, 46–59).

The alteration seems to be part of a wider process of diminishing the French connection. In the Quarto we have a scene in which Shakespeare feels compelled to explain away the absence of the King of France—why isn't he leading his own army?

KENT   Why the King of France is so suddenly gone back, know you no reason?

GENTLEMAN   Something he left imperfect in the state, which since his coming forth is thought of, which imports to the kingdom

so much fear and danger that his personal return was most
required and necessary. (Quarto Passages, 168–73)

It is, to say the least, a halting explanation, which is perhaps one reason why Shakespeare cut the whole of this scene, Act 4 Scene 3 in
the received editorial tradition, from the Folio text. Theater audiences tend to think most about the things that are mentioned: by
drawing attention to the king's absence, the dramatist in a curious
way establishes his presence. Better just to keep quiet about him,
which is what happens in Folio—since he's not mentioned, the audience forgets him.

Who, then, is to lead the French army? In Quarto, the Gentleman
informs Kent that the Marshall of France, Monsieur La Far, has been
left in charge. By omitting the scene in question, Folio obliterates
Monsieur La Far; it compensates by altering the staging of the next
scene (Act 4 scene 4 in the received editorial tradition, Act 4 Scene 3
in ours). In Quarto, the scene begins "*Enter Cordelia, Doctor and others,*" whereas in Folio it begins "*Enter with Drum and Colours Cordelia,
Gentleman and Soldiers.*" Where in Quarto Cordelia is a daughter
seeking medical attention for her father, in Folio she is a general leading an army. She has replaced Monsieur La Far. This alteration is part
of a broad shift of emphasis from family to state in the revision—
Folio makes less of the familial love trial and more of the fractured
internal politics of the divided kingdom. So it is that the later version
adds some crucial lines in the opening scene, giving a stronger political justification for the division of the kingdom:

We have this hour a constant will to publish
Our daughters' several dowers, that future strife
May be prevented now. . . . (1.1.41–43)

Furthermore, Folio cuts the so-called arraignment of Goneril, the
mock trial in the hovel scene that is the quid pro quo for the show
trial of love in the opening scene. This has the effect of retrospec-
tively rendering the opening more political and less personal.

Other Folio cuts include the passage at the end of the blinding
scene when loyal servants promise to apply flax and whites of egg to

Gloucester's bleeding eye sockets. When Peter Brook cut this from his famous 1962 RSC production, critics rebuked him for imposing on the play his own theater of cruelty. But now we know that Brook's cut was made in Shakespeare's own theater.

A further intensification of the play's moral bleakness is brought about by a series of cuts to Albany's role: his castigations of Goneril in Act 4 Scene 2 are severely trimmed back, considerably reducing his moral force. Quarto Albany is a well-developed character who closes the play as a mature and victorious duke assuming responsibility for the kingdom. In Folio he is weaker, he stands by as his wife walks all over both him and the moral order, he avoids responsibility. His ultimate vacation of power is such that the revision ends at the point where my discussion began: with Edgar having no choice but to take over as sustainer of the gored state.

If you look at printers' handbooks from the age of Shakespeare, you quickly discover that one of the first rules was that, whenever possible, compositors were recommended to set their type from existing printed books rather than manuscripts. This was the age before mechanical typesetting, where each individual letter had to be picked out by hand from the compositor's case and placed on a stick (upside down and back to front) before being laid on the press. It was an age of murky rushlight and of manuscripts written in a secretary hand that had dozens of different, hard-to-decipher forms. Printers' lives were a lot easier when they were reprinting existing books rather than struggling with handwritten copy. Easily the quickest way to have created the First Folio would have been simply to reprint those eighteen plays that had already appeared in Quarto and only work from manuscript on the other eighteen.

But that is not what happened. Whenever Quartos were used, playhouse "promptbooks" were also consulted and stage directions copied in from them. And in the case of several major plays where a reasonably well-printed Quarto was available, *Lear* notable among them, the Folio printers were instructed to work from an alternative, playhouse-derived manuscript. This meant that the whole process of producing the first complete Shakespeare took months, even years, longer than it might have done. But for the men overseeing the project, John Hemings and Henry Condell, friends and fellow actors who had been remembered in Shakespeare's will, the additional labor and cost were worth the effort for the sake of producing an edition that was close to the practice of the theater. They wanted all the plays in print so that people could, as they wrote in their prefatory address to the reader, "read him and again and again," but they also wanted "the great variety of readers" to work from texts that were close to the theater-life for which Shakespeare originally intended them. For this reason, the *RSC Shakespeare*, in both *Complete Works* and individual volumes, uses the Folio as base text wherever possible. Significant Quarto variants are, however, noted in the Textual Notes and Quarto-only passages are appended after the text of *King Lear*.

The following notes highlight various aspects of the editorial process and indicate conventions used in the text of this edition:

Lists of Parts are supplied in the First Folio for only six plays, not including *Lear,* so the list at the beginning of the play is provided by the editors, arranged by groups of character. Capitals indicate that part of the name which is used for speech headings in the script (thus "LEAR, King of Britain").

Locations are provided by the Folio for only two plays. Eighteenth-century editors, working in an age of elaborately realistic stage sets, were the first to provide detailed locations. Given that Shakespeare wrote for a bare stage and often an imprecise sense of place, we have relegated locations to the explanatory notes at the foot of the page, where they are given at the beginning of each scene where the imaginary location is different from the one before. We have emphasized broad geographical settings rather than specifics of the kind that suggest anachronistically realistic staging. We have therefore avoided such niceties as "another room in the palace."

Act and Scene Divisions were provided in the Folio in a much more thoroughgoing way than in the Quartos. Sometimes, however, they were erroneous or omitted; corrections and additions supplied by editorial tradition are indicated by square brackets. Five-act division is based on a classical model, and act breaks provided the opportunity to replace the candles in the indoor Blackfriars playhouse, which the King's Men used after 1608, but Shakespeare did not necessarily think in terms of a five-part structure of dramatic composition. The Folio convention is that a scene ends when the stage is empty. Nowadays, partly under the influence of film, we tend to consider a scene to be a dramatic unit that ends with either a change of imaginary location or a significant passage of time within the narrative. Shakespeare's fluidity of composition accords well with this convention, so in addition to act and scene numbers we provide a **running scene** count in the right margin at the beginning of each new scene, in the typeface used for editorial directions. Where there is a scene break caused by a momentary bare stage, but the location does not change and extra time does not pass, we use the convention **running scene continues.** There is inevitably a degree of editorial judgment in making such calls, but the system is very valuable in suggesting the pace of the plays.

Speakers' Names are often inconsistent in Folio. We have regularized speech headings, but retained an element of deliberate inconsistency in entry directions, in order to give the flavor of Folio.

Verse is indicated by lines that do not run to the right margin and by capitalization of each line. The Folio printers sometimes set verse as prose, and vice versa (either out of misunderstanding or for reasons of space). We have silently corrected in such cases, although in some instances there is ambiguity, in which case we have leaned toward the preservation of Folio layout. Folio sometimes uses contraction ("turnd" rather than "turned") to indicate whether or not the final "-ed" of a past participle is sounded, an area where there is variation for the sake of the five-beat iambic pentameter rhythm. We use the convention of a grave accent to indicate sounding (thus "turnèd" would be two syllables), but would urge actors not to overstress. In cases where one speaker ends with a verse half-line and the next begins with the other half of the pentameter, editors since the late eighteenth century have indented the second line. We have abandoned this convention, since the Folio does not use it, and nor did actors' cues in the Shakespearean theater. An exception is made when the second speaker actively interrupts or completes the first speaker's sentence.

Spelling is modernized, but older forms are occasionally maintained where necessary for rhythm or aural effect.

Punctuation in Shakespeare's time was as much rhetorical as grammatical. "Colon" was originally a term for a unit of thought in an argument. The semicolon was a new unit of punctuation (some of the Quartos lack them altogether). We have modernized punctuation throughout but have given more weight to Folio punctuation than many editors, since, though not Shakespearean, it reflects the usage of his period. In particular, we have used the colon far more than many editors: it is exceptionally useful as a way of indicating how many Shakespearean speeches unfold clause by clause in a developing argument that gives the illusion of enacting the process of thinking in the moment. We have also kept in mind the origin of punctuation in classical times as a way of assisting the actor and orator: the comma suggests the briefest of pauses for breath, the colon a middling one, and a full stop or period a longer pause. Semicolons, by contrast, belong to an era of punctuation that was only just coming in during Shakespeare's time and that is coming to an end now: we have accordingly only used them where they occur in our copy texts (and not always then). Dashes are sometimes used for parenthetical interjections where the Folio has brackets. They are also used for interruptions and changes in train of thought. Where a change of addressee occurs within a speech, we have used a dash preceded by a full stop (or occasionally another form of punctuation). Often the identity of the respective addressees is obvious from the context. When it is not, this has been indicated in a marginal stage direction.

Entrances and Exits are fairly thorough in Folio, which has accordingly been followed as faithfully as possible. Where characters are omitted or corrections are necessary, this is indicated by square brackets (e.g. "[and Attendants]"). Exit is sometimes silently normalized to *Exeunt* and *Manet* anglicized to "remains." We trust Folio positioning of entrances and exits to a greater degree than most editors.

Editorial Stage Directions such as stage business, asides, indications of addressee and of characters' position on the gallery stage are only used sparingly in Folio. Other editions mingle directions of this kind with original Folio and Quarto directions, sometimes marking them by means of square brackets. We have sought to distinguish what could be described as *directorial* interventions of this kind from Folio-style directions (either original or supplied) by placing them in the right margin in a different typeface. There is a degree of subjectivity about which directions are of which kind, but the procedure is intended as a reminder to the reader and the actor that Shakespearean stage directions are often dependent upon editorial inference alone and are not set in stone. We also depart from editorial tradition in sometimes admitting uncertainty and thus printing permissive stage directions, such as an **Aside?** (often a line may be equally effective as an aside or a direct address—it is for each production or reading to make its own decision) or a **may exit** or a piece of business placed between arrows to indicate that it may occur at various moments within a scene.

Line Numbers in the left margin are editorial, for reference and to key the explanatory and textual notes.

Explanatory Notes at the foot of each page explain allusions and gloss obsolete and difficult words, confusing phraseology, occasional major textual cruces, and so on. Particular attention is given to nonstandard usage, bawdy innuendo, and technical terms (e.g. legal and military language). Where more than one sense is given, commas indicate shades of related meaning, slashes alternative or double meanings.

Textual Notes at the end of the play indicate major departures from the Folio. They take the following form: the reading of our text is given in bold and its source given after an equals sign, with "Q" indicating one that derives from the principal Quarto, "F2" one that derives from the Second Folio of 1632, and "Ed" one that derives from the editorial tradition. The rejected Folio ("F") reading is then given. A selection of Quarto variants and plausible unadopted editorial readings are also included. Thus, for example, at Act 1 Scene 1 line 299, "**plighted** = F. Q = pleated." This indicates that we have retained the Folio reading "plighted" and that "pleated" is an interestingly different reading in the Quarto.

KEY FACTS

MAJOR PARTS: (*with percentage of lines/number of speeches/scenes on stage*) Lear (22%/188/10), Edgar (11%/98/10), Earl of Kent (11%/127/12), Earl of Gloucester (10%/118/12), Edmund (9%/79/9), Fool (7%/58/6), Goneril (6%/53/8), Regan (5%/73/8), Duke of Albany (5%/58/5), Cordelia (3%/31/4), Duke of Cornwall (3%/63/5), Oswald (2%/38/7).

LINGUISTIC MEDIUM: 75% verse, 25% prose.

DATE: 1605–6. Performed at court December 1606; draws on old *Leir* play (published 1605); seems to refer to eclipses of September and October 1605; borrows from books by Samuel Harsnett and John Florio that were published in 1603.

SOURCES: Based on *The True Chronicle Historie of King Leir and his Three Daughters,* an old play of unknown authorship that was in the London theatrical repertoire in the early 1590s, but makes many changes, including alteration of providential Christian to pagan language and the introduction of a tragic ending. The Lear story also appeared in other sources familiar to Shakespeare: *The Mirrour for Magistrates* (edition of 1574), Holinshed's *Chronicles* (1587), and book 2 canto 10 of Edmund Spenser's epic poem *The Faerie Queene* (1590). In all versions of the story before Shakespeare's, there is a "romance" ending whereby the old king is restored to his daughter Cordelia and to the throne. The Gloucester subplot is derived from the story of the Paphlagonian king in book 2 chapter 10 of *The Countess of Pembroke's Arcadia* by Sir Philip Sidney (1590): a blind old man is led to the top of a cliff from where he contemplates suicide because he has been deceived by his bastard son; the good son returns and encounters the bad one in a chivalric duel. The story was intended to exemplify both "true natural goodness" and "wretched ungratefulness"; a few chapters later (2.15), Sidney tells of a different credulous king who is tricked into mistrusting his virtuous son. The characters of "Poor Tom" and the Fool are entirely Shakespearean creations, though some of the language of demonic possession feigned by Edgar is borrowed from Samuel Harsnett's *Declaration of Egregious Popish Impostures* (1603), a work of propaganda about Catholic plots and faked exorcisms that Shakespeare probably read because of the Stratford origins of one of the exorcizing priests, Robert Debdale. The language of the play and some of its philosophical ideas reveal that Shakespeare had also been reading *The Essayes of Montaigne* in John Florio's English translation (1603).

TEXT: Published in Quarto in 1608 under the title *M. William Shakspeare: HIS True Chronicle Historie of the life and death of King LEAR and his three Daughters. With the vnfortunate life of Edgar, sonne and heire to the Earle of Gloster, and his sullen and assumed humor of TOM of Bedlam: As it was played before the Kings Maiestie at Whitehall vpon S. Stephans night in Christmas Hollidayes. By his Maiesties seruants playing vsually at the Gloabe on the Bancke-side.* This text was very poorly printed, partly because its printer (Nicholas Okes) was unaccustomed to setting plays and also because it seems to derive from Shakespeare's own working manuscript, which would have been difficult to read. Quarto includes about 300 lines that are not in the 1623 Folio text, which was entitled "The Tragedy of King Lear," and has clear signs of derivation from the theatrical playbook (though, to complicate matters, the Folio printing was also influenced by a reprint of the Quarto that appeared in 1619 as one of the ten plays published by Thomas Pavier in an attempt to produce a collected Shakespeare). The Folio in turn has about 100 lines that are not in the Quarto, and nearly 1,000 lines have variations of word or phrase. The two early texts thus represent two different stages in the life of the play, with extensive revision having been carried out, either systematically or incrementally. Revisions include diminution of the prominence given to the invading French army (perhaps for political reasons), clarification of Lear's motives for dividing his kingdom, and weakening of the role of Albany (including reassignment from him to Edgar of the play's closing speech, and thus by implication—since it was a convention of Shakespearean tragedy that the new man in power always has the last word—of the right to rule Britain). Among the more striking cuts are the mock trial of Goneril in the hovel and the moment of compassion when loyal servants apply a palliative to Gloucester's bleeding eyes. For centuries, editors have conflated the Quarto and Folio texts, creating a play that Shakespeare never wrote. We endorse the body of scholarship since the 1980s and the new editorial tradition in which Folio and Quarto are regarded as discrete entities. We have edited the more theatrical Folio text but have corrected its errors (which are plentiful, since much of it was set in type by "Compositor E," the apprentice who was by far the worst printer in Isaac Jaggard's shop). The influence of Quarto copy on the Folio is of great assistance in making these corrections. Textual notes are perforce more numerous than for any other work by Shakespeare; several hundred Quarto variants are listed. All the most significant Quarto-only passages are printed at the end of the play.

THE TRAGEDY
OF KING LEAR

LIST OF PARTS

LEAR, King of Britain

GONERIL, Lear's eldest daughter

REGAN, Lear's middle daughter

CORDELIA, Lear's youngest daughter

Duke of ALBANY, Goneril's husband

Duke of CORNWALL, Regan's husband

King of FRANCE, suitor and later husband to Cordelia

Duke of BURGUNDY, suitor to Cordelia

Earl of KENT, later disguised as Caius

Earl of GLOUCESTER

EDGAR, Gloucester's son, later disguised as Poor Tom

EDMUND, Gloucester's illegitimate son

OLD MAN, Gloucester's tenant

CURAN, Gloucester's retainer

Lear's FOOL

OSWALD, Goneril's steward

GENTLEMAN, a Knight serving Lear

GENTLEMAN, attendant on Cordelia

SERVANT of Cornwall

HERALD

CAPTAIN

Knights attendant upon Lear, other Attendants, Messengers, Soldiers, Servants, and Trumpeters

Act 1 Scene 1

Enter Kent, Gloucester and Edmund

KENT   I thought the king had more affected the Duke of Albany than Cornwall.

GLOUCESTER It did always seem so to us: but now in the division of the kingdom it appears not which of the dukes he values

5   most, for qualities are so weighed that curiosity in neither can make choice of either's moiety.

KENT   Is not this your son, my lord?

GLOUCESTER His breeding, sir, hath been at my charge. I have so often blushed to acknowledge him that now I am brazed to't.

10   KENT   I cannot conceive you.

GLOUCESTER Sir, this young fellow's mother could; whereupon she grew round-wombed and had indeed, sir, a son for her cradle ere she had a husband for her bed. Do you smell a fault?

15   KENT   I cannot wish the fault undone, the issue of it being so proper.

GLOUCESTER But I have a son, sir, by order of law, some year elder than this, who yet is no dearer in my account, though this knave came something saucily to the world before he was

20   sent for: yet was his mother fair, there was good sport at his making and the whoreson must be acknowledged.— Do you know this noble gentleman, Edmund?

EDMUND   No, my lord.

GLOUCESTER My lord of Kent: remember him hereafter as my

25   honourable friend.

EDMUND   My services to your lordship.

1.1 ***Location: the royal court, Britain*** **1 affected** favored   **5 qualities . . . moiety** their qualities are so evenly balanced that the most careful scrutiny cannot distinguish between either man's share   **8 breeding** upbringing (plays on the sense of "conception")   **charge** cost (plays on the sense of "accusation, blame")   **9 brazed** made brazen, hardened **10 conceive** understand (Gloucester then plays on sense of "become pregnant")   **13 ere** before   **14 fault** transgression/loss of scent during a hunt/vagina   **15 undone** plays on the sense of "not copulated with"   **issue** outcome/child   **16 proper** handsome/worthy/rightful **17 by . . . law** legitimate   **some year** about a year   **18 dearer** more beloved (plays on the sense of "more expensive")   **account** estimation (plays on the financial sense)   **21 whoreson** i.e. bastard (here used affectionately)

KENT   I must love you, and sue to know you better.

EDMUND   Sir, I shall study deserving.

GLOUCESTER   He hath been out nine years, and away he shall
30   again. The king is coming.

Sennet. Enter [one bearing a coronet, then] King Lear, Cornwall,
Albany, Goneril, Regan, Cordelia and Attendants

LEAR   Attend the lords of France and Burgundy,
Gloucester.

GLOUCESTER   I shall, my lord.   *Exit*

LEAR   Meantime we shall express our darker purpose.
35   Give me the map there.   *Kent or an Attendant gives Lear a map*
Know that we have divided
In three our kingdom, and 'tis our fast intent
To shake all cares and business from our age,
Conferring them on younger strengths while we
Unburdened crawl toward death. Our son of
Cornwall,
40   And you our no less loving son of Albany,
We have this hour a constant will to publish
Our daughters' several dowers, that future strife
May be prevented now. The princes, France and
Burgundy,
Great rivals in our youngest daughter's love,
45   Long in our court have made their amorous sojourn
And here are to be answered. Tell me, my
daughters —
Since now we will divest us both of rule,
Interest of territory, cares of state —

---

27 sue entreat, seek   **28 deserving** to be worthy of (your esteem)   **29 out** away (perhaps abroad or in the house of another nobleman; it was common for a nobleman's son to be educated in the house of another important family)   *Sennet* trumpet call signaling a procession   *bearing a coronet* carrying a small crown denoting inferior rank/wearing a wreath or garland about the head (must be of material that can be broken in half)   **31 Attend** wait on, look after   **34 darker** secret (with sinister connotations)   **36 fast intent** firm intention   **37 business** official duties/exertion/anxiety   **39 son** i.e. son-in-law (like Albany)   **41 constant will** unshakable intention   **publish** proclaim, make public   **42 several dowers** individual dowries   **that** so that   **45 sojourn** stay   **48 Interest** possession

Which of you shall we say doth love us most,
50   That we our largest bounty may extend
Where nature doth with merit challenge? Goneril,
Our eldest born, speak first.

GONERIL   Sir, I love you more than word can wield the matter,
·Dearer than eyesight, space and liberty,
55   Beyond what can be valued rich or rare,
No less than life, with grace, health, beauty, honour:
As much as child e'er loved or father found:
A love that makes breath poor and speech unable:
Beyond all manner of so much I love you.

60   CORDELIA   What shall Cordelia speak? Love and be silent.   *Aside*

LEAR   Of all these bounds, even from this line to this,   *Points*
With shadowy forests and with champaigns riched,   *to the map*
With plenteous rivers and wide-skirted meads,
We make thee lady. To thine and Albany's issues
65   Be this perpetual.— What says our second daughter?
Our dearest Regan, wife of Cornwall?

REGAN   I am made of that self-mettle as my sister,
And prize me at her worth. In my true heart,
I find she names my very deed of love:
70   Only she comes too short, that I profess
Myself an enemy to all other joys
Which the most precious square of sense professes,
And find I am alone felicitate
In your dear highness' love.

75   CORDELIA   Then poor Cordelia: *Aside*
And yet not so, since I am sure my love's
More ponderous than my tongue.

---

50 **bounty** generosity/gift   51 **nature . . . challenge** natural affection, combined with merit,
makes a claim   53 **wield** express   56 **grace** virtue   58 **makes breath poor** makes words
insufficient/renders one breathless (in the attempt to express it)   **unable** inadequate
59 **all . . . much** i.e. all possible expressions of the amount of love   61 **bounds** territories
62 **shadowy** shady   **champaigns riched** rich open countryside   63 **wide-skirted meads**
extensive meadows   67 **self-mettle** same temperament/same substance ("metal")
68 **prize . . . worth** value myself in equal terms   69 **deed** action, performance/bond,
legal document   70 **that** in that   72 **square of sense** guiding principle governing the
senses/(physical or mental) region of the senses   73 **alone felicitate** only happy
77 **ponderous** weighty

LEAR   To thee and thine hereditary ever
Remain this ample third of our fair kingdom,
80   No less in space, validity and pleasure
Than that conferred on Goneril.— Now, our joy,   *To Cordelia*
Although our last and least, to whose young love
The vines of France and milk of Burgundy
Strive to be interested, what can you say to draw
85   A third more opulent than your sisters'? Speak.

CORDELIA   Nothing, my lord.

LEAR   Nothing?

CORDELIA   Nothing.

LEAR   Nothing will come of nothing; speak again.

CORDELIA   Unhappy that I am, I cannot heave
90   My heart into my mouth: I love your majesty
According to my bond, no more nor less.

LEAR   How, how, Cordelia? Mend your speech a little,
Lest you may mar your fortunes.

CORDELIA   Good my lord,
95   You have begot me, bred me, loved me:
I return those duties back as are right fit,
Obey you, love you and most honour you.
Why have my sisters husbands if they say
100   They love you all? Happily when I shall wed,
That lord whose hand must take my plight shall
    carry
Half my love with him, half my care and duty:
Sure I shall never marry like my sisters.

LEAR   But goes thy heart with this?

105   CORDELIA   Ay, my good lord.

LEAR   So young and so untender?

---

78 hereditary by inheritance   **80 validity** value   **83 vines . . . Burgundy** Lear characterizes
France and Burgundy by their assets: vineyards and cattle pastures   **84 interested** admitted,
given a share   **draw** attract/receive, collect/pull forth (as one "draws lots")   **92 bond** duty
(with connotations both of a binding legal agreement and of restrictive shackles)   **93 Mend**
improve   **94 mar** spoil   **96 begot** conceived, fathered   **bred** raised, brought up   **101 plight**
pledge, promise   **106 untender** hard/cruel (plays on the sense of "not young")

CORDELIA   So young, my lord, and true.

LEAR   Let it be so: thy truth then be thy dower,
For by the sacred radiance of the sun,
110   The mysteries of Hecate and the night,
By all the operation of the orbs
From whom we do exist and cease to be,
Here I disclaim all my paternal care,
Propinquity and property of blood,
115   And as a stranger to my heart and me
Hold thee from this for ever. The barbarous Scythian,
Or he that makes his generation messes
To gorge his appetite, shall to my bosom
Be as well neighboured, pitied and relieved
120   As thou my sometime daughter.

KENT   Good my liege—

LEAR   Peace, Kent:
Come not between the dragon and his wrath.
I loved her most, and thought to set my rest
125   On her kind nursery.— Hence, and avoid my sight!—   *To*
So be my grave my peace, as here I give   *Cordelia*
Her father's heart from her. Call France. Who stirs?
Call Burgundy.— Cornwall and Albany,

                                            [*Exit Attendant*]

With my two daughters' dowers digest the third.
130   Let pride, which she calls plainness, marry her.
I do invest you jointly with my power,

---

110 **Hecate** Greek goddess of witchcraft and the moon   111 **operation** movement and astrological influence   **orbs** planets   114 **Propinquity . . . blood** close ties of kinship
116 **this** this time (or Lear gestures toward himself)   **Scythian** person from Scythia, an ancient region extending over much of eastern Europe and Asiatic Russia, notorious for its **barbarous** inhabitants   117 **generation** children/own people   **messes** small groups of people who eat together/portions of food, meals/disgusting concoctions/troubled, confused conditions   119 **neighboured** treated with hospitable kindness   120 **sometime** former
121 **liege** lord, one to whom feudal duty and service was owed   124 **set my rest** stake everything (card-playing term)/repose, be at ease   125 **kind** affectionate (in the manner of a family member)   **nursery** care   **avoid** leave   127 **Who stirs?** Get on with it!/Why don't you move?   129 **digest** absorb, incorporate   130 **plainness** frankness, plain speaking   **marry her** be her dowry/get her a husband

Pre-eminence, and all the large effects

That troop with majesty. Ourself by monthly course,

With reservation of an hundred knights — *still wants 100 knights*

135   By you to be sustained, shall our abode

Make with you by due turn: only we shall retain

The name and all th'addition to a king: the sway,

Revenue, execution of the rest,

Belovèd sons, be yours, which to confirm,

140   This coronet part between you.   *Gives them coronet to break in half*

KENT   Royal Lear,

Whom I have ever honoured as my king,

Loved as my father, as my master followed,

As my great patron thought on in my prayers—

145   LEAR   The bow is bent and drawn, make from the shaft.

KENT   Let it fall rather, though the fork invade

The region of my heart: be Kent unmannerly

When Lear is mad. What wouldst thou do, old man?

Think'st thou that duty shall have dread to speak

150   When power to flattery bows? To plainness honour's
            bound

When majesty falls to folly. Reserve thy state,   *speaking to Curney*

And in thy best consideration check

This hideous rashness. Answer my life my
            judgement:

Thy youngest daughter does not love thee least,

155   Nor are those empty-hearted whose low sounds

Reverb no hollowness.

LEAR   Kent, on thy life, no more.

---

132 **large effects** extensive trappings   133 **troop with** accompany   134 **With reservation of**
reserving the right to have (legal language)   135 **sustained** maintained, supported
137 **th'addition to** the title and honors of   **sway** authority, rule   145 **make . . . shaft** avoid
the arrow (of my anger)   146 **fork** barbed arrowhead   148 **thou** kings are almost always
addressed, respectfully, as "you"; Kent is **unmannerly** in his use of the familiar "thou"
151 **Reserve thy state** retain your sovereignty   152 **in . . . consideration** with wise and
careful reflection   153 **Answer . . . judgement** I'll stake my life on my opinion   156 **Reverb
no hollowness** do not reverberate hollowly (i.e. emptily/insincerely)

KENT   My life I never held but as pawn
To wage against thine enemies, ne'er fear to lose it,
160   Thy safety being motive.

LEAR   Out of my sight!

KENT   See better, Lear, and let me still remain
The true blank of thine eye.

LEAR   Now, by Apollo—

165   KENT   Now, by Apollo, king,
Thou swear'st thy gods in vain.

LEAR   O, vassal! Miscreant!   *Puts his hand on his sword or attacks Kent*

ALBANY *AND* CORDELIA   Dear sir, forbear.

KENT   Kill thy physician, and thy fee bestow
170   Upon the foul disease. Revoke thy gift,
Or whilst I can vent clamour from my throat,
I'll tell thee thou dost evil.

LEAR   Hear me, recreant, on thine allegiance hear me!
That thou hast sought to make us break our vows,
175   Which we durst never yet, and with strained pride
To come betwixt our sentences and our power,
Which nor our nature nor our place can bear,
Our potency made good, take thy reward:
Five days we do allot thee for provision
180   To shield thee from disasters of the world,
And on the sixth to turn thy hated back
Upon our kingdom: if on the next day following
Thy banished trunk be found in our dominions,
The moment is thy death. Away! By Jupiter,
185   This shall not be revoked.

---

158 held regarded, valued   **pawn** a pledge, surety   **159 wage** deposit as security   **163 blank** center of a target/line of sight (Kent asks to be the means to help Lear see better)   **164 Apollo** Greek and Roman sun god   **167 vassal** servant/wretch   **Miscreant** villain (literally, "infidel, unbeliever")   **168 forbear** stop, desist   **169 Kill . . . disease** i.e. Lear has got things the wrong way round   **170 foul disease** loathsome, festering disease/syphilis   **173 recreant** traitor **174 That** in that, since   **175 durst** dared   **strained** excessive/unnatural   **176 sentences** pronouncements, decisions   **177 nor . . . nor** neither . . . nor   **place** status, rank **178 potency** power   **made good** being carried into effect/shown to be valid/secured, defended   **180 disasters** misfortunes   **183 trunk** body   **184 Jupiter** supreme Roman god

KENT Fare thee well, king: sith thus thou wilt appear,
Freedom lives hence and banishment is here.—
The gods to their dear shelter take thee, maid, *To Cordelia*
That justly think'st, and hast most rightly said.—
190 And your large speeches may your deeds approve, *To Goneril*
That good effects may spring from words of love. *and Regan*
Thus Kent, O princes, bids you all adieu.
He'll shape his old course in a country new. *Exit*

Flourish. Enter Gloucester with France and Burgundy, Attendants

CORDELIA Here's France and Burgundy, my noble lord.
195 LEAR My lord of Burgundy,
We first address toward you, who with this king
Hath rivalled for our daughter: what in the least
Will you require in present dower with her,
Or cease your quest of love?
200 BURGUNDY Most royal majesty,
I crave no more than hath your highness offered,
Nor will you tender less.
LEAR Right noble Burgundy,
When she was dear to us, we did hold her so,
205 But now her price is fallen. Sir, there she stands:
If aught within that little seeming substance,
Or all of it, with our displeasure pieced,
And nothing more, may fitly like your grace,
She's there, and she is yours.
210 BURGUNDY I know no answer.
LEAR Will you, with those infirmities she owes,
Unfriended, new-adopted to our hate,

---

186 sith since **190 your . . . approve** may your actions prove the truth of your grand statements **193 shape . . . course** behave in his usual manner *Flourish* trumpet fanfare signaling the arrival of an important person **197 rivalled** competed **in the least** at the lowest **198 present dower** immediately available dowry **202 tender** offer **204 hold her so** consider her to be **dear** (i.e. beloved/worth a great deal) **206 aught** anything **little seeming substance** insignificant (or physically small) thing/one who totally refuses to play a part **207 pieced** augmented, increased **208 fitly like** justly please **211 infirmities** deficiencies **owes** owns

Dowered with our curse and strangered with our
 oath,
Take her or leave her?

215 BURGUNDY Pardon me, royal sir:
Election makes not up in such conditions.

LEAR Then leave her, sir, for by the power that made me,
I tell you all her wealth.— For you, great king, *To France*
I would not from your love make such a stray
220 To match you where I hate, therefore beseech you
T'avert your liking a more worthier way
Than on a wretch whom nature is ashamed
Almost t'acknowledge hers.

FRANCE This is most strange,
225 That she whom even but now was your object,
The argument of your praise, balm of your age,
The best, the dearest, should in this trice of time
Commit a thing so monstrous to dismantle
So many folds of favour. Sure her offence
230 Must be of such unnatural degree
That monsters it, or your fore-vouched affection
Fall into taint, which to believe of her
Must be a faith that reason without miracle
Should never plant in me.

235 CORDELIA I yet beseech your majesty —
If for I want that glib and oily art
To speak and purpose not, since what I will intend
I'll do't before I speak — that you make known
It is no vicious blot, murder, or foulness,
240 No unchaste action or dishonoured step

---

213 Dowered with given as a dowry **strangered** made a stranger, disowned
216 Election . . . up choice is impossible **218 tell you** inform you of/enumerate
219 from . . . stray stray so far from your love as **225 your object** your focus, the object of
your sight (the apple of your eye) **226 argument** theme **balm** soothing ointment
227 trice mere moment **228 monstrous** unnatural **dismantle** strip off (the **folds** of the
metaphorical cloth of favor) **231 monsters it** it becomes monstrous **fore-vouched**
previously sworn **232 Fall into taint** (must) come under suspicion **which . . . me** i.e. and to
believe in all reason that she had committed such a monstrous offense would require a miracle
236 for (your anger is) because **want** lack **237 purpose not** not intend to do what I say
239 foulness wickedness/moral impurity

That hath deprived me of your grace and favour,
But even for want of that for which I am richer:
A still-soliciting eye and such a tongue
That I am glad I have not, though not to have it
245   Hath lost me in your liking.

LEAR   Better thou hadst
Not been born than not t'have pleased me better.

FRANCE   Is it but this? A tardiness in nature,
Which often leaves the history unspoke
250   That it intends to do? My lord of Burgundy,
What say you to the lady? Love's not love
When it is mingled with regards that stands
Aloof from th'entire point. Will you have her?
She is herself a dowry.

255   BURGUNDY   Royal king,   *To Lear*
Give but that portion which yourself proposed,
And here I take Cordelia by the hand,
Duchess of Burgundy.

LEAR   Nothing: I have sworn: I am firm.

260   BURGUNDY   I am sorry, then, you have so lost a father   *To Cordelia*
That you must lose a husband.

CORDELIA   Peace be with Burgundy.
Since that respect and fortunes are his love,
I shall not be his wife.

265   FRANCE   Fairest Cordelia, that art most rich being poor,
Most choice forsaken, and most loved despised,
Thee and thy virtues here I seize upon:
Be it lawful, I take up what's cast away.   *Takes her hand*
Gods, gods! 'Tis strange that from their cold'st neglect
270   My love should kindle to inflamed respect.—

---

242 for which i.e. for lack of which   **243 still-soliciting** constantly entreating, self-seeking
248 tardiness in nature natural slowness   **249 history** account (of an action)
252 regards . . . point irrelevant concerns   **263 respect and fortunes** status and wealth
266 Most choice forsaken most desirable when rejected   **267 seize upon** take possession of
(legal term)   **268 be it lawful** provided it is lawful   **269 their** may refer to either the gods or to
Lear and Burgundy   **270 inflamed** glowing, ardent

Thy dowerless daughter, king, thrown to my chance,
Is queen of us, of ours and our fair France:
Not all the dukes of wat'rish Burgundy
Can buy this unprized precious maid of me.—
275   Bid them farewell, Cordelia, though unkind.
Thou losest here, a better where to find.

LEAR   Thou hast her, France: let her be thine, for we
Have no such daughter, nor shall ever see
That face of hers again. Therefore be gone
280   Without our grace, our love, our benison.
Come, noble Burgundy.

Flourish. Exeunt. [France and the sisters remain]

FRANCE   Bid farewell to your sisters.

CORDELIA   The jewels of our father, with washèd eyes
Cordelia leaves you. I know you what you are,
285   And like a sister am most loath to call
Your faults as they are named. Love well our father:
To your professèd bosoms I commit him,
But yet, alas, stood I within his grace,
I would prefer him to a better place.
290   So farewell to you both.

REGAN   Prescribe not us our duty.

GONERIL   Let your study
Be to content your lord who hath received you
At fortune's alms. You have obedience scanted,
295   And well are worth the want that you have wanted.

---

271 **thrown . . . chance** cast to my luck (gambling metaphor)   273 **wat'rish** well-watered
(with rivers)/wet, feeble   274 **unprized** unvalued (may play on a sense of "priceless")
275 **though unkind** though they are cruel (or "lacking in natural familial affection")
276 **where** somewhere, place   280 **grace** favor (with connotations of "divinely sanctioned
mercy")   **benison** blessing   283 **washèd** i.e. wet with tears   286 **as . . . named** by their
true names   287 **your professèd bosoms** i.e. the love you claim to have for him   **commit**
entrust; perhaps with connotations of "confine (to prison)"   289 **prefer** advance, promote
292 **study** concern, endeavor   294 **At fortune's alms** as a charitable gift from fortune
scanted stinted, withheld/slighted, neglected   295 **are . . . wanted** deserve to be deprived of
the love you have failed to show (to others)

CORDELIA   Time shall unfold what plighted cunning hides:
Who covers faults, at last with shame derides.
Well may you prosper.

FRANCE   Come, my fair Cordelia.   *Exit France and Cordelia*

300   GONERIL   Sister, it is not little I have to say of what most nearly
appertains to us both. I think our father will hence tonight.

REGAN   That's most certain, and with you: next month with
us.

GONERIL   You see how full of changes his age is: the
305   observation we have made of it hath not been little. He
always loved our sister most, and with what poor judgement
he hath now cast her off appears too grossly.

REGAN   'Tis the infirmity of his age; yet he hath ever but
slenderly known himself.

310   GONERIL   The best and soundest of his time hath been but
rash. Then must we look from his age to receive not alone the
imperfections of long-engrafted condition, but therewithal
the unruly waywardness that infirm and choleric years
bring with them.

315   REGAN   Such unconstant starts are we like to have from him
as this of Kent's banishment.

GONERIL   There is further compliment of leave-taking
between France and him. Pray you let us sit together: if our
father carry authority with such disposition as he bears, this
320   last surrender of his will but offend us.

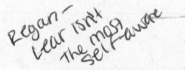

Regan -
Lear isn't
The most
self aware

296 **plighted cunning** secret cunning/deceitful promises   297 **Who . . . derides** those who
hide their faults will in the end be shamed and mocked   300 **nearly** closely   307 **grossly**
obviously   308 **ever** always   309 **slenderly** slightly   310 **The . . . rash** even at his best and
healthiest he was impulsive   311 **look** expect   312 **long-engrafted condition** long-implanted
tendencies   **therewithal** in addition to that   313 **choleric** irascible, hot-tempered, impulsive/
bilious; one of the four "humors" or temperaments thought to be related to an excess of bile in
the constitution   315 **unconstant starts** unpredictable fits   317 **compliment** etiquette,
ceremony   318 **sit together** i.e. get together, confer   319 **carry** maintain, manage
disposition frame of mind   320 **last surrender** recent yielding (of authority)   **offend** harm

REGAN	We shall further think of it.
GONERIL	We must do something, and i'th'heat.

Exeunt

Act 1 Scene 2

running scene 2

Enter Bastard [Edmund]   *With a letter*

EDMUND   Thou, nature, art my goddess: to thy law
My services are bound. Wherefore should I
Stand in the plague of custom and permit
The curiosity of nations to deprive me
5   For that I am some twelve or fourteen moonshines
Lag of a brother? Why bastard? Wherefore base?
When my dimensions are as well compact,
My mind as generous, and my shape as true,
As honest madam's issue? Why brand they us
10   With base? With baseness? Bastardy? Base, base?
Who in the lusty stealth of nature take
More composition and fierce quality
Than doth within a dull, stale, tirèd bed,
Go to th'creating a whole tribe of fops
15   Got 'tween a sleep and wake? Well then,
Legitimate Edgar, I must have your land:
Our father's love is to the bastard Edmund
As to th'legitimate — fine word, 'legitimate' —
Well, my legitimate, if this letter speed
20   And my invention thrive, Edmund the base
Shall to th'legitimate. I grow, I prosper:
Now, gods, stand up for bastards!

---

322 **i'th'heat** immediately   **1.2** *Location: the Earl of Gloucester's residence*
2 **Wherefore** why   3 **Stand in** endure/stand still under   4 **curiosity** scruples, fussiness
nations i.e. society   5 **moonshines** months   6 **Lag of** behind (i.e. younger than)   **base**
illegitimate (also low/unworthy/dishonorable)   7 **dimensions** physical proportions
compact composed   8 **generous** noble   **true** well-proportioned/authentic, true to his
father's likeness   9 **honest madam's issue** a legitimate child   11 **Who** i.e. we bastards who
take require/receive   12 **More . . . quality** a more complex creation and more vigorous
disposition   14 **fops** weak fools   15 **Got** conceived   18 **As** the same as   19 **speed** succeed
20 **invention** scheme   21 **to th'legitimate** advance to (or "take over") the place of the
legitimate son; editors sometimes emend this to "top the legitimate"

Enter Gloucester

GLOUCESTER Kent banished thus? And France in choler parted?
And the king gone tonight? Prescribed his power,
25   Confined to exhibition? All this done
Upon the gad? Edmund, how now? What news?

EDMUND So please your lordship, none.   *Hides the letter*

GLOUCESTER Why so earnestly seek you to put up that letter?

EDMUND I know no news, my lord.

30   GLOUCESTER What paper were you reading?

EDMUND Nothing, my lord.

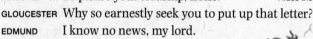

GLOUCESTER No? What needed, then, that terrible dispatch of it
into your pocket? The quality of nothing hath not such need
to hide itself. Let's see: come, if it be nothing I shall not need
35   spectacles.

EDMUND I beseech you, sir, pardon me: it is a letter from my
brother that I have not all o'er-read; and for so much as I
have perused, I find it not fit for your o'erlooking.

GLOUCESTER Give me the letter, sir.

40   EDMUND I shall offend either to detain or give it: the contents,
as in part I understand them, are to blame.

GLOUCESTER Let's see, let's see.   *Edmund gives the letter*

EDMUND I hope for my brother's justification he wrote this
but as an essay or taste of my virtue.

45   GLOUCESTER *Reads* 'This policy and reverence of age makes the
world bitter to the best of our times, keeps our fortunes from
us till our oldness cannot relish them. I begin to find an idle
and fond bondage in the oppression of aged tyranny, who
sways, not as it hath power, but as it is suffered. Come to me,
50   that of this I may speak more. If our father would sleep till I
waked him, you should enjoy half his revenue for ever and
live the beloved of your brother, Edgar.'

23 **choler** anger   **parted** departed   24 **Prescribed** restricted, limited   25 **exhibition** an
allowance, maintenance   26 **gad** spur of the moment   28 **up** away   32 **terrible dispatch**
fearful and hasty stowing away   37 **for** as for   38 **o'erlooking** reading   44 **essay or taste**
test   45 **policy . . . age** policy of revering the old (**policy** also suggests the "strategic cunning"
of the elderly)   46 **the . . . times** i.e. our youth, our prime   **fortunes** inheritance   47 **relish**
savor, enjoy   **idle** useless   48 **fond** foolish   49 **sways** rules   **as . . . suffered** only insofar as
it is allowed to do so

Hum! Conspiracy! 'Sleep till I wake him, you should enjoy
half his revenue.' My son Edgar? Had he a hand to write this?
55   A heart and brain to breed it in? When came you to this?
Who brought it?

EDMUND   It was not brought me, my lord; there's the cunning
of it: I found it thrown in at the casement of my closet.

GLOUCESTER   You know the character to be your brother's?

60   EDMUND   If the matter were good, my lord, I durst swear it
were his, but in respect of that I would fain think it were not.

GLOUCESTER   It is his.

EDMUND   It is his hand, my lord, but I hope his heart is not in
the contents.

65   GLOUCESTER   Has he never before sounded you in this business?

EDMUND   Never, my lord: but I have heard him oft maintain it
to be fit that, sons at perfect age and fathers declined, the
father should be as ward to the son, and the son manage his
revenue.

70   GLOUCESTER   O, villain, villain! His very opinion in the letter!
Abhorred villain! Unnatural, detested, brutish villain! Worse
than brutish! Go, sirrah, seek him: I'll apprehend him.
Abominable villain, where is he?

EDMUND   I do not well know, my lord. If it shall please you to
75   suspend your indignation against my brother till you can
derive from him better testimony of his intent, you should
run a certain course, where, if you violently proceed against
him, mistaking his purpose, it would make a great gap in
your own honour and shake in pieces the heart of his
80   obedience. I dare pawn down my life for him, that he hath
writ this to feel my affection to your honour, and to no other
pretence of danger.

---

58 casement window   **closet** private room   **59 character** handwriting   **60 matter** subject
matter   **61 in . . . that** given the contents   **fain** willingly   **67 at perfect age** being mature
declined old/ill   **72 sirrah** sir (used to social inferiors and children)   **apprehend** arrest
73 Abominable often, popularly, "inhuman, unnatural" (from the incorrect belief that the
word was derived from the Latin *ab homine*, i.e. "away from man")   **77 run . . . course** proceed
securely   **where** whereas   **proceed** perhaps with legal connotations (in keeping with
apprehend and **testimony**)   **80 pawn down** pledge   **81 feel** test, feel out   **82 pretence**
intention, purpose

GLOUCESTER Think you so?

EDMUND   If your honour judge it meet, I will place you where
85   you shall hear us confer of this, and by an auricular
assurance have your satisfaction, and that without any
further delay than this very evening.

GLOUCESTER He cannot be such a monster. Edmund, seek him
out: wind me into him, I pray you: frame the business after
90   your own wisdom. I would unstate myself to be in a due
resolution.

EDMUND   I will seek him, sir, presently: convey the business as
I shall find means and acquaint you withal.

GLOUCESTER These late eclipses in the sun and moon portend no
95   good to us: though the wisdom of nature can reason it thus
and thus, yet nature finds itself scourged by the sequent
effects: love cools, friendship falls off, brothers divide: in
cities, mutinies; in countries, discord; in palaces, treason;
and the bond cracked 'twixt son and father. This villain of
100   mine comes under the prediction; there's son against father.
The king falls from bias of nature; there's father against
child. We have seen the best of our time: machinations,
hollowness, treachery, and all ruinous disorders follow us
disquietly to our graves. Find out this villain, Edmund: it
105   shall lose thee nothing. Do it carefully.— And the noble and
true-hearted Kent banished! His offence, honesty! 'Tis
strange.   Exit

EDMUND   This is the excellent foppery of the world, that when
we are sick in fortune — often the surfeits of our own
110   behaviour — we make guilty of our disasters the sun, the

---

84 meet suitable   85 auricular assurance i.e. by hearing for yourself   86 have your
satisfaction resolve yourself of any doubt   89 wind . . . him insinuate yourself into his
confidence for me   frame devise, arrange   90 unstate . . . resolution give up my rank and
wealth to be resolved on this matter   92 presently immediately   convey manage, undertake
93 withal therewith   94 late recent   95 wisdom of nature human reason/natural science
96 scourged punished   sequent effects subsequent events   101 bias of nature natural
inclination (a bowling image: the bias refers to the curving path taken by a weighted ball)
104 it . . . nothing i.e. it will advantage you   108 excellent foppery supreme foolishness
109 surfeits excesses   110 disasters misfortunes

moon and stars, as if we were villains on necessity, fools by
heavenly compulsion, knaves, thieves and treachers by
spherical predominance, drunkards, liars and adulterers
by an enforced obedience of planetary influence, and all that
115   we are evil in, by a divine thrusting on: an admirable evasion
of whoremaster man, to lay his goatish disposition on the
charge of a star! My father compounded with my mother
under the dragon's tail and my nativity was under Ursa
Major, so that it follows I am rough and lecherous. I should
120   have been that I am had the maidenliest star in the
firmament twinkled on my bastardizing.

Enter Edgar

Pat he comes like the catastrophe of the old comedy: my cue
is villainous melancholy, with a sigh like Tom o'Bedlam.—
O, these eclipses do portend these divisions! Fa, sol, la, mi.

125   EDGAR   How now, brother Edmund, what serious
contemplation are you in?

EDMUND   I am thinking, brother, of a prediction I read this
other day, what should follow these eclipses.

EDGAR   Do you busy yourself with that?

130   EDMUND   I promise you, the effects he writes of succeed
unhappily. When saw you my father last?

EDGAR   The night gone by.

EDMUND   Spake you with him?

EDGAR   Ay, two hours together.

---

111 on i.e. by   112 treachers traitors   113 spherical predominance the dominant influence
of a particular planet at one's birth   115 divine celestial, supernatural   evasion shuffling
excuse   116 whoremaster i.e. lecherous, whore-using   goatish lustful   117 charge
responsibility   compounded had sex   118 the dragon's tail the constellation Draco
Ursa Major (constellation of) the Great Bear (or Plough)   119 rough cruel, violent
120 maidenliest most virginal   121 firmament sky, heavens   bastardizing conception out of
wedlock   122 Pat on cue   catastrophe conclusion   'comedy play   my cue could also
mean "designated role"   123 Tom o'Bedlam i.e. a madman (from the Saint Mary of
Bethlehem hospital in London, an institution for the insane)   124 divisions conflicts, discords
(plays on the sense of "musical variations")   Fa . . . mi Edmund hums a musical scale to
himself   127 this the   130 succeed follow   131 unhappily unluckily, by misfortune

135 EDMUND Parted you in good terms? Found you no displeasure
in him by word nor countenance?

EDGAR None at all.

EDMUND Bethink yourself wherein you may have offended
him, and at my entreaty forbear his presence until some little
140 time hath qualified the heat of his displeasure, which at this
instant so rageth in him that with the mischief of your
person it would scarcely allay.

EDGAR Some villain hath done me wrong.

EDMUND That's my fear. I pray you have a continent
145 forbearance till the speed of his rage goes slower: and, as I
say, retire with me to my lodging, from whence I will fitly
bring you to hear my lord speak. Pray ye go.   *Gives a key*
There's my key: if you do stir abroad, go armed.

EDGAR Armed, brother?

150 EDMUND Brother, I advise you to the best: I am no honest
man if there be any good meaning toward you: I have told
you what I have seen and heard, but faintly, nothing like the
image and horror of it. Pray you away.

EDGAR Shall I hear from you anon?   *Exit*

155 EDMUND I do serve you in this business.—
A credulous father and a brother noble,
Whose nature is so far from doing harms
That he suspects none: on whose foolish honesty
My practices ride easy. I see the business.
160 Let me, if not by birth, have lands by wit:
All with me's meet that I can fashion fit.   *Exit*

---

136 countenance bearing, demeanor/facial expression   **139 forbear** avoid   **140 qualified** cooled, lessened   **141 mischief . . . person** harm caused by your presence   **142 allay** abate, calm   **144 have . . . forbearance** i.e. restrain yourself and stay away from him   **146 fitly** at an appropriate time   **148 abroad** out of the house   **151 meaning** intention   **153 image and horror** horrific true picture   **154 anon** soon   **155 serve** help/trick, deceive   **159 practices** plots   **160 wit** intelligence, ingenuity   **161 meet** fitting   **fashion fit** shape to my purposes

Act 1 Scene 3

Enter Goneril and Steward [Oswald]

GONERIL   Did my father strike my gentleman for chiding of his
fool?

OSWALD   Ay, madam.

GONERIL   By day and night he wrongs me: every hour

5   He flashes into one gross crime or other
That sets us all at odds. I'll not endure it.
His knights grow riotous, and himself upbraids us
On every trifle. When he returns from hunting
I will not speak with him: say I am sick.

10   If you come slack of former services
You shall do well: the fault of it I'll answer.

OSWALD   He's coming, madam: I hear him.   *Horns within*

GONERIL   Put on what weary negligence you please,
You and your fellows: I'd have it come to question:

15   If he distaste it, let him to my sister,
Whose mind and mine, I know, in that are one.
Remember what I have said.

OSWALD   Well, madam.

GONERIL   And let his knights have colder looks among you:

20   what grows of it, no matter: advise your fellows so. I'll write
straight to my sister, to hold my course. Prepare for dinner.

Exeunt

Act 1 Scene 4

Enter Kent   *Disguised*

KENT   If but as will I other accents borrow,
That can my speech defuse, my good intent

1.3 *Location: Goneril and the Duke of Albany's residence*   **1 gentleman** man of gentle
(i.e. noble) birth attached to a royal household   **chiding** rebuking   **5 flashes** breaks out
10 come slack fall short   **11 answer** be answerable for   **14 fellows** fellow servants
question conflict, a dispute   **15 distaste** dislike   **21 straight** straight away   **to** i.e. and tell
her to   **1.4**   **1 as will I** perhaps "as I intend" (but most editors opt for the Quarto "well"—
i.e. "as well as being disguised")   **2 defuse** confuse, disorder

May carry through itself to that full issue
For which I razed my likeness. Now, banished Kent,
5   If thou canst serve where thou dost stand condemned,
So may it come thy master whom thou lov'st,
Shall find thee full of labours.

Horns within. Enter Lear and Attendants [his Knights]

LEAR   Let me not stay a jot for dinner: go get it ready.

[Exit a Knight]

To Kent

How now, what art thou?

10   KENT   A man, sir.

LEAR   What dost thou profess? What wouldst thou with us?

KENT   I do profess to be no less than I seem; to serve him truly that will put me in trust, to love him that is honest, to
15   converse with him that is wise and says little, to fear judgement, to fight when I cannot choose and to eat no fish.

LEAR   What art thou?

KENT   A very honest-hearted fellow, and as poor as the king.

20   LEAR   If thou be'st as poor for a subject as he's for a king, thou art poor enough. What wouldst thou?

KENT   Service.

LEAR   Who wouldst thou serve?

KENT   You.

25   LEAR   Dost thou know me, fellow?

KENT   No, sir, but you have that in your countenance which I would fain call master.

LEAR   What's that?

KENT   Authority.

30   LEAR   What services canst thou do?

---

3 full issue complete outcome   **4 razed my likeness** erased my true appearance   **8 stay** wait
11 What . . . profess? What is your occupation? (Kent shifts the sense of **profess** to "claim, declare")   **wouldst thou** do you want   **12 us** Lear continues to use the royal plural pronoun
16 judgement i.e. God's judgment/the judgment of fellow men   **cannot choose** have no other
option   **to eat . . . fish** i.e. only to eat a hearty diet of meat/not to eat fish on Fridays like a
Roman Catholic/not to have sex with prostitutes

KENT   I can keep honest counsel, ride, run, mar a curious tale in telling it, and deliver a plain message bluntly: that which ordinary men are fit for, I am qualified in, and the best of me is diligence.

35   LEAR   How old art thou?

KENT   Not so young, sir, to love a woman for singing, nor so old to dote on her for anything: I have years on my back forty-eight.

LEAR   Follow me, thou shalt serve me: if I like thee no
40   worse after dinner, I will not part from thee yet.— Dinner, ho, dinner! Where's my knave? My fool? Go you and call my fool hither.   [*Exit another Knight*]

Enter Steward [*Oswald*]

You, you, sirrah, where's my daughter?

OSWALD   So please you—   *Exit*

45   LEAR   What says the fellow there? Call the clotpoll back.—   [*Exit another Knight*]

Where's my fool? Ho, I think the world's asleep.—

[*Enter a Knight*]

How now? Where's that mongrel?

KNIGHT   He says, my lord, your daughter is not well.

LEAR   Why came not the slave back to me when I called
50   him?

KNIGHT   Sir, he answered me in the roundest manner, he would not.

LEAR   He would not?

KNIGHT   My lord, I know not what the matter is, but to my
55   judgement your highness is not entertained with that ceremonious affection as you were wont: there's a great abatement of kindness appears as well in the general dependants as in the duke himself also and your daughter.

---

31 **keep honest counsel** keep secrets like an honorable man/keep secrets that are honorable
mar . . . tale spoil an elaborate story   37 **anything** "thing" plays on the sense of "vagina"
41 **knave** rogue/servant   44 **So if it**   45 **clotpoll** idiot   49 **slave** servant/villain
51 **roundest** bluntest   55 **entertained** received, treated hospitably   56 **wont** accustomed (to receive)   57 **general dependants** servants as a whole

LEAR   Ha? Say'st thou so?

60 KNIGHT   I beseech you pardon me, my lord, if I be mistaken,
for my duty cannot be silent when I think your highness
wronged.

LEAR   Thou but rememb'rest me of mine own conception:
I have perceived a most faint neglect of late, which I have
65 rather blamed as mine own jealous curiosity than as a very
pretence and purpose of unkindness. I will look further
into't. But where's my fool? I have not seen him this two
days.

KNIGHT   Since my young lady's going into France, sir, the
70 fool hath much pined away.

LEAR   No more of that, I have noted it well.— Go you and
tell my daughter I would speak with her.—   [*Exit a Knight*]
Go you, call hither my fool.—   [*Exit another Knight*]
Enter Steward [Oswald]
O, you sir, you, come you hither, sir. Who am I, sir?

75 OSWALD   My lady's father.

LEAR   'My lady's father'? My lord's knave: you whoreson
dog, you slave, you cur!

OSWALD   I am none of these, my lord, I beseech your pardon.

LEAR   Do you bandy looks with me, you rascal?   *Strikes him*

80 OSWALD   I'll not be strucken, my lord.

KENT   Nor tripped neither, you base football player.   *Trips him*

LEAR   I thank thee, fellow: thou serv'st me and I'll love
thee.

KENT   Come, sir, arise, away! I'll teach you differences:
85 away, away! If you will measure your lubber's length again,
tarry: but away, go to. Have you wisdom? So.   *Pushes Oswald out*

---

63 rememb'rest remind   **conception** notion, thought   **64 faint** slight/lazy, half-hearted
65 jealous curiosity mistrustful fastidiousness   **very pretence** real intention   **77 cur** dog
79 bandy exchange looks as an equal (literally, "bat to and fro" as in tennis)   **80 strucken**
struck, beaten   **81 football** played by the lower classes (unlike tennis)   **84 differences** class
distinctions   **85 measure . . . length** be knocked flat to the floor   **lubber** clumsy lout
86 tarry stay   **go to** an expression of impatient dismissal

LEAR   Now, my friendly knave, I thank thee.   *Gives money*
There's earnest of thy service.

Enter Fool

FOOL   Let me hire him too: here's my   *Offers Kent his cap*
90   coxcomb.

LEAR   How now, my pretty knave, how dost thou?

FOOL   Sirrah, you were best take my coxcomb.   *To Kent*

LEAR   Why, my boy?

FOOL   Why? For taking one's part that's out of favour: nay,
95   an thou canst not smile as the wind sits, thou'lt catch cold
shortly. There, take my coxcomb. Why, this fellow has
banished two on's daughters and did the third a blessing
against his will: if thou follow him, thou must needs wear
my coxcomb.— How now, nuncle? Would I had two
100   coxcombs and two daughters.

LEAR   Why, my boy?

FOOL   If I gave them all my living, I'd keep my coxcombs
myself. There's mine: beg another of thy daughters.

LEAR   Take heed, sirrah: the whip.

105   FOOL   Truth's a dog must to kennel: he must be whipped
out when the Lady Brach may stand by th'fire and stink.

LEAR   A pestilent gall to me!

FOOL   Sirrah, I'll teach thee a speech.

LEAR   Do.

110   FOOL   Mark it, nuncle:
Have more than thou showest,
Speak less than thou knowest,
Lend less than thou owest,
Ride more than thou goest,
115   Learn more than thou trowest,
Set less than thou throwest;

88 **earnest** part-payment in advance   90 **coxcomb** fool's headgear with a crest like a cock's
comb   91 **pretty** fine-looking/clever   95 **an . . . sits** i.e. if you cannot please those in power
97 **on's** of his   98 **needs** necessarily   99 **nuncle** contraction of "mine uncle"   **Would I
wish**   102 **living** property, possessions   106 **Brach** bitch   107 **pestilent gall** troublesome
irritation   110 **Mark** pay attention to   113 **owest** own   114 **goest** walk   115 **trowest**
believe   116 **Set . . . throwest** don't stake everything on the throw of the dice

FOOL = WISE

Leave thy drink and thy whore,
And keep in-a-door,
And thou shalt have more
120   Than two tens to a score.

KENT   This is nothing, fool.

FOOL   Then 'tis like the breath of an unfee'd   *To Lear*
lawyer; you gave me nothing for't.— Can you make no use
of nothing, nuncle?

125 LEAR   Why, no, boy: nothing can be made out of nothing.

FOOL   Prithee tell him, so much the rent of his land *To Kent*
comes to: he will not believe a fool.

LEAR   A bitter fool!

FOOL   Dost thou know the difference, my boy, between a
130 bitter fool and a sweet one?

LEAR   No, lad, teach me.

FOOL   Nuncle, give me an egg and I'll give thee two
crowns.

LEAR   What two crowns shall they be?

135 FOOL   Why, after I have cut the egg i'th'middle and eat up
the meat, the two crowns of the egg. When thou clovest thy
crowns i'th'middle and gav'st away both parts, thou bor'st
thine ass on thy back o'er the dirt: thou hadst little wit in thy
bald crown when thou gav'st thy golden one away. If I speak
140 like myself in this, let him be whipped that first finds it so:

    Fools had ne'er less grace in a year,   *Sings*
    For wise men are grown foppish
    And know not how their wits to wear,
    Their manners are so apish.

145 LEAR   When were you wont to be so full of songs, sirrah?

FOOL   I have used it, nuncle, e'er since thou mad'st thy
daughters thy mothers: for when thou gav'st them the rod

nothing comes from nothing

---

119 have . . . score i.e. make a profit   120 score twenty   122 unfee'd unpaid   123 use
employment/profit   134 crowns coins (the sense then shifts to "eggshells," "royal headgear,"
and "head")   136 meat edible contents   clovest split   140 like myself i.e. foolishly
141 grace favor, patronage   142 foppish foolish   144 apish silly   146 used it made it my
custom   147 rod punishment cane

and put'st down thine own breeches,

Then they for sudden joy did weep, *Sings*

150 And I for sorrow sung,

That such a king should play bo-peep

And go the fool among.

Prithee, nuncle, keep a schoolmaster that can teach thy fool

to lie: I would fain learn to lie.

155 **LEAR** An you lie, sirrah, we'll have you whipped.

FOOL I marvel what kin thou and thy daughters are:
they'll have me whipped for speaking true, thou'lt have me
whipped for lying, and sometimes I am whipped for holding
my peace. I had rather be any kind o'thing than a fool. And

160 yet I would not be thee, nuncle: thou hast pared thy wit
o'both sides and left nothing i'th'middle. Here comes one
o'the parings.

Enter Goneril

LEAR How now, daughter? What makes that frontlet on?
You are too much of late i'th'frown.

165 **FOOL** Thou wast a pretty fellow when thou hadst no need
to care for her frowning: now thou art an O without a figure.
I am better than thou art now: I am a fool, thou art
nothing.— Yes, forsooth, I will hold my tongue, so *To Goneril*
your face bids me, though you say nothing.

170 Mum, mum, *Sings*

He that keeps nor crust nor crumb,

Weary of all, shall want some.

That's a shelled peascod. *Points to Lear*

GONERIL Not only, sir, this your all-licensed fool,

175 But other of your insolent retinue

---

151 bo-peep a child's game (in which an adult alternately conceals and reveals his or her face)
152 the fool among among fools **154 fain** gladly **155 An** if **156 marvel** wonder
160 pared trimmed **163 frontlet** ornamental headband/band worn round forehead at night
to smooth wrinkles **166 figure** accompanying digit (to make it a number higher than zero)
168 forsooth in truth **171 nor . . . crumb** i.e. no part of the loaf **172 want some** need
something/experience need **173 peascod** peapod **174 all-licensed** licensed to speak
entirely freely

Do hourly carp and quarrel, breaking forth
In rank and not-to-be endured riots, sir.
I had thought by making this well known unto you
To have found a safe redress, but now grow fearful,
180   By what yourself too late have spoke and done.
That you protect this course and put it on
By your allowance, which if you should, the fault
Would not scape censure, nor the redresses sleep
Which in the tender of a wholesome weal
185   Might in their working do you that offence,
Which else were shame, that then necessity
Will call discreet proceeding.

FOOL   For you know, nuncle,
       The hedge-sparrow fed the cuckoo so long,
190   That it's had it head bit off by it young.
So, out went the candle, and we were left darkling.

LEAR   Are you our daughter?   *To Goneril*

GONERIL   I would you would make use of your good
       wisdom —
Whereof I know you are fraught — and put away
195   These dispositions which of late transport you
From what you rightly are.

FOOL   May not an ass know when the cart draws the
       horse?
Whoop, Jug! I love thee.

LEAR   Does any here know me? This is not Lear.
200   Does Lear walk thus? Speak thus? Where are his
       eyes?

---

176 **carp** complain   177 **rank** excessive, uncontrolled   179 **safe** certain   180 **too late** all too recently   181 **course** behavior   **put it on** encourage it   183 **scape** escape   **redresses sleep** punishments be neglected   184 **in . . . proceeding** might offend and shame you but which, in the interests of maintaining a healthy state, must be deemed a prudent course of action   189 **cuckoo** young cuckoo, hatched from an egg its mother had laid in another bird's nest   190 **it's had it** it had its   **it young** the young cuckoo   191 **darkling** in darkness   194 **fraught** equipped (literally "freighted")   195 **dispositions** moods   198 **Jug** a form of "Joan," often used as a generic name for a prostitute

Either his notion weakens, his discernings
Are lethargied — Ha! Waking? 'Tis not so?
Who is it that can tell me who I am?

FOOL   Lear's shadow.

205 LEAR   Your name, fair gentlewoman?

GONERIL   This admiration, sir, is much o'th'savour
Of other your new pranks. I do beseech you
To understand my purposes aright:
As you are old and reverend, should be wise.
210 Here do you keep a hundred knights and squires,
Men so disordered, so debauched and bold,
That this our court, infected with their manners,
Shows like a riotous inn: epicurism and lust
Makes it more like a tavern or a brothel
215 Than a graced palace. The shame itself doth speak
For instant remedy. Be then desired
By her, that else will take the thing she begs,
A little to disquantity your train,
And the remainders, that shall still depend
220 To be such men as may besort your age,
Which know themselves and you.

LEAR   Darkness and devils!—
Saddle my horses, call my train together.—   *To a Servant*
Degenerate bastard! I'll not trouble thee.   *To Goneril*
225 Yet have I left a daughter.

GONERIL   You strike my people, and your disordered
rabble
Make servants of their betters.

Enter Albany

201 **notion** understanding   **discernings Are lethargied** power of discernment is asleep
202 **Waking?** Am I awake?   204 **shadow** reflection/ghost/shadow cast by the sun/imitator,
actor   206 **admiration** air of wonder   **o'th'savour** of the flavor   209 **should** i.e. you should
211 **bold** presumptuous, audacious   213 **epicurism** gluttony/pleasure-seeking   215 **graced**
honorable   **speak** call   216 **desired** requested, entreated   218 **disquantity your train**
reduce your retinue   219 **depend** be your dependants, serve you   220 **besort** befit, suit
221 **know . . . you** i.e. know their place, and yours   224 **Degenerate** having lost the qualities
proper to a family member

LEAR   Woe that too late repents!— Is it your will?   *To Albany*
              Speak, sir.— Prepare my horses.   *To a Servant*
230   Ingratitude, thou marble-hearted fiend,
              More hideous when thou show'st thee in a child
              Than the sea-monster!

ALBANY   Pray, sir, be patient.

LEAR   Detested kite, thou liest.   *To Goneril*
235   My train are men of choice and rarest parts,
              That all particulars of duty know
              And in the most exact regard support
              The worships of their name. O, most small fault,
              How ugly didst thou in Cordelia show!
240   Which, like an engine, wrenched my frame of nature
              From the fixed place, drew from my heart all love,
              And added to the gall. O Lear, Lear, Lear!
              Beat at this gate, that let thy folly in,   *Hits his head*
              And thy dear judgement out!— Go, go, my people.

245 ALBANY   My lord, I am guiltless as I am ignorant
              Of what hath moved you.

LEAR   It may be so, my lord.—
              Hear, nature, hear, dear goddess, hear!
              Suspend thy purpose if thou didst intend
250   To make this creature fruitful: *— wishes Goneril to be childless*
              Into her womb convey sterility,
              Dry up in her the organs of increase,
              And from her derogate body never spring
              A babe to honour her: if she must teem,
255   Create her child of spleen, that it may live
              And be a thwart disnatured torment to her:
              Let it stamp wrinkles in her brow of youth,
              With cadent tears fret channels in her cheeks,

---

228 that to he who   **234 kite** bird of prey, scavenger   **235 rarest parts** splendid qualities
237 in . . . name uphold the honor of their names with the most careful consideration (or
" . . . in every respect")   **240 engine** piece of machinery   **242 gall** bitterness   **246 moved**
provoked, angered   **252 increase** procreation   **253 derogate** degenerate, debased
254 teem be fertile, have children   **255 spleen** malice   **256 thwart** perverse, obstinate
disnatured unnatural   **258 cadent** falling   **fret** erode, wear

Turn all her mother's pains and benefits
260   To laughter and contempt, that she may feel
How sharper than a serpent's tooth it is
To have a thankless child!— Away, away!   *Exit*   *Perhaps with Kent*

ALBANY   Now, gods that we adore, whereof comes   *and Knights*
this?

GONERIL   Never afflict yourself to know more of it,
265   But let his disposition have that scope
As dotage gives it.

Enter Lear

LEAR   What, fifty of my followers at a clap?
Within a fortnight?

ALBANY   What's the matter, sir?

270   LEAR   I'll tell thee:— Life and death! I am ashamed   *To Goneril*
That thou hast power to shake my manhood thus,
That these hot tears, which break from me perforce,
Should make thee worth them. Blasts and fogs upon
thee!
Th'untented woundings of a father's curse
275   Pierce every sense about thee! Old fond eyes,
Beweep this cause again, I'll pluck ye out
And cast you, with the waters that you loose,
To temper clay. Ha? Let it be so.
I have another daughter,   — He will go see Regan
280   Who, I am sure, is kind and comfortable:
When she shall hear this of thee, with her nails
She'll flay thy wolvish visage. Thou shalt find
That I'll resume the shape which thou dost think
I have cast off for ever.

Exeunt [Lear, perhaps with Kent and Knights]

---

259 **pains** efforts (also suggests labor pains)   **benefits** kindnesses   266 **dotage** foolish old age
267 **at a clap** with one blow   272 **perforce** by force, uncontrollably   273 **Blasts** violent gusts
of winds   274 **Th'untented** the festering (literally, not probed and cleaned surgically)
275 **fond** foolish/doting   277 **waters . . . loose** i.e. tears   278 **temper** moisten   **clay** i.e.
earth, the ground   280 **kind** benevolent/possessed of natural familial love   **comfortable**
comforting   282 **visage** face

285 GONERIL   Do you mark that?

ALBANY   I cannot be so partial, Goneril,
To the great love I bear you—

GONERIL   Pray you, content.— What, Oswald, ho!—
You, sir, more knave than fool, after your master.   *To Fool*

290 FOOL   Nuncle Lear, nuncle Lear, tarry, take the fool with
thee.

A fox, when one has caught her,   *Sings*
And such a daughter
Should sure to the slaughter,
295 If my cap would buy a halter:
So the fool follows after.   *Exit*

GONERIL   This man hath had good counsel. A hundred
knights?
'Tis politic and safe to let him keep
At point a hundred knights: yes, that on every
dream,
300 Each buzz, each fancy, each complaint, dislike,
He may enguard his dotage with their powers
And hold our lives in mercy.— Oswald, I say!

ALBANY   Well, you may fear too far.

GONERIL   Safer than trust too far:
305 Let me still take away the harms I fear,
Not fear still to be taken. I know his heart.
What he hath uttered I have writ my sister:
If she sustain him and his hundred knights
When I have showed th'unfitness—
Enter Steward [Oswald]
310   How now, Oswald?
What, have you writ that letter to my sister?

OSWALD   Ay, madam.

---

281 partial biased   **288 content** content yourself, i.e. be quiet   **295 halter** hangman's noose
298 politic prudent, shrewd   **299 At point** armed and ready   **that** so that   **300 buzz** rumor
fancy whim   **301 enguard** protect, defend   **302 in** at (his)   **305 still** always   **306 taken**
defeated, captured

GONERIL   Take you some company and away to horse:
Inform her full of my particular fear,
And thereto add such reasons of your own
315   As may compact it more. Get you gone,
And hasten your·return.—   [*Exit Oswald*]
                                        No, no, my lord,
This milky gentleness and course of yours
Though I condemn not, yet, under pardon,
You are much more at task for want of wisdom
320   Than praised for harmful mildness.
ALBANY   How far your eyes may pierce I cannot tell:
Striving to better, oft we mar what's well.
GONERIL   Nay, then—
ALBANY   Well, well, th'event.   *Exeunt*

Act 1 Scene 5   *running scene 3 continues*

Enter Lear, Kent, Gentleman and Fool   *Kent disguised as Caius*

LEAR   Go you before to Gloucester with these letters. *To Kent*
Acquaint my daughter no further with anything you know
than comes from her demand out of the letter. If your
diligence be not speedy, I shall be there afore you.
5   KENT   I will not sleep, my lord, till I have delivered your
letter.   *Exit*
FOOL   If a man's brains were in's heels, were't not in
danger of kibes?
LEAR   Ay, boy.
10   FOOL   Then, I prithee be merry: thy wit shall not go slip-
shod.
LEAR   Ha, ha, ha!

---

315 **compact** confirm, consolidate   318 **under pardon** if you'll pardon my saying so   319 **at
task** taken to task, blamed   324 **th'event** the outcome (will tell)   **1.5   1 before** ahead
3 **demand out of** questions prompted by   8 **kibes** chilblains   10 **wit** intellect   **slip-shod** in
slippers (worn for chilblains)

FOOL   Shalt see thy other daughter will use thee kindly, for
           though she's as like this as a crab's like an apple, yet I can tell
15   what I can tell.

LEAR   What canst tell, boy?

FOOL   She will taste as like this as a crab does to a crab.
           Thou canst tell why one's nose stands i'th'middle on's face?

LEAR   No.

20 FOOL   Why, to keep one's eyes of either side's nose, that
           what a man cannot smell out he may spy into.

LEAR   I did her wrong—

FOOL   Canst tell how an oyster makes his shell?

LEAR   No.

25 FOOL   Nor I neither; but I can tell why a snail has a house.

LEAR   Why?

FOOL   Why, to put's head in, not to give it away to his
           daughters and leave his horns without a case.

LEAR   I will forget my nature. So kind a father!— Be my
30   horses ready?

FOOL   Thy asses are gone about 'em. The reason why the
           seven stars are no more than seven is a pretty reason.

LEAR   Because they are not eight.

FOOL   Yes, indeed: thou wouldst make a good fool.

35 LEAR   To take't again perforce. Monster ingratitude!

FOOL   If thou wert my fool, nuncle, I'd have thee beaten
           for being old before thy time.

LEAR   How's that?

FOOL   Thou shouldst not have been old till thou hadst
40   been wise.

LEAR   O, let me not be mad, not mad, sweet heaven!
           Keep me in temper: I would not be mad!—
           How now, are the horses ready?   *To Gentleman*

---

13 **Shalt** i.e. thou shalt   14 **crab** sour-tasting crab apple   18 **on's** of his   20 **side's** side of his
22 **her** i.e. Cordelia (though Goneril is just possible)   31 **asses** idiots/donkeys (i.e. Lear's
servants)   31 **the seven stars** the Pleiades   32 **pretty** ingenious   35 **again** back again
(refers either to an intention to reclaim sovereignty, or to Goneril's withdrawal of Lear's
privileges)   42 **temper** my right state of mind

GENTLEMAN	Ready, my lord.	

45 LEAR   Come, boy.

FOOL   She that's a maid now, and laughs at my departure,
Shall not be a maid long, unless things be cut shorter.

Exeunt

Act 2 Scene 1   *running scene 4*

Enter Bastard [Edmund] and Curan, severally

EDMUND   Save thee, Curan.

CURAN   And you, sir. I have been with your father, and given
him notice that the Duke of Cornwall and Regan his duchess
will be here with him this night.

5 EDMUND   How comes that?

CURAN   Nay, I know not. You have heard of the news
abroad: I mean the whispered ones, for they are yet but ear-
kissing arguments?

EDMUND   Not I: pray you, what are they?

10 CURAN   Have you heard of no likely wars toward 'twixt the
dukes of Cornwall and Albany?

EDMUND   Not a word.

CURAN   You may do then in time. Fare you well, sir.   *Exit*

EDMUND   The duke be here tonight? The better — best!

15 This weaves itself perforce into my business.
My father hath set guard to take my brother,
And I have one thing, of a queasy question,
Which I must act. Briefness and fortune, work!—

Enter Edgar   *Appears above and then enters below*

Brother, a word: descend, brother, I say!

20 My father watches: O sir, fly this place.
Intelligence is given where you are hid;

---

46 maid virgin   **47 things** penises   **2.1**   *Location: the Earl of Gloucester's residence*
severally separately   **1 Save thee** God save thee (a common greeting)   **7 abroad** out there,
in circulation   **ones** i.e. the **news**, regarded as plural   **ear-kissing arguments** rumored,
whispered topics, not established truths   **10 toward** impending   **15 perforce** of necessity
16 take arrest   **17 queasy question** dangerous, uncertain nature   **20 watches** is on guard,
on the lookout   **21 Intelligence** information

You have now the good advantage of the night.
Have you not spoken gainst the Duke of Cornwall?
He's coming hither, now, i'th'night, i'th'haste,
25   And Regan with him: have you nothing said
Upon his party gainst the Duke of Albany?
Advise yourself.

EDGAR   I am sure on't, not a word.

EDMUND   I hear my father coming, pardon me:
30   In cunning I must draw my sword upon you: *Draws*
Draw, seem to defend yourself. Now quit you well.   *Edgar draws*
Yield: come before my father.— Light, ho, here!—
Fly, brother.— Torches, torches!— So, farewell.

Exit Edgar

Some blood drawn on me would beget opinion   *Wounds his arm*
35   Of my more fierce endeavour: I have seen drunkards
Do more than this in sport.— Father, father!
Stop, stop! No help?

Enter Gloucester and Servants with torches

GLOUCESTER   Now, Edmund, where's the villain?

EDMUND   Here stood he in the dark, his sharp sword out,
40   Mumbling of wicked charms, conjuring the moon
To stand auspicious mistress—

GLOUCESTER   But where is he?

EDMUND   Look, sir, I bleed.

GLOUCESTER   Where is the villain, Edmund?

45   EDMUND   Fled this way, sir. When by no means he
could—

GLOUCESTER   Pursue him, ho! Go after.   [*Exeunt Servants*]
By no means what?

---

24 i'th'haste in haste   **25 have . . . Albany** i.e. have you spoken in support of Cornwall and against Albany/have you spoken critically about Cornwall's hostility to Albany   **27 Advise yourself** consider   **30 In cunning** to deceive (Gloucester; though playing on the fact that it is Edgar who is being tricked)   **31 quit you** acquit yourself   **34 beget . . . endeavour** give the impression that I fought more fiercely   **35 fierce** violent/brave/zealous   **40 conjuring** invoking   **the moon** i.e. Hecate, goddess of the moon and of witchcraft   **41 stand auspicious mistress** favor him as his patroness *saying that Edgar was trying to convince Edmund to kill Lear*

EDMUND   Persuade me to the murder of your lordship,
          But that I told him the revenging gods
50   Gainst parricides did all the thunder bend,
          Spoke with how manifold and strong a bond
          The child was bound to th'father; sir, in fine,
          Seeing how loathly opposite I stood
          To his unnatural purpose, in fell motion
55   With his preparèd sword, he charges home
          My unprovided body, latched mine arm;
          And when he saw my best alarumed spirits,
          Bold in the quarrel's right, roused to th'encounter,
          Or whether ghasted by the noise I made,
60   Full suddenly he fled.

says Edgar stabbed him then ran away

GLOUCESTER Let him fly far:
          Not in this land shall he remain uncaught,
          And found — dispatch. The noble duke my master,
          My worthy arch and patron, comes tonight:
65   By his authority I will proclaim it,
          That he which finds him shall deserve our thanks,
          Bringing the murderous coward to the stake:
          He that conceals him, death.

catch + kill Edgar

EDMUND   When I dissuaded him from his intent
70   And found him pight to do it, with curst speech
          I threatened to discover him: he replied,
          'Thou unpossessing bastard, dost thou think,
          If I would stand against thee, would the reposal
          Of any trust, virtue, or worth in thee
75   Make thy words faithed? No: what should I deny —
          As this I would, though thou didst produce

Edmund i. e. Iago

---

50 **bend** direct   52 **fine** conclusion   53 **loathly opposite** deeply opposed, horrified   54 **fell** savage, ruthless   55 **preparèd** unsheathed   **charges home** makes a direct attack on   56 **unprovided** unprotected   **latched** caught   57 **alarumed** stirred, roused   58 **quarrel's right** rightfulness of my cause   **th'encounter** the fight   59 **ghasted** frightened   60 **Full** very   63 **found — dispatch** once found, he shall be killed   64 **arch and patron** chief patron   67 **stake** i.e. place of execution   70 **pight** determined   **curst** angry   71 **discover** reveal his plans   72 **unpossessing** unable to take possession of land and property (illegitimate children could not legally inherit)   73 **would stand against** stood against, contradicted   **reposal** placing   75 **faithed** believed

My very character — I'd turn it all
To thy suggestion, plot, and damnèd practice,
And thou must make a dullard of the world,
80 If they not thought the profits of my death
Were very pregnant and potential spirits
To make thee seek it.'   *Tucket within*

GLOUCESTER O, strange and fastened villain!
Would he deny his letter, said he?
85 Hark, the duke's trumpets! I know not where he
    comes.
All ports I'll bar: the villain shall not scape:
The duke must grant me that. Besides, his picture
I will send far and near, that all the kingdom
May have due note of him, and of my land,
90 Loyal and natural boy, I'll work the means
To make thee capable.

Enter Cornwall, Regan and Attendants

CORNWALL How now, my noble friend? Since I came
    hither —
Which I can call but now — I have heard
    strangeness.

REGAN   If it be true, all vengeance comes too short
95 Which can pursue th'offender. How dost, my lord?

GLOUCESTER O, madam, my old heart is cracked, it's cracked!

REGAN   What, did my father's godson seek your life?
He whom my father named? Your Edgar?

GLOUCESTER O, lady, lady, shame would have it hid!

100 REGAN   Was he not companion with the riotous knights
That tended upon my father?

---

77 character handwriting   **78 suggestion** incitement to evil   **practice** scheme
79 make . . . world think the world very stupid   **80 not thought** did not think   **profits** i.e.
benefits to Edmund   **81 pregnant . . . spirits** fertile and powerful temptations (literally, evil
spirits)   *Tucket* personal trumpet call, here signaling the arrival of Cornwall   **83 strange**
unnatural   **fastened** confirmed, determined   **85 where** why   **86 ports** seaports/gates of
walled towns   **87 picture** could also mean "description"   **90 natural** naturally loyal and
loving to one's family (plays on the sense of "illegitimate")   **work the means** find a way
91 capable able to inherit   **101 tended upon** attended, waited on

GLOUCESTER I know not, madam: 'tis too bad, too bad.

EDMUND   Yes, madam, he was of that consort.

REGAN   No marvel, then, though he were ill affected:
105   'Tis they have put him on the old man's death,
       To have th'expense and waste of his revenues.
       I have this present evening from my sister
       Been well informed of them, and with such cautions
       That if they come to sojourn at my house,
110   I'll not be there.

CORNWALL   Nor I, assure thee, Regan.—
       Edmund, I hear that you have shown your father
       A child-like office.

EDMUND   It was my duty, sir.

115 GLOUCESTER He did bewray his practice and received   *To Cornwall*
       This hurt you see striving to apprehend him.

CORNWALL   Is he pursued?

GLOUCESTER Ay, my good lord.

CORNWALL   If he be taken, he shall never more
120   Be feared of doing harm: make your own purpose,
       How in my strength you please. For you, Edmund,
       Whose virtue and obedience doth this instant
       So much commend itself, you shall be ours:
       Natures of such deep trust we shall much need:
125   You we first seize on.

EDMUND   I shall serve you, sir, truly, however else.

GLOUCESTER For him I thank your grace.

CORNWALL   You know not why we came to visit you?

REGAN   Thus out of season, threading dark-eyed night:
130   Occasions, noble Gloucester, of some prize,
       Wherein we must have use of your advice:

---

103 consort company (often pejorative)   **104 though . : . affected** if he is ill-disposed
105 put him on incited him to   **106 th'expense** the spending   **113 child-like** i.e. obedient,
loving   **office** duty/service   **115 bewray** inform on, expose   **his practice** Edgar's plot
120 make . . . please to achieve your ends, use my means and authority in any way you wish
121 For as for   **123 be ours** i.e. work for us, join our household   **125 seize on** take
possession of (legal term)   **129 out of season** inconveniently, unconventionally   **threading**
finding a way through (sewing image)   **dark-eyed** quibbling on the idea of a needle's eye
130 Occasions events/circumstances   **prize** importance

Our father he hath writ, so hath our sister,
Of differences, which I best thought it fit
To answer from our home: the several messengers
135 From hence attend dispatch. Our good old friend,
Lay comforts to your bosom, and bestow
Your needful counsel to our businesses,
Which craves the instant use.

GLOUCESTER I serve you, madam: — *loyal to Regan*
140 Your graces are right welcome.   *Exeunt. Flourish*

Act 2 Scene 2 *Caius*   running scene 5

Enter Kent and Steward [Oswald], severally   Kent disguised as Caius

OSWALD Good dawning to thee, friend: art of this house?

KENT Ay.

OSWALD Where may we set our horses?

KENT I'th'mire.

5 OSWALD Prithee, if thou lov'st me, tell me.

KENT I love thee not.

OSWALD Why then, I care not for thee.

KENT If I had thee in Lipsbury pinfold, I would make thee
care for me.

10 OSWALD Why dost thou use me thus? I know thee not.

KENT Fellow, I know thee.

OSWALD What dost thou know me for?

KENT A knave, a rascal, an eater of broken meats, a base,
proud, shallow, beggarly, three-suited, hundred-pound,

---

133 **differences** disputes   134 **from** away from   135 **attend dispatch** wait to be dispatched
138 **craves . . . use** requires immediate action   **2.2** *Location: outside the Earl of
Gloucester's residence*   **severally** separately   1 **dawning** it is actually before dawn; we
later learn that the moon shines   2 **Ay** in fact, Kent is not a servant at this house; perhaps
Kent opens up an opportunity to abuse Oswald   3 **set** put, lodge (Kent plays on the sense of
"fix, make stuck")   4 **mire** mud   5 **if . . . me** i.e. if you would be so kind (Kent pretends to take
the expression literally)   8 **Lipsbury pinfold** the pound for stray animals in Lips-town (i.e.
"between my teeth")   10 **use** treat   12 **for** as   13 **knave** rogue (two lines later the sense
shifts to "servant")   **broken meats** scraps of food   14 **three-suited** servingmen were
permitted to have three outfits a year   **hundred-pound** far more than a servingman's income;
possibly a contemptuous reference to those who bought knighthoods from James I for £100

15　filthy, worsted-stocking knave, a lily-livered, action-taking,
whoreson, glass-gazing, super-serviceable finical rogue:
one-trunk-inheriting slave: one that wouldst be a bawd in
way of good service, and art nothing but the composition of
a knave, beggar, coward, pander, and the son and heir of a
20　mongrel bitch: one whom I will beat into clamorous
whining if thou deny'st the least syllable of thy addition.

OSWALD　Why, what a monstrous fellow art thou thus to rail
on one that is neither known of thee nor knows thee!

KENT　What a brazen-faced varlet art thou to deny thou
25　knowest me! Is it two days since I tripped up thy heels and beat
thee before the king? Draw, you rogue, for though it be night,
yet the moon shines: I'll make a sop o'th'moonshine of you,
you whoreson cullionly barber-monger. Draw.　*Draws his sword*

OSWALD　Away! I have nothing to do with thee.

30　KENT　Draw, you rascal: you come with letters against the
king, and take vanity the puppet's part against the royalty of
her father: draw, you rogue, or I'll so carbonado your
shanks: draw, you rascal, come your ways.

OSWALD　Help, ho! Murder! Help!

35　KENT　Strike, you slave! Stand, rogue, stand, you neat
slave, strike!　*Beats him*

OSWALD　Help, ho! Murder! Murder!

Enter Bastard [Edmund], Cornwall, Regan, Gloucester, Servants

---

15 worsted-stocking i.e. servant/unable to afford silk stockings (worsted is a woollen fabric)
lily-livered cowardly, with a bloodless liver (the organ thought to be the seat of strong
emotions)　**action-taking** litigious　**16 whoreson** bastard　**glass-gazing** vain　**glass**
mirror　**super-serviceable** ready to do any kind of service　**finical** fussy　**17 one-trunk-
inheriting** owner (or heir to) no more than would fit in a single trunk　**bawd** pimp
18 service plays on the sense of "sex"　**composition** combination　**19 pander** go-
between/pimp　**21 addition** attributes/title/mark of honor added to a coat of arms (ironic)
22 rail rant, heap abuse　**24 varlet** rogue　**26 Draw** draw your sword　**27 sop**
o'th'moonshine i.e. beat you to a pulp (so that you resemble either a soggy piece of bread lying
under the moon's light, or the blancmange pudding called moonshine)　**28 cullionly** rascally
barber-monger frequenter of barbers (i.e. vain fop)　**31 vanity the puppet** i.e. Goneril,
imagined as a puppet (or dressed-up woman) who is the personification of vanity
32 carbonado slash diagonally, like meat prepared for broiling or grilling　**33 come your
ways** come on then　**35 neat** trim, foppish

EDMUND   How now, what's the matter? Part!

KENT   With you, Goodman boy, if you please: come, I'll

40   flesh ye: come on, young master.

GLOUCESTER   Weapons? Arms? What's the matter here?

CORNWALL   Keep peace, upon your lives: he dies that strikes
again. What is the matter?

REGAN   The messengers from our sister and the king.

45   CORNWALL   What is your difference? Speak.

OSWALD   I am scarce in breath, my lord.

KENT   No marvel, you have so bestirred your valour. You
cowardly rascal, nature disclaims in thee: a tailor made thee.

CORNWALL   Thou art a strange fellow — a tailor make a man?

50   KENT   A tailor, sir: a stone-cutter or a painter could not
have made him so ill, though they had been but two years
o'th'trade.

CORNWALL   Speak yet, how grew your quarrel?

OSWALD   This ancient ruffian, sir, whose life I have spared at
55   suit of his grey beard—

KENT   Thou whoreson zed, thou unnecessary letter!— My
lord, if you will give me leave, I will tread this unbolted
villain into mortar and daub the wall of a jakes with him.—
Spare my grey beard, you wagtail?

60   CORNWALL   Peace, sirrah!
You beastly knave, know you no reverence?

KENT   Yes, sir, but anger hath a privilege.

CORNWALL   Why art thou angry?

---

39 With you i.e. I'll fight with you   **Goodman boy** a contemptuous and belittling form of
address (used to Edmund)   **Goodman** a man below the rank of gentleman   **40 flesh ye**
initiate you (into fighting; from the practice of feeding dogs bits of freshly killed meat in order
to excite them for prey)   **45 difference** argument   **47 bestirred your valour** worked up your
courage (ironic)   **48 disclaims in** disowns   **tailor made thee** i.e. his only worth lies in his
fancy clothes   **51 ill** badly   **55 suit . . . beard** his own request, because his old age required it
56 zed . . . letter "z" was regarded as **unnecessary** because "s" could be used instead and there
was no "z" in the Latin alphabet   **57 unbolted** unsifted (plays on the sense of "unmanly/
impotent"—a "bolt" was a term for the penis)   **58 jakes** privy, toilet   **59 wagtail** tail-wagger,
obsequious person/womanizer   **61 beastly** brutish   **62 a privilege** license to express itself

KENT   That such a slave as this should wear a sword,
Who wears no honesty. Such smiling rogues as
          these,
Like rats, oft bite the holy cords a-twain
Which are too intrinse t'unloose, smooth every
          passion
That in the natures of their lords rebel,
Being oil to fire, snow to the colder moods,
Revenge, affirm, and turn their halcyon beaks
With every gall and vary of their masters,
Knowing naught, like dogs, but following.—
A plague upon your epileptic visage!   *To Oswald*
Smile you my speeches, as I were a fool?
Goose, if I had you upon Sarum plain,
I'd drive ye cackling home to Camelot.

CORNWALL   What, art thou mad, old fellow?

GLOUCESTER How fell you out? Say that.

KENT   No contraries hold more antipathy
Than I and such a knave.

CORNWALL   Why dost thou call him knave? What is his fault?

KENT   His countenance likes me not.

CORNWALL   No more, perchance, does mine, nor his, nor hers—

KENT   Sir, 'tis my occupation to be plain:
I have seen better faces in my time
Than stands on any shoulder that I see
Before me at this instant.

---

65 honesty honor, integrity   **66 holy cords** sacred bonds (family or matrimonial ties)
a-twain in two   **67 too intrinse t'unloose** too intertwined to be disentangled   **smooth** flatter,
indulge   **68 rebel** i.e. against reason   **69 Being . . . fire** i.e. feed the fire of their masters'
passions   **70 halcyon beaks** the kingfisher (**halcyon**) was thought to act as a weather vane if
dried and hung up   **71 gall** irritation   **vary** change   **73 epileptic visage** seeing Oswald
smiling away his insults, Kent compares his expression to that of an epileptic, grimacing
involuntarily   **74 my** at my   **as** as if   **75 Goose** proverbially stupid bird; **cackling** suggests
that Oswald may be laughing   **if . . . Camelot** i.e. if I had you at my mercy, I'd send you
running home in fright; the exact nature of this reference is unclear, though, as Camelot was
sometimes identified with Winchester, some suspect a jibe about a "Winchester goose" (i.e. a
prostitute/venereal disease)   **Sarum** Salisbury, in Wiltshire   **76 Camelot** legendary city that
was home to King Arthur   **82 likes** pleases   **84 occupation** habit, business

CORNWALL   This is some fellow
Who, having been praised for bluntness, doth affect
90 A saucy roughness, and constrains the garb
Quite from his nature. He cannot flatter, he:
An honest mind and plain, he must speak truth!
An they will take it, so: if not, he's plain.
These kind of knaves I know, which in this plainness
95 Harbour more craft and more corrupter ends
Than twenty silly ducking observants
That stretch their duties nicely.

KENT   Sir, in good faith, in sincere verity,
Under th'allowance of your great aspect,
100 Whose influence, like the wreath of radiant fire
On flickering Phoebus' front—

CORNWALL   What mean'st by this?

KENT   To go out of my dialect, which you discommend so
much. I know, sir, I am no flatterer: he that beguiled you in a
105 plain accent was a plain knave, which for my part I will not
be, though I should win your displeasure to entreat me to't.

CORNWALL   What was th'offence you gave him?   *To Oswald*

OSWALD   I never gave him any.
It pleased the king his master very late
110 To strike at me, upon his misconstruction:
When he, compact and flattering his displeasure,
Tripped me behind, being down, insulted, railed,
And put upon him such a deal of man
That worthied him, got praises of the king

---

90 saucy insolent   **constrains . . . nature** forces the style (of speaking) away from its true
purpose   **93 An** if   **so** so be it   **plain** honest (his excuse for his rudeness)   **95 craft** cunning
corrupter corrupt   **96 ducking observants** bowing attendants   **97 stretch . . . nicely** strain
to perform their duties to the last detail   **98 verity** truth   **99 th'allowance** the approval
aspect face/planetary position (in comparing Cornwall to a powerful planet, Kent mocks a
courtier's flattery)   **100 influence** astrological influence   **101 Phoebus** the Greek and
Roman sun god   **front** forehead   **103 dialect** usual manner of speaking   **104 beguiled**
deceived   **106 though . . . to't** even if I should incur your displeasure by refusing (to be a
knave) when asked   **110 misconstruction** misinterpretation   **111 compact** colluding (with
the king)   **112 being** and I being   **113 deal of man** great show of manliness   **114 worthied**
him earned him honor/made him a hero

115 For him attempting who was self-subdued:
     And, in the fleshment of this dread exploit,
     Drew on me here again.

KENT   None of these rogues and cowards
     But Ajax is their fool.

120 CORNWALL   Fetch forth the stocks!—
     You stubborn ancient knave, you reverent braggart,
     We'll teach you.

KENT   Sir, I am too old to learn.
     Call not your stocks for me: I serve the king,
125 On whose employment I was sent to you:
     You shall do small respects, show too bold malice
     Against the grace and person of my master,
     Stocking his messenger.

CORNWALL   Fetch forth the stocks! As I have life and
     honour,
130 There shall he sit till noon.

REGAN   Till noon? Till night, my lord, and all night too.

KENT   Why, madam, if I were your father's dog
     You should not use me so.

REGAN   Sir, being his knave, I will.

     Stocks brought out

135 CORNWALL   This is a fellow of the self-same colour
     Our sister speaks of. Come, bring away the stocks!

GLOUCESTER Let me beseech your grace not to do so:
     The king his master needs must take it ill
     That he so slightly valued in his messenger,
140 Should have him thus restrained.

CORNWALL   I'll answer that.

---

115 attempting . . . self-subdued attacking one who offered no resistance   **116 fleshment**
excitement of a first success   **dread exploit** fearsome military enterprise (sarcastic)
118 None . . . fool there is not one of these rogues and cowards who cannot make a fool of a
man like **Ajax** (the great Greek warrior was famously stupid; Cornwall is the subject of this dig)
120 stocks instrument of public punishment in which the offender sat with his ankles and
sometimes wrists confined   **121 reverent** old and revered (sarcastic)   **braggart** boaster
126 bold malice impudent hostility   **127 grace** sovereignty   **133 use** treat   **135 colour** type
136 sister sister-in-law, i.e. Goneril   **away** here/there (Cornwall directs where the stocks are
to be placed)   **141 answer** be responsible for

REGAN   My sister may receive it much more worse
　　　　To have her gentleman abused, assaulted.   *Kent put in the stocks*

CORNWALL   Come, my lord, away.

　　　　　　　　　　　　Exeunt. [Gloucester and Kent remain]

145 GLOUCESTER   I am sorry for thee, friend: 'tis the duke's
　　　　pleasure,
　　　　Whose disposition all the world well knows
　　　　Will not be rubbed nor stopped. I'll entreat for thee.

KENT   Pray do not, sir. I have watched and travelled
　　　　hard:
　　　　Some time I shall sleep out, the rest I'll whistle.
150 　　　A good man's fortune may grow out at heels.
　　　　Give you good morrow.

GLOUCESTER   The duke's to blame in this: 'twill be ill
　　　　taken.   *Exit*

KENT   Good king, that must approve the common saw,
　　　　Thou out of heaven's benediction com'st
155 　To the warm sun.   *Pulls out a letter*
　　　　Approach, thou beacon to this under globe,
　　　　That by thy comfortable beams I may
　　　　Peruse this letter. Nothing almost sees miracles
　　　　But misery. I know 'tis from Cordelia,
160 　Who hath most fortunately been informed
　　　　Of my obscurèd course, and shall find time
　　　　From this enormous state, seeking to give
　　　　Losses their remedies. All weary and o'erwatched,
　　　　Take vantage, heavy eyes, not to behold

---

145 pleasure will   **147 rubbed** deflected (from bowling where the "rub" is the obstacle that disrupts the path of the ball)   **148 watched** gone without sleep   **150 out at heels** worn out (literally, coming through one's stockings or shoes; an appropriate phrase for one whose feet are poking out of the stocks)   **151 Give . . . morrow** Good-bye   **153 approve** prove   **saw** saying   **154 out . . . sun** proverbial for going from good to bad; Kent means that Regan will prove worse than Goneril   **156 beacon** i.e. the sun   **this under globe** i.e. the earth **157 comfortable** comforting, encouraging   **158 Nothing . . . misery** the miserable are almost the only people to see miracles   **161 obscurèd course** secret (and "disguised") course of action/dimmed fortunes   **162 From** away from (i.e. in France)   **enormous state** disordered situation (or country)   **163 o'erwatched** worn out by lack of sleep   **164 vantage** advantage

165   This shameful lodging.
        Fortune, goodnight: smile once more, turn thy wheel!   *Sleeps*
Enter Edgar
        EDGAR   I heard myself proclaimed,
        And by the happy hollow of a tree
        Escaped the hunt. No port is free, no place
170   That guard and most unusual vigilance
        Does not attend my taking. Whiles I may scape,
        I will preserve myself, and am bethought
        To take the basest and most poorest shape
        That ever penury in contempt of man
175   Brought near to beast: my face I'll grime with filth,
        Blanket my loins, elf all my hairs in knots,
        And with presented nakedness outface
        The winds and persecutions of the sky.
        The country gives me proof and precedent
180   Of Bedlam beggars, who with roaring voices
        Strike in their numbed and mortifièd arms
        Pins, wooden pricks, nails, sprigs of rosemary,
        And with this horrible object, from low farms,
        Poor pelting villages, sheepcotes, and mills,
185   Sometimes with lunatic bans, sometime with prayers,
        Enforce their charity. Poor Turlygod, poor Tom!
        That's something yet: Edgar I nothing am.   *Exit*
Enter Lear, Fool and Gentleman

---

166 Fortune . . . wheel! Fortune was traditionally depicted as a woman turning a wheel that raised humans up and cast them down   **167 proclaimed** publicly declared an outlaw
168 happy opportune, fortunate   **171 attend my taking** wait to catch me   **172 am bethought** have decided   **174 in . . . man** despising mankind (in particular, man's claim to be superior to beasts)   **176 elf** tangle (into "elflocks" or messy knots of hair)   **177 presented** openly displayed   **180 Bedlam** the Saint Mary of Bethlehem hospital in London; a number of those who were released became **beggars**   **181 mortifièd** deadened   **182 pricks** spikes
183 object sight   **low** humble, lowly   **184 pelting** paltry, insignificant   **185 bans** curses
186 Poor . . . Tom! the sorts of cries the beggars would utter; several sixteenth-century accounts refer to beggars calling themselves "Poor Tom"   **Turlygod** unexplained; perhaps a deliberately nonsensical name   **187 That's something yet** i.e. at least as Poor Tom I have some form of existence   **Edgar . . . am** as Edgar I do not exist/I renounce my identity as Edgar
Gentleman presumably one of Lear's reduced retinue of knights

LEAR   'Tis strange that they should so depart from home
And not send back my messengers.

190 GENTLEMAN   As I learned,
The night before there was no purpose in them
Of this remove.

KENT   Hail to thee, noble master!   *Wakes*

LEAR   Ha? Mak'st thou this shame thy pastime?

195 KENT   No, my lord.

FOOL   Ha, ha, he wears cruel garters. Horses are tied by
the heads, dogs and bears by th'neck, monkeys by th'loins,
and men by th'legs: when a man's over-lusty at legs, then he
wears wooden nether-stocks.

200 LEAR   What's he that hath so much thy place mistook
To set thee here?

KENT   It is both he and she:
Your son and daughter.

LEAR   No.

205 KENT   Yes.

LEAR   No, I say.

KENT   I say, yea.

LEAR   By Jupiter, I swear, no.

KENT   By Juno, I swear, ay.

210 LEAR   They durst not do't:
They could not, would not do't: 'tis worse than
murder
To do upon respect such violent outrage.
Resolve me with all modest haste which way
Thou might'st deserve or they impose this usage,

215 Coming from us.

---

188 **they** i.e. Regan and Cornwall   196 **cruel** puns on "crewel" (i.e. wool used for stockings)
198 **over-lusty at legs** as a servant, too ready to run away (perhaps plays on the sense of "too
eager for sex")   199 **nether-stocks** stockings   200 **place** position (as Lear's messenger)
201 **To** as to   203 **son** son-in-law   209 **Juno** wife of **Jupiter**, the supreme Roman god
212 **upon respect** upon consideration/against the respect due to a king and his representatives
213 **Resolve** make clear to, inform   **modest** moderate, reasonable   **which way** why, how
214 **usage** treatment   215 **Coming from us** when you were sent by me

KENT   My lord, when at their home
             I did commend your highness' letters to them,
             Ere I was risen from the place that showed
             My duty kneeling, came there a reeking post,
220   Stewed in his haste, half breathless, panting forth
             From Goneril his mistress salutations,
             Delivered letters, spite of intermission,
             Which presently they read: on those contents
             They summoned up their meiny, straight took horse,
225   Commanded me to follow and attend
             The leisure of their answer, gave me cold looks:
             And meeting here the other messenger,
             Whose welcome I perceived had poisoned mine —
             Being the very fellow which of late
230   Displayed so saucily against your highness —
             Having more man than wit about me, drew.
             He raised the house with loud and coward cries:
             Your son and daughter found this trespass worth
             The shame which here it suffers.
235   FOOL   Winter's not gone yet if the wild geese fly that way.
             Fathers that wear rags   *Sings*
             Do make their children blind,
             But fathers that bear bags
             Shall see their children kind.
240   Fortune, that arrant whore,
             Ne'er turns the key to th' poor.
             But, for all this, thou shalt have as many dolours for thy
             daughters as thou canst tell in a year.

---

217 **commend** deliver   219 **reeking** steaming (with sweat)   **post** messenger   220 **Stewed**
hot and drenched in sweat   222 **spite of intermission** in spite of interrupting me/in spite of
his halting breath   223 **presently** immediately   224 **meiny** retinue   **straight** straight away
225 **attend . . . answer** wait until they had time to answer   230 **Displayed . . . against** openly
behaved so impudently toward   231 **man than wit** courage than sense   **drew** drew my sword
235 **Winter's . . . way** i.e. there is more stormy weather (trouble) on the way   237 **blind** i.e. to
their father's needs   238 **bags** moneybags   240 **arrant** downright/notorious   241 **turns the
key** opens the door/provides sexual favors   242 **dolours** griefs (puns on "dollar," a silver coin)
243 **tell** relate/count

LEAR   O, how this mother swells up toward my heart!

245   *Hysterica passio,* down, thou climbing sorrow:

Thy element's below!— Where is this daughter?

KENT   With the earl, sir, here within.

LEAR   Follow me not: stay here.   *Exit*

GENTLEMAN   Made you no more offence but what you speak of?

250   KENT   None. How chance the king comes with so small a
number?

FOOL   An thou had'st been set i'th'stocks for that
question, thou'dst well deserved it.

KENT   Why, fool?

255   FOOL   We'll set thee to school to an ant to teach thee
there's no labouring i'th'winter. All that follow their noses
are led by their eyes but blind men, and there's not a nose
among twenty but can smell him that's stinking. Let go thy
hold when a great wheel runs down a hill lest it break thy

260   neck with following: but the great one that goes upward, let
him draw thee after. When a wise man gives thee better
counsel, give me mine again: I would have none but knaves
follow it, since a fool gives it.

That sir which serves and seeks for gain,   *Sings*

265   And follows but for form,

Will pack when it begins to rain,

And leave thee in the storm.

But I will tarry, the fool will stay,

And let the wise man fly:

270   The knave turns fool that runs away,

The fool no knave, perdy.

Enter Lear and Gloucester

---

244 mother i.e. hysteria (frequently a female affliction thought to arise from the womb or, in men, the abdomen; characterized by breathlessness and agitation)   **245 *Hysterica passio*** the Latin term for hysteria   **246 element** rightful environment   **below** i.e. in the womb   **255 to school to** i.e. to learn from   **ant . . . i'th'winter** i.e. the ant gathers food only in the summer when it is abundant; similarly, men work only when there is profit to be gained from a patron who is at the height of his fortunes   **258 stinking** i.e. with the stench of decaying fortunes   **262 again** back again   **264 sir** man   **265 form** appearances, outward show   **266 pack** pack up, be off   **271 perdy** by God (from the French *par dieu*)

KENT   Where learned you this, fool?

FOOL   Not i'th'stocks, fool.

LEAR   Deny to speak with me? They are sick, they are
weary,
275   They have travelled all the night? Mere fetches,
The images of revolt and flying off.
Fetch me a better answer.

GLOUCESTER My dear lord,
You know the fiery quality of the duke,
280   How unremovable and fixed he is
In his own course.

LEAR   Vengeance, plague, death, confusion!
Fiery? What quality? Why, Gloucester, Gloucester,
I'd speak with the Duke of Cornwall and his wife.

285 GLOUCESTER Well, my good lord, I have informed them so.

LEAR   Informed them? Dost thou understand me, man?

GLOUCESTER Ay, my good lord.

LEAR   The king would speak with Cornwall: the dear
father
Would with his daughter speak, commands, tends,
service.
290   Are they informed of this? My breath and blood!
Fiery? The fiery duke? Tell the hot duke that —
No, but not yet: maybe he is not well.
Infirmity doth still neglect all office
Whereto our health is bound: we are not ourselves
295   When nature, being oppressed, commands the mind
To suffer with the body. I'll forbear,
And am fallen out with my more headier will,
To take the indisposed and sickly fit

---

274 **Deny** refuse   275 **fetches** tricks, stratagems (Lear goes on to employ the sense of "bring")
276 **flying off** desertion   282 **confusion** destruction, overthrow   289 **tends** attends, awaits
293 **Infirmity . . . bound** illness always makes us neglect the duties which, when healthy, we are
bound to carry out   295 **oppressed** overwhelmed/afflicted   297 **fallen . . . will** angry with
my more headstrong impulse

For the sound man. Death on my state! Wherefore   *Sees Kent*
300 Should he sit here? This act persuades me
That this remotion of the duke and her
Is practice only. Give me my servant forth.
Go tell the duke and's wife I'd speak with them,
Now, presently: bid them come forth and hear me,
305 Or at their chamber-door I'll beat the drum
Till it cry sleep to death.

GLOUCESTER I would have all well betwixt you.   *Exit*

LEAR   O me, my heart, my rising heart! But, down!

FOOL   Cry to it, nuncle, as the cockney did to the eels when
310 she put 'em i'th'paste alive: she knapped 'em o'th'coxcombs
with a stick and cried 'Down, wantons, down!' 'Twas her
brother that, in pure kindness to his horse, buttered his hay.

Enter Cornwall, Regan, Gloucester, Servants

LEAR   Good morrow to you both.

CORNWALL   Hail to your grace!

Kent here set at liberty

315 REGAN   I am glad to see your highness.

LEAR   Regan, I think you are. I know what reason
I have to think so: if thou shouldst not be glad,
I would divorce me from thy mother's tomb,
Sepulch'ring an adult'ress.— O, are you free?   *To Kent*
320 Some other time for that.— Belovèd Regan,
Thy sister's naught: O Regan, she hath tied
Sharp-toothed unkindness, like a vulture, here.   *Points to his heart*
I can scarce speak to thee. Thou'lt not believe
With how depraved a quality — O Regan!

---

299 sound healthy   **my state** royal state   **301 remotion** removal   **302 practice** deceit,
cunning   **Give . . . forth** release my servant   **303 and's** and his   **309 cockney** squeamish or
affected woman/town-dweller not used to hardier country ways   **310 i'th'paste alive** alive
into the pie (being too squeamish to kill them first)   **knapped** hit   **o'th'coxcombs** on the
heads   **311 wantons** frisky creatures   **312 buttered his hay** another example of misguided
kindness (horses dislike grease)   **319 Sepulch'ring** entombing   **adult'ress** i.e. as you could
not possibly be my daughter if you were not glad to see me   **321 naught** wicked/worthless
322 vulture recalls the Greek legend of Prometheus, who was punished for stealing fire from
the gods by having his liver perpetually gnawed by vultures

325 REGAN   I pray you, sir, take patience: I have hope
            You less know how to value her desert
            Than she to scant her duty.

    LEAR   Say? How is that?

    REGAN   I cannot think my sister in the least
330   Would fail her obligation: if, sir, perchance
            She have restrained the riots of your followers,
            'Tis on such ground and to such wholesome end
            As clears her from all blame.

    LEAR   My curses on her!

335 REGAN   O, sir, you are old:
            Nature in you stands on the very verge
            Of her confine: you should be ruled and led
            By some discretion that discerns your state
            Better than you yourself. Therefore, I pray you,
340   That to our sister you do make return;
            Say you have wronged her. —→ wants Lear
                                         to apologize

    LEAR   Ask her forgiveness?
            Do you but mark how this becomes the house:
            Dear daughter, I confess that I am old: *Kneels*
345   Age is unnecessary. On my knees I beg
            That you'll vouchsafe me raiment, bed and food.

    REGAN   Good sir, no more: these are unsightly tricks:
            Return you to my sister. → Regan doesn't
                                      want Lear to stay

    LEAR   Never, Regan: *Rises*
350   She hath abated me of half my train,
            Looked black upon me, struck me with her tongue
            Most serpent-like upon the very heart.
            All the stored vengeances of heaven fall
            On her ingrateful top! Strike her young bones,
355   You taking airs, with lameness—

326 **You . . . duty** you are more likely to undervalue her worth than she is to neglect her duty
336 **verge . . . confine** limit of her domain (i.e. you are near death)   338 **discretion** (person of)
good judgment   **state** personal condition (imaged as a country; ironic glance at the sense of
"kingship")   343 **becomes the house** befits the royal line or family   345 **unnecessary**
superfluous, useless   346 **vouchsafe** permit   **raiment** clothing   350 **abated** deprived
354 **top** head   355 **taking** infectious

CORNWALL   Fie, sir, fie!

LEAR   You nimble lightnings, dart your blinding flames
Into her scornful eyes! Infect her beauty,
You fen-sucked fogs drawn by the powerful sun
360 To fall and blister!

REGAN   O the blest gods! So will you wish on me
When the rash mood is on.

LEAR   No, Regan, thou shalt never have my curse:
Thy tender-hafted nature shall not give
365 Thee o'er to harshness. Her eyes are fierce, but thine
Do comfort and not burn. 'Tis not in thee
To grudge my pleasures, to cut off my train,
To bandy hasty words, to scant my sizes,
And, in conclusion, to oppose the bolt
370 Against my coming in: thou better know'st
The offices of nature, bond of childhood,
Effects of courtesy, dues of gratitude:
Thy half o'th'kingdom hast thou not forgot,
Wherein I thee endowed.

375 REGAN   Good sir, to th'purpose.   *Tucket within*

LEAR   Who put my man i'th'stocks?

Enter Steward [Oswald]

CORNWALL   What trumpet's that?

REGAN   I know't my sister's: this approves her letter,
That she would soon be here.— Is your lady come?   *To Oswald*

380 LEAR   This is a slave, whose easy-borrowed pride
Dwells in the sickly grace of her he follows.—
Out, varlet, from my sight!

CORNWALL   What means your grace?

---

359 fen-sucked . . . blister noxious vapors produced by sunshine on swampy ground were
considered to be infectious and so to cause blistering   **364 tender-hafted** delicately framed,
gently disposed   **368 scant my sizes** reduce my allowances (of food and drink etc.)
369 oppose the bolt lock the door   **371 offices of nature** natural filial duties   **372 Effects**
outward marks   **375 to th'purpose** get to the point   **378 approves** confirms, bears out
380 easy-borrowed easily assumed   **381 sickly** diseased, corrupt   **grace** favor/royalty

Enter Goneril

LEAR   Who stocked my servant? Regan, I have good hope
385   Thou didst not know on't. Who comes here? O heavens,
          If you do love old men, if your sweet sway
          Allow obedience, if you yourselves are old,
          Make it your cause, send down, and take my part!—
          Art not ashamed to look upon this beard?—   *To Goneril*
390   O Regan, will you take her by the hand?   *Regan and Goneril join hands*

GONERIL   Why not by th'hand, sir? How have I offended?
          All's not offence that indiscretion finds
          And dotage terms so.

LEAR   O sides, you are too tough!
395   Will you yet hold?— How came my man i'th'stocks?

CORNWALL   I set him there, sir: but his own disorders
          Deserved much less advancement.

LEAR   You? Did you?

REGAN   I pray you, father, being weak, seem so.
400   If till the expiration of your month,
          You will return and sojourn with my sister,
          Dismissing half your train, come then to me:
          I am now from home, and out of that provision
          Which shall be needful for your entertainment.

405 LEAR   Return to her? And fifty men dismissed?
          No, rather I abjure all roofs, and choose
          To wage against the enmity o'th'air,
          To be a comrade with the wolf and owl,
          Necessity's sharp pinch! Return with her?
410   Why, the hot-blooded France, that dowerless took
          Our youngest born, I could as well be brought
          To knee his throne and, squire-like, pension beg

---

385 on't of it   386 sway authority, rule   387 Allow sanctions, approves   389 beard gray
beard, symbol of his age   392 indiscretion poor judgment   394 sides bodily frame, rib cage
396 disorders misconduct   397 much less advancement less favorable treatment
404 entertainment hospitable reception   406 abjure renounce   407 wage . . . o'th'air battle
against the hostility of the open air   409 Necessity's need's, deprivation's   412 knee kneel
before   squire-like like a servant or follower   pension financial allowance

To keep base life afoot. Return with her?
Persuade me rather to be slave and sumpter
415   To this detested groom.

refuses to go with Goneril

Points at Oswald

GONERIL   At your choice, sir.

LEAR   I prithee, daughter, do not make me mad.
I will not trouble thee, my child, farewell:
We'll no more meet, no more see one another.
420   But yet thou art my flesh, my blood, my daughter —
Or rather a disease that's in my flesh,
Which I must needs call mine: thou art a boil,
A plague-sore, or embossèd carbuncle,
In my corrupted blood. But I'll not chide thee:
425   Let shame come when it will, I do not call it:
I do not bid the thunder-bearer shoot,
Nor tell tales of thee to high-judging Jove.
Mend when thou canst, be better at thy leisure:
I can be patient, I can stay with Regan,
430   I and my hundred knights.

disowns Goneril

REGAN   Not altogether so:
I looked not for you yet, nor am provided
For your fit welcome. Give ear, sir, to my sister,
For those that mingle reason with your passion
435   Must be content to think you old, and so —
But she knows what she does.

LEAR   Is this well spoken?

REGAN   I dare avouch it, sir: what, fifty followers?
Is it not well? What should you need of more?
440   Yea, or so many, sith that both charge and danger
Speak gainst so great a number? How in one house
Should many people under two commands
Hold amity? 'Tis hard, almost impossible.

— he can keep 50 men

---

413 afoot going   **414 sumpter** packhorse, beast of burden   **415 groom** manservant
423 embossèd carbuncle swollen tumor   **424 corrupted blood** diseased lineage
428 Mend improve   **432 looked not for** did not expect   **434 mingle . . . passion** apply
rational judgment to your impulsive behavior   **438 avouch** declare, affirm   **440 sith that**
since   **charge and danger** expense and the risk of riotous behavior

GONERIL   Why might not you, my lord, receive attendance
445   From those that she calls servants, or from mine?

REGAN   Why not, my lord? If then they chanced to slack ye,
We could control them. If you will come to me —
For now I spy a danger — I entreat you
To bring but five-and-twenty: to no more
450   Will I give place or notice.

LEAR   I gave you all—

REGAN   And in good time you gave it.

LEAR   Made you my guardians, my depositaries,
But kept a reservation to be followed
455   With such a number. What, must I come to you
With five-and-twenty? Regan, said you so?

REGAN   And speak't again, my lord: no more with me.

LEAR   Those wicked creatures yet do look well-favoured
When others are more wicked: not being the worst
460   Stands in some rank of praise.— I'll go with thee: *To Goneril*
Thy fifty yet doth double five-and-twenty,
And thou art twice her love.

GONERIL   Hear me, my lord:
What need you five-and-twenty, ten, or five,
465   To follow in a house where twice so many
Have a command to tend you?

REGAN   What need one?

LEAR   O, reason not the need! Our basest beggars
Are in the poorest thing superfluous:
470   Allow not nature more than nature needs,
Man's life is cheap as beast's. Thou art a lady;
If only to go warm were gorgeous,

---

446 **slack ye** treat you negligently   447 **control** discipline   450 **place or notice** room or
acknowledgment   452 **in . . . it** it was about time you did so   453 **guardians, my
depositaries** trustees   454 **kept a reservation** reserved the right   458 **well-favoured** good-
looking   460 **Stands . . . praise** is, in relative terms, worthy of some praise   468 **Our . . .
superfluous** even our most wretched beggars have something, however poor, that is more than
they absolutely need   470 **Allow not** if you do not allow   472 **If . . . gorgeous** if being
sumptuously dressed simply entailed wearing sufficiently warm clothes

Why, nature needs not what thou gorgeous wear'st,
Which scarcely keeps thee warm. But for true
   need —
475 You heavens, give me that patience, patience I need!
You see me here, you gods, a poor old man,
As full of grief as age, wretched in both.
If it be you that stirs these daughters' hearts
Against their father, fool me not so much
480 To bear it tamely: touch me with noble anger,
And let not women's weapons, water drops,
Stain my man's cheeks! No, you unnatural hags,
I will have such revenges on you both,
That all the world shall — I will do such things —
485 What they are yet I know not, but they shall be
The terrors of the earth! You think I'll weep:
No, I'll not weep: I have full cause of weeping,

Storm and tempest

But this heart shall break into a hundred thousand flaws,
Or ere I'll weep. O fool, I shall go mad!

                Exeunt [Lear, Gloucester, Kent and Fool]

490 CORNWALL Let us withdraw: 'twill be a storm.

REGAN   This house is little: the old man and's people
Cannot be well bestowed.

GONERIL   'Tis his own blame hath put himself from rest
And must needs taste his folly.

495 REGAN   For his particular, I'll receive him gladly,
But not one follower.

GONERIL   So am I purposed.
Where is my lord of Gloucester?

Enter Gloucester

---

473 what . . . wear'st your magnificent clothes   479 fool . . . much don't make me such a fool
as   488 flaws fragments   489 Or ere before   491 and's and his   492 bestowed lodged,
accommodated   493 blame fault (that he)   put . . . rest turned himself away from
repose/deprived himself of peace of mind   495 his particular him individually

CORNWALL   Followed the old man forth: he is returned.

500   GLOUCESTER   The king is in high rage.

CORNWALL   Whither is he going?

GLOUCESTER   He calls to horse, but will I know not whither.

CORNWALL   'Tis best to give him way: he leads himself.

GONERIL   My lord, entreat him by no means to stay.

505   GLOUCESTER   Alack, the night comes on, and the high
winds
Do sorely ruffle, for many miles about
There's scarce a bush.

REGAN   O, sir, to wilful men
The injuries that they themselves procure

510   Must be their schoolmasters. Shut up your doors:
He is attended with a desperate train,
And what they may incense him to, being apt
To have his ear abused, wisdom bids fear.

CORNWALL   Shut up your doors, my lord, 'tis a wild
night.

515   My Regan counsels well: come out o'th'storm.   *Exeunt*

Act 3 Scene 1   *running scene 6*

Storm still. Enter Kent and a Gentleman, severally

KENT   Who's there, besides foul weather?

GENTLEMAN   One minded like the weather, most unquietly.

KENT   I know you. Where's the king?

GENTLEMAN   Contending with the fretful elements;

5   Bids the wind blow the earth into the sea
Or swell the curlèd waters 'bove the main,
That things might change or cease.

---

502 **will** will go   503 **give him way** let him go, give him scope   506 **ruffle** rage, bluster
509 **themselves procure** bring on themselves   511 **desperate train** retinue of dangerous men
513 **have . . . abused** be misled by what he is told   **3.1**   *Location: somewhere out in the
open, not far from the Earl of Gloucester's residence*   **severally** separately
2 **minded . . . unquietly** in the same restless and disturbed mood as the storm   4 **Contending**
battling against/competing with   6 **main** mainland

KENT   But who is with him?

GENTLEMAN   None but the fool, who labours to out-jest
10   His heart-struck injuries.

KENT   Sir, I do know you.
And dare, upon the warrant of my note
Commend a dear thing to you. There is division —
Although as yet the face of it is covered
15   With mutual cunning — 'twixt Albany and
        Cornwall,
Who have — as who have not, that their great stars
Throned and set high? — servants, who seem no less,
Which are to France the spies and speculations
Intelligent of our state. What hath been seen,
20   Either in snuffs and packings of the dukes,
Or the hard rein which both of them hath borne
Against the old kind king, or something deeper,
Whereof perchance these are but furnishings.

GENTLEMAN   I will talk further with you.

25   **KENT**   No, do not.
For confirmation that I am much more
Than my out-wall, open this purse and take   *Gives a purse*
What it contains. If you shall see Cordelia —
As fear not but you shall — show her this ring,   *Gives a ring*
30   And she will tell you who that fellow is
That yet you do not know. Fie on this storm!
I will go seek the king.

GENTLEMAN   Give me your hand. Have you no more to
        say?

---

9 out-jest drive out with jokes   **10 heart-struck injuries** injuries that strike to the heart
12 warrant . . . note basis of what I have observed (about you)   **13 Commend . . . you** entrust
you with an important matter   **16 as . . . high** i.e. like anyone to whom fortune has given
power and royal authority   **17 seem no less** seem to be only servants (but are really spies)
18 France the King of France   **speculations** observers   **19 Intelligent of** bearing information
about   **20 snuffs** resentments   **packings** plots   **21 hard rein** harsh curbing (equestrian
metaphor; puns on "reign")   **borne** maintained   **23 furnishings** superficial trappings
27 out-wall outward appearance   **30 that fellow** i.e. Kent

KENT   Few words, but, to effect, more than all yet:
35   That when we have found the king — in which your
                  pain
        That way, I'll this — he that first lights on him
        Holla the other.   *Exeunt* [*separately*]

Act 3 Scene 2   *running scene 6 continues*

Storm still. Enter Lear and Fool

LEAR   Blow winds and crack your cheeks! Rage, blow,
        You cataracts and hurricanoes, spout
        Till you have drenched our steeples, drown the cocks!
        You sulphurous and thought-executing fires,
5   Vaunt-couriers of oak-cleaving thunderbolts,
        Singe my white head! And thou, all-shaking thunder,
        Strike flat the thick rotundity o'th'world!
        Crack nature's moulds, all germens spill at once
        That makes ingrateful man!
10 FOOL   O, nuncle, court holy-water in a dry house is better
        than this rain-water out o'door. Good nuncle, in, ask thy
        daughters' blessing: here's a night pities neither wise men
        nor fools.
    LEAR   Rumble thy bellyful! Spit fire! Spout rain!
15   Nor rain, wind, thunder, fire, are my daughters.
        I tax not you, you elements, with unkindness:
        I never gave you kingdom, called you children;
        You owe me no subscription. Then let fall
        Your horrible pleasure: here I stand, your slave,
20   A poor, infirm, weak and despised old man:
        But yet I call you servile ministers,

---

34 to effect in importance   **35 in . . . this** to which end you employ your efforts that way
while I go this way   **37 Holla** shout to   **3.2   2 cataracts** floods/waterspouts   **hurricanoes**
waterspouts   **3 cocks** weathercocks   **4 thought-executing fires** i.e. lightning (as swift as
thought/thought-destroying)   **5 Vaunt-couriers** forerunners   **8 nature's moulds** the molds
in which nature makes living creatures   **germens** seeds   **10 court holy-water** courtly
flattery   **16 tax . . . with** accuse . . . of   **18 subscription** allegiance   **21 ministers** agents

That will with two pernicious daughters join
Your high-engendered battles gainst a head
So old and white as this. O, ho, 'tis foul!

25 FOOL   He that has a house to put's head in has a good
head-piece:

    The codpiece that will house   *Sings*
    Before the head has any,
    The head and he shall louse,
30   So beggars marry many.
    The man that makes his toe
    What he his heart should make
    Shall of a corn cry woe,
    And turn his sleep to wake.

35 For there was never yet fair woman, but she made mouths
in a glass.

Enter Kent   *Disguised as Caius*

LEAR   No, I will be the pattern of all patience:
I will say nothing.

KENT   Who's there?

40 FOOL   Marry, here's grace and a codpiece: that's a wise
man and a fool.

KENT   Alas, sir, are you here? Things that love night
Love not such nights as these: the wrathful skies
Gallow the very wanderers of the dark
45 And make them keep their caves. Since I was man,
Such sheets of fire, such bursts of horrid thunder,
Such groans of roaring wind and rain, I never

---

22 **pernicious** destructive/wicked   23 **high-engendered battles** battalions created in the heavens   **head** plays on the sense of "army"   24 **foul** wicked/bad (weather)   25 **put's** put his   26 **head-piece** helmet/brain   27 **codpiece** penis (literally, appendage worn on the front of a man's breeches to cover and emphasize the genitals)   **house** find a house for itself, i.e. have sex   28 **any** i.e. any shelter   29 **louse** get lice (in pubic and head hair)   30 **So . . . many** in this way beggars end up with a string of mistresses (or "end up not only with a woman but a quantity of lice")   31 **makes . . . make** values most what he should value least/considers his penis (sex) more important than his heart (love/moral integrity)   33 **corn** may suggest a syphilitic sore   35 **made . . . glass** practiced smiling or pouting in a mirror   40 **grace . . . codpiece** royalty and a fool (fools sometimes wore exaggerated codpieces and were proverbially well-endowed)   44 **Gallow** gally, i.e. frighten   **wanderers . . . dark** nocturnal animals

Remember to have heard: man's nature cannot carry
Th'affliction nor the fear.

50 LEAR   Let the great gods,
That keep this dreadful pudder o'er our heads,
Find out their enemies now. Tremble, thou wretch,
That hast within thee undivulgèd crimes
Unwhipped of justice: hide thee, thou bloody hand,
55 Thou perjured, and thou simular of virtue
That art incestuous: caitiff, to pieces shake,
That under covert and convenient seeming
Has practised on man's life: close pent-up guilts,
Rive your concealing continents and cry
60 These dreadful summoners grace. I am a man
More sinned against than sinning.

KENT   Alack, bare-headed?
Gracious my lord, hard by here is a hovel:
Some friendship will it lend you gainst the tempest.
65 Repose you there while I to this hard house —
More harder than the stones whereof 'tis raised,
Which even but now, demanding after you,
Denied me to come in — return and force
Their scanted courtesy.

70 LEAR   My wits begin to turn.
Come on, my boy: how dost, my boy? Art cold?
I am cold myself.— Where is this straw, my fellow?
The art of our necessities is strange,
And can make vile things precious. Come, your
            hovel.—
75 Poor fool and knave, I have one part in my heart
That's sorry yet for thee.

---

51 **pudder** pother, tumult   54 **Unwhipped of** unpunished by   55 **simular** faker, pretender
56 **caitiff** villain, wretch   57 **seeming** false appearances, deception   58 **practised on** plotted
against   59 **Rive** split open   **continents** containers   **cry . . . grace** beg for mercy from these
terrifying **summoners** (officers who summoned the accused to court)   65 **hard** near   **hard
house** pitiless household (Gloucester's house, under the authority of Cornwall and Regan)
67 **demanding** (when I was) asking urgently   69 **scanted** withheld   72 **fellow** servant (but
with connotations of "companion")   73 **The . . . strange** necessity has a strange skill

FOOL   He that has and a little tiny wit,   *Sings*
         With hey, ho, the wind and the rain,
         Must make content with his fortunes fit,
80   Though the rain it raineth every day.
LEAR   True, boy.— Come, bring us to this hovel.

Exeunt [*Lear and Kent*]

FOOL   This is a brave night to cool a courtesan.
         I'll speak a prophecy ere I go:
         When priests are more in word than matter;
85   When brewers mar their malt with water;
         When nobles are their tailors' tutors;
         No heretics burned, but wenches' suitors;
         When every case in law is right;
         No squire in debt, nor no poor knight;
90   When slanders do not live in tongues;
         Nor cutpurses come not to throngs;
         When usurers tell their gold i'th'field,
         And bawds and whores do churches build,
         Then shall the realm of Albion
95   Come to great confusion:
         Then comes the time, who lives to see't,
         That going shall be used with feet.
         This prophecy Merlin shall make, for I live before his time.

Exit

---

77 He . . . day adapted from Feste's song at the end of *Twelfth Night*   **and a** a very   **wit**
possibly plays on the sense of "penis"   **79 make . . . fit** make his happiness fit his
fortunes/be content with the fortune that he deserves   **82 brave** fine   **cool** i.e. cool the lust
of   **courtesan** courtier's mistress, high-class prostitute   **84 in . . . matter** more concerned
with words than substance (i.e. do not practice what they preach)   **85 mar** spoil (i.e. water
down for their own profit)   **86 are . . . tutors** i.e. teach their tailors about fashion
87 heretics religious dissenters, conventionally punished with burning at the stake
wenches' suitors i.e. who are afflicted with the burning effects of syphilis   **88 right** just
91 cutpurses thieves who cut the strings of moneybags hanging at their victims' waists
throngs crowds   **92 usurers** moneylenders, notorious for charging excessively high interest
tell . . . i'th'field count their money openly   **93 bawds** pimps   **94 Albion** ancient name for
Britain   **95 confusion** destruction, overthrow   **96 who** whoever   **97 going . . . feet** walking
will be done on foot (perhaps simply meaning "things will return to normal")   **98 Merlin** in
the legendary history of Britain, the reign of Lear precedes that of Arthur by centuries

Act 3 Scene 3   *running scene 7*

Enter Gloucester and Edmund   *Carrying torches*

GLOUCESTER Alack, alack, Edmund, I like not this unnatural
dealing. When I desired their leave that I might pity him,
they took from me the use of mine own house, charged me
on pain of perpetual displeasure neither to speak of him,
5   entreat for him, or any way sustain him.

EDMUND   Most savage and unnatural.

GLOUCESTER Go to; say you nothing. There is division between
the dukes, and a worse matter than that. I have received a
letter this night — 'tis dangerous to be spoken — I have
10   locked the letter in my closet. These injuries the king now
bears will be revenged home; there is part of a power already
footed. We must incline to the king: I will look him and
privily relieve him. Go you and maintain talk with the duke,
that my charity be not of him perceived: if he ask for me, I
15   am ill and gone to bed: if I die for it — as no less is threatened
me — the king my old master must be relieved. There is
strange things toward, Edmund: pray you be careful.

Exit

EDMUND   This courtesy forbid thee shall the duke
Instantly know, and of that letter too:
20   This seems a fair deserving and must draw me
That which my father loses: no less than all.
The younger rises when the old doth fall.   *Exit*

3.3   *Location: the Earl of Gloucester's residence*   **2 leave . . . pity** permission to help,
take pity on   **7 Go to** expression of impatient dismissal   **10 closet** private room/cabinet
11 home thoroughly   **power** army   **12 footed** ashore   **incline to** support, side with   **look**
look for   **13 privily relieve** secretly help   **14 that** so that   **of** by   **17 toward** imminent
18 courtesy forbid thee forbidden kindness (to Lear)   **20 This . . . deserving** i.e. my action
should be worth a good reward

Act 3 Scene 4

Enter Lear, Kent and Fool   *Kent disguised as Caius*

	KENT	Here is the place, my lord. Good my lord, enter:
		The tyranny of the open night's too rough
		For nature to endure.

Storm still

	LEAR	Let me alone.
5	KENT	Good my lord, enter here.
	LEAR	Will't break my heart?
	KENT	I had rather break mine own. Good my lord, enter.
	LEAR	Thou think'st 'tis much that this contentious storm
		Invades us to the skin so: 'tis to thee,
10		But where the greater malady is fixed
		The lesser is scarce felt. Thou'dst shun a bear,
		But if thy flight lay toward the roaring sea
		Thou'dst meet the bear i'th'mouth. When the mind's
		free,
		The body's delicate: the tempest in my mind
15		Doth from my senses take all feeling else
		Save what beats there. Filial ingratitude!
		Is it not as this mouth should tear this hand
		For lifting food to't? But I will punish home.
		No, I will weep no more. In such a night
20		To shut me out? Pour on, I will endure.
		In such a night as this? O Regan, Goneril,
		Your old kind father, whose frank heart gave all —
		O, that way madness lies: let me shun that:
		No more of that.
25	KENT	Good my lord, enter here.
	LEAR	Prithee go in thyself: seek thine own ease:
		This tempest will not give me leave to ponder

3.4 *Location: outside a hovel somewhere out in the open, not far from the Earl of Gloucester's residence*   **3 nature** human nature   **10 greater malady** i.e. mental suffering **13 i'th'mouth** face to face   **free** free of worry, untroubled   **14 delicate** sensitive   **17 as** as if **18 home** soundly   **22 frank** generous

On things would hurt me more. But I'll go in.—
In, boy, go first.—   *To the Fool*

            You houseless poverty—
30 Nay, get thee in.— I'll pray, and then I'll sleep.

                                        Exit [*Fool*]

Poor naked wretches, wheresoe'er you are,   *Kneels*
That bide the pelting of this pitiless storm,
How shall your houseless heads and unfed sides,
Your lopped and windowed raggedness, defend you
35 From seasons such as these? O, I have ta'en
Too little care of this! Take physic, pomp,
Expose thyself to feel what wretches feel,
That thou mayst shake the superflux to them
And show the heavens more just.

Enter Edgar and Fool   *Within the hovel*
40 EDGAR   Fathom and half, fathom and half! Poor Tom!
    FOOL   Come not in here, nuncle, here's a spirit. Help me,
    help me!
    KENT   Give me thy hand. Who's there?
    FOOL   A spirit, a spirit: he says his name's poor Tom.
45 KENT   What art thou that dost grumble there i'th'straw?
    Come forth.

                      Edgar comes out, disguised as a mad beggar

    EDGAR   Away! The foul fiend follows me! Through the sharp
    hawthorn blow the winds. Hum! Go to thy bed and warm
    thee.
50 LEAR   Did'st thou give all to thy daughters? And art thou
    come to this?
    EDGAR   Who gives anything to poor Tom? Whom the foul
    fiend hath led through fire and through flame, through ford

---

32 bide endure   **33 sides** bodies (with visible ribs)   **34 lopped and windowed** full of holes
36 physic medicine (often a purgative)   **pomp** splendor, ostentatious display (i.e. rich and
powerful people)   **38 superflux** superfluity, excess (**flux** was used for a discharge of excrement
from the bowels, the result of a purgative)   **40 Fathom and half** Edgar calls as though he is
measuring the depth of the water in the hovel, as a sailor might in a leaking ship   **Fathom**
about six feet   **41 spirit** evil spirit, demon   **45 grumble** mutter, mumble   **52 foul** wicked

and whirlpool, o'er bog and quagmire, that hath laid knives
55   under his pillow, and halters in his pew, set ratsbane by his
porridge, made him proud of heart, to ride on a bay trotting-
horse over four-inched bridges, to course his own shadow for
a traitor. Bless thy five wits! Tom's a-cold. O, do de, do de, do
de. Bless thee from whirlwinds, star-blasting and taking! Do
60   poor Tom some charity, whom the foul fiend vexes: there
could I have him now — and there — and there again, and
there.

Storm still

LEAR   Has his daughters brought him to this pass?
Couldst thou save nothing? Wouldst thou give 'em all?

65   FOOL   Nay, he reserved a blanket, else we had been all
shamed.

LEAR   Now, all the plagues that in the pendulous air
Hang fated o'er men's faults light on thy daughters!

KENT   He hath no daughters, sir.

70   LEAR   Death, traitor! Nothing could have subdued nature
To such a lowness but his unkind daughters.
Is it the fashion that discarded fathers
Should have thus little mercy on their flesh?
Judicious punishment! 'Twas this flesh begot
75   Those pelican daughters.

EDGAR   Pillicock sat on Pillicock-hill: alow, alow, loo, loo!

---

54 knives . . . pew the devil was believed to tempt men to damnation by leaving them the
means of committing suicide (even in church)   55 ratsbane rat poison   56 porridge
vegetable or meat soup   bay reddish-brown   57 four-inched four inches wide (the devil gives
one the arrogance to try and perform extremely difficult feats)   course hunt   for as
58 five wits five mental faculties (common wit, imagination, fantasy, estimation, and memory)
do . . . de the sound of chattering teeth?   59 star-blasting being afflicted by the malign
influence of the stars   taking being infected with disease/malign influence of the stars
60 vexes torments   there . . . there perhaps Edgar snatches at parts of his body as he tries to
catch lice or the devil; or he may grab or point at the air around him   63 pass state,
predicament   65 reserved a blanket kept a blanket (to cover himself)   67 pendulous
overhanging   68 fated . . . faults destined to punish men's faults   70 subdued nature
reduced human nature   73 thus . . . flesh refers to Edgar's self-mutilation   75 pelican young
pelicans supposedly fed on their mother's blood; they were proverbial for filial cruelty
76 Pillicock . . . Pillicock-hill possibly part of an old nursery rhyme, but Pillicock is slang for
penis and Pillycock-hill the female genitals   alow . . . loo possibly from "halloo" (cry to incite
dogs in a hunt), perhaps an imitation of a cock's crow, or simply a nonsensical sound

FOOL   This cold night will turn us all to fools and madmen.

EDGAR   Take heed o'th'foul fiend: obey thy parents, keep thy
                word's justice, swear not, commit not with man's sworn
80   spouse, set not thy sweetheart on proud array. Tom's a-cold.

LEAR   What hast thou been?

EDGAR   A servingman, proud in heart and mind, that
                curled my hair, wore gloves in my cap, served the lust of my
                mistress' heart, and did the act of darkness with her: swore
85   as many oaths as I spake words, and broke them in the sweet
                face of heaven: one that slept in the contriving of lust, and
                waked to do it: wine loved I dearly, dice dearly, and in woman
                out-paramoured the Turk: false of heart, light of ear, bloody
                of hand: hog in sloth, fox in stealth, wolf in greediness, dog
90   in madness, lion in prey. Let not the creaking of shoes nor
                the rustling of silks betray thy poor heart to woman: keep
                thy foot out of brothels, thy hand out of plackets, thy pen
                from lenders' books, and defy the foul fiend. Still through the
                hawthorn blows the cold wind, says suum, mun, nonny,
95   Dolphin my boy, boy sessa! Let him trot by.

                Storm still

LEAR   Thou wert better in a grave than to answer with thy
                uncovered body this extremity of the skies. Is man no more
                than this? Consider him well. Thou ow'st the worm no silk,
                the beast no hide, the sheep no wool, the cat no perfume. Ha?
100   Here's three on's are sophisticated. Thou art the thing itself:
                unaccommodated man is no more but such a poor bare,

---

78 **obey** Edgar begins a paraphrased version of five of the Ten Commandments   79 **commit
not** i.e. do not commit adultery   80 **on proud array** in overly fine clothes   83 **gloves** i.e. a
mistress' gift, displayed by being worn in one's **cap**   86 **slept in** i.e. dreamed of   87 **dice** i.e.
gambling   88 **out-paramoured the Turk** had more lovers than the Turkish Sultan, famous for
his harem   **light of ear** eager to listen to gossip   90 **creaking . . . silks** i.e. the sounds of a
fashionable woman walking   92 **plackets** openings in skirts/vaginas   **pen . . . books** i.e. do
not sign a loan agreement   94 **suum, mun** presumably Edgar imitates the sounds of the wind
nonny often used as part of a refrain in popular songs   95 **Dolphin . . . by** perhaps Edgar
addresses an imaginary horse; **sessa** is a cry of encouragement used in hunting or may derive
from the French *cessez* ("stop")   96 **answer** face, encounter   99 **cat no perfume** the
secretions of the anal glands of the civet cat are used to make perfume   100 **on's** of us
sophisticated not simple or natural   101 **unaccommodated** unprovided for (i.e. not wearing
clothes)

forked animal as thou art. Off, off, you lendings! Come,
unbutton here.   *Tears off his clothes*

Enter Gloucester with a torch

FOOL   Prithee, nuncle, be contented: 'tis a naughty night
105   to swim in. Now a little fire in a wild field were like an old
lecher's heart, a small spark, all the rest on's body cold. Look,
here comes a walking fire.

EDGAR   This is the foul Flibbertigibbet: he begins at curfew
and walks till the first cock: he gives the web and the pin,
110   squints the eye and makes the hare-lip, mildews the white
wheat, and hurts the poor creature of earth.

Swithold footed thrice the old,   *Chants?*
He met the nightmare and her nine-fold;
Bid her alight,
115   And her troth plight,
And, aroint thee, witch, aroint thee!

KENT   How fares your grace?

LEAR   What's he?

KENT   Who's there? What is't you seek?

120   GLOUCESTER What are you there? Your names?

EDGAR   Poor Tom, that eats the swimming frog, the toad,
the tadpole, the wall-newt and the water, that in the fury of
his heart, when the foul fiend rages, eats cow-dung for
salads, swallows the old rat and the ditch-dog, drinks the
125   green mantle of the standing pool, who is whipped from
tithing to tithing, and stocked, punished and imprisoned,
who hath had three suits to his back, six shirts to his body:

---

102 lendings clothes that are "lent" only, not part of him   **104 naughty** nasty, wicked
107 walking fire i.e. Gloucester and his torch   **108 Flibbertigibbet** the name of a devil (all of
the devils Edgar mentions are to be found in Samuel Harsnett's 1603 *Declaration of Egregious
Popish Impostures*)   **curfew** i.e. nightfall   **109 cock** cockcrow   **web . . . pin** cataract of the
eye   **110 squints** causes to squint   **112 Swithold** probably Saint Withold, apparently a
protector from harm   **footed thrice** walked three times   **old** wold, downs   **113 nightmare**
evil female spirit supposed to settle upon a sleeper's chest, inducing bad dreams and feelings of
suffocation   **nine-fold** perhaps the imps who attend her   **115 her troth plight** give a solemn
promise (to do no more harm)   **116 aroint** begone (used to witches and demons)
118 What's who's   **122 wall-newt** i.e. lizard on the wall   **water** i.e. water newt   **124 ditch-
dog** i.e. dead dog in a ditch   **125 mantle** scum   **standing** stagnant   **whipped** the standard
punishment for vagabonds   **126 tithing** parish   **127 three . . . shirts** the clothing allowance
of a servant

Horse to ride, and weapon to wear,

But mice and rats and such small deer

130   Have been Tom's food for seven long year.

Beware my follower. Peace, Smulkin, peace, thou fiend!

GLOUCESTER What, hath your grace no better company?

EDGAR   The prince of darkness is a gentleman: Modo he's

called, and Mahu.

135   GLOUCESTER Our flesh and blood, my lord, is grown so   *To Lear*

vile,

That it doth hate what gets it.

EDGAR   Poor Tom's a-cold.

GLOUCESTER Go in with me: my duty cannot suffer

T'obey in all your daughters' hard commands:

140   Though their injunction be to bar my doors

And let this tyrannous night take hold upon you,

Yet have I ventured to come seek you out

And bring you where both fire and food is ready.

LEAR   First let me talk with this philosopher.—

145   What is the cause of thunder?   *To Edgar*

KENT   Good my lord, take his offer: go into th'house.

LEAR   I'll talk a word with this same learnèd Theban.—

What is your study?   *To Edgar*

EDGAR   How to prevent the fiend and to kill vermin.

150   LEAR   Let me ask you one word in private.   *They talk apart*

KENT   Importune him once more to go, my lord: *To Gloucester*

His wits begin t'unsettle.

GLOUCESTER Canst thou blame him?

Storm still

His daughters seek his death. Ah, that good Kent!

155   He said it would be thus, poor banished man!

---

129 deer animals   **131 Smulkin** the name of a devil (that, according to Harsnett, took the
form of a mouse)   **133 The . . . darkness** the devil   **Modo . . . Mahu** the names of two devils
135 flesh and blood i.e. children (Gloucester is thinking of Edgar, Goneril, and Regan)   **vile**
debased, corrupted   **136 gets** begets, conceives   **147 Theban** i.e. Greek philosopher (from
Thebes)   **149 prevent** forestall, thwart   **151 Importune** urge   **152 t'unsettle** to be disturbed

Thou sayest the king grows mad: I'll tell thee, friend,
I am almost mad myself. I had a son,
Now outlawed from my blood: he sought my life
But lately, very late. I loved him, friend:

160 No father his son dearer. True to tell thee,
The grief hath crazed my wits. What a night's this!—
I do beseech your grace—   *To Lear*

LEAR   O, cry you mercy, sir.—
Noble philosopher, your company.   *To Edgar*

165 EDGAR   Tom's a-cold.

GLOUCESTER In, fellow, there, into th'hovel: keep thee   *To Edgar*
warm.

LEAR   Come let's in all.

KENT   This way, my lord.

LEAR   With him;

170 I will keep still with my philosopher.

KENT   Good my lord, soothe him: let him take   *To Gloucester*
the fellow.

GLOUCESTER Take him you on.   *To Kent*

KENT   Sirrah, come on: go along with us.   *To Edgar*

LEAR   Come, good Athenian.

175 GLOUCESTER No words, no words: hush.

EDGAR   Child Rowland to the dark tower came,
His word was still: fie, foh and fum,
I smell the blood of a British man.   *Exeunt*

---

158 blood lineage, family   **163 cry you mercy** excuse me   **170 keep still** remain
171 soothe indulge, humor   **172 him you on** him along with you   **174 Athenian** i.e. Greek
philosopher (from Athens)   **176 Child . . . came** perhaps a line from a lost ballad about the
legendary French hero Roland (**Child** was the title for a young man seeking knighthood)
177 word password/customary saying   **still** always   **fie . . . man** the cry of the giant in the
children's tale of Jack the giant-killer

Act 3 Scene 5

Enter Cornwall and Edmund

CORNWALL   I will have my revenge ere I depart his house.

EDMUND   How, my lord, I may be censured, that nature thus
gives way to loyalty, something fears me to think of.

5   CORNWALL   I now perceive it was not altogether your brother's
evil disposition made him seek his death, but a provoking
merit set a-work by a reprovable badness in himself.

EDMUND   How malicious is my fortune — that I must repent
to be just! This is the letter which he spoke of   *Shows a letter*
which approves him an intelligent party to the advantages of

10   France. O heavens! That this treason were not, or not I the
detector!

CORNWALL   Go with me to the duchess.

EDMUND   If the matter of this paper be certain, you have
mighty business in hand.

15   CORNWALL   True or false, it hath made thee Earl of Gloucester.
Seek out where thy father is, that he may be ready for our
apprehension.

EDMUND   If I find him comforting the king, it will stuff   *Aside*
his suspicion more fully.— I will persevere in my course of

20   loyalty, though the conflict be sore between that and my
blood.

CORNWALL   I will lay trust upon thee, and thou shalt find a dear
father in my love.

Exeunt

3.5   *Location: the Earl of Gloucester's residence*   **1 his** i.e. Gloucester's   **2 nature**
natural familial affection   **3 something fears** somewhat frightens   **5 his** i.e. Gloucester's
provoking . . . himself Edgar's sense of his own worth, provoked into action by Gloucester's
reprehensible badness/a provoking quality in Gloucester, which incited Edgar's reprehensible
wickedness   **8 to be** of being   **9 approves** proves   **an intelligent party** a spy, an informer
17 apprehension arrest   **19 his suspicion** suspicion of Gloucester

Act 3 Scene 6

Enter Kent and Gloucester

GLOUCESTER Here is better than the open air, take it thankfully. I
will piece out the comfort with what addition I can: I will not
be long from you.   *Exit*

KENT   All the power of his wits have given way to his
5   impatience: the gods reward your kindness!

Enter Lear, Edgar and Fool   *Edgar disguised as Poor Tom*

EDGAR   Frateretto calls me, and tells me Nero is an angler in
the lake of darkness. Pray, innocent, and beware the foul
fiend.

FOOL   Prithee, nuncle, tell me whether a madman be a
10   gentleman or a yeoman?

LEAR   A king, a king!

FOOL   No, he's a yeoman that has a gentleman to his son,
for he's a mad yeoman that sees his son a gentleman before
him.

15 LEAR   To have a thousand with red burning spits
Come hizzing in upon 'em—

EDGAR   Bless thy five wits!

KENT   O pity! Sir, where is the patience now
That you so oft have boasted to retain?

20 EDGAR   My tears begin to take his part so much   *Aside*
They mar my counterfeiting.

**3.6   Location: unspecified; presumably an outbuilding on the Earl of Gloucester's
estate   2 piece out** supplement   **5 impatience** anger/inability to bear suffering
6 Frateretto the name of a devil; in Harsnett he is associated with a "fiddler," which perhaps
suggests **Nero**, the first-century Roman emperor who famously played the fiddle while Rome
burned   **angler** fisherman/thief   **7 lake of darkness** presumably the Stygian lake of the
classical underworld, but a phallic fishing rod and vaginal dark lake may also be implied;
perhaps Nero's murder of his own mother is glanced at—she reportedly asked to be stabbed in
the womb as this was where her son had grown   **10 yeoman** land owner below the rank of
gentleman   **12 to** as   **13 mad** sense now shifts to "angry"   **15 a thousand** i.e. a thousand
devils   **16 hizzing** hissing   **'em** them i.e. Goneril and Regan; the Quarto text continues at
this point with an imaginary "arraignment" of Goneril (see "Quarto Passages That Do Not
Appear in the Folio," p. 132)   **21 mar my counterfeiting** spoil my pretense

LEAR   The little dogs and all,
          Trey, Blanch and Sweetheart, see, they bark at me.

EDGAR   Tom will throw his head at them. Avaunt, you curs!
25   Be thy mouth or black or white,
          Tooth that poisons if it bite,
          Mastiff, greyhound, mongrel grim,
          Hound or spaniel, brach or him,
          Or bobtail tyke or trundle-tail,
30   Tom will make him weep and wail:
          For, with throwing thus my head,
          Dogs leapt the hatch, and all are fled.
     Do de, de, de. Sessa! Come, march to wakes and fairs and
     market towns. Poor Tom, thy horn is dry.

35   LEAR   Then let them anatomize Regan: see what breeds
     about her heart. Is there any cause in nature that make
     these hard hearts?— You, sir, I entertain for one of   *To Edgar*
     my hundred; only I do not like the fashion of your garments:
     you will say they are Persian; but let them be changed.

Enter Gloucester   *At a distance*

40   KENT   Now, good my lord, lie here and rest awhile.

     LEAR   Make no noise, make no noise: draw the curtains.
     So, so, we'll go to supper i'th'morning.   *Sleeps*

     FOOL   And I'll go to bed at noon.

     GLOUCESTER   Come hither, friend: where is the king my   *To Kent*
          master?

45   KENT   Here, sir, but trouble him not: his wits are gone.

---

23 Trey . . . Sweetheart names for bitches—even his female dogs, he imagines, have turned
against him; their names may suggest Lear's daughters ("tray" can mean "pain, affliction,"
"blanch" can mean "to deceive," "to flatter")   **24 throw his head** unclear; presumably a
threatening gesture of some sort   **Avaunt** begone   **25 or black or** either black or
26 poisons i.e. with rabies   **27 grim** fierce   **28 brach** bitch   **him** male   **29 bobtail tyke**
small dog with a tail that has been bobbed (cut short)   **trundle-tail** dog with a long, curling
tail   **32 hatch** lower half of a divided door   **33 Do . . . de** apparently the sound of chattering
teeth again   **Sessa!** cry of encouragement used in hunting or may derive from the French
cessez ("stop")   **wakes** annual parish fairs (frequented by beggars)   **34 horn** beggars carried
drinking horns on strings round their necks   **35 anatomize** dissect   **37 entertain** employ
39 Persian i.e. gorgeous, luxurious   **41 curtains** Lear imagines that he is in a curtained bed

GLOUCESTER Good friend, I prithee take him in thy
     arms;
    I have o'erheard a plot of death upon him:
    There is a litter ready, lay him in't
    And drive toward Dover, friend, where thou shalt
     meet
50   Both welcome and protection. Take up thy master:
    If thou shouldst dally half an hour, his life,
    With thine and all that offer to defend him,
    Stand in assurèd loss. Take up, take up,
    And follow me, that will to some provision   *They carry Lear*
55   Give thee quick conduct. Come, come, away.   *Exeunt*

Act 3 Scene 7   *running scene 11*

Enter Cornwall, Regan, Goneril, Bastard [Edmund] and Servants

CORNWALL Post speedily to my lord your husband;   *To Goneril*
    show him this letter: the army of France is   *Gives a letter*
    landed.— Seek out the traitor Gloucester.

                        [Exeunt some Servants]

REGAN   Hang him instantly.
5 GONERIL   Pluck out his eyes.
CORNWALL Leave him to my displeasure. Edmund, keep you our
    sister company: the revenges we are bound to take upon
    your traitorous father are not fit for your beholding. Advise
    the duke where you are going, to a most festinate
10   preparation: we are bound to the like. Our posts shall be swift
    and intelligent betwixt us. Farewell, dear sister: farewell, my
    lord of Gloucester.

---

48 litter vehicle containing a bed, here apparently drawn by horses   **49 Dover** port on the
south coast   **54 to . . . conduct** i.e. hastily guide you to the necessary supplies for your
journey   **3.7   *Location: the Earl of Gloucester's residence*   1 Post** travel swiftly
7 sister sister-in-law, i.e. Goneril   **8 Advise** counsel, urge   **9 duke** i.e. the Duke of Albany
festinate preparation hasty preparation of troops   **10 posts** messengers   **11 intelligent**
possessed of information   **12 lord of Gloucester** Edmund's new title (though when Oswald
uses it, he refers to Edmund's father)

Enter Oswald

How now? Where's the king?

15 OSWALD   My lord of Gloucester hath conveyed him
       hence:
    Some five- or six-and-thirty of his knights,
    Hot questrists after him, met him at gate,
    Who, with some other of the lord's dependants,
    Are gone with him toward Dover, where they boast
20 To have well-armèd friends.

CORNWALL   Get horses for your mistress.

GONERIL   Farewell, sweet lord, and sister.

                    Exeunt [Goneril, Edmund and Oswald]

CORNWALL   Edmund, farewell.—
    Go seek the traitor Gloucester,
25 Pinion him like a thief, bring him before us.

                    [Exeunt other Servants]

    Though well we may not pass upon his life
    Without the form of justice, yet our power
    Shall do a court'sy to our wrath, which men
    May blame but not control.

Enter Gloucester and Servants

                    Who's there? The traitor?

30 REGAN   Ingrateful fox! 'Tis he.

CORNWALL   Bind fast his corky arms.

GLOUCESTER   What means your graces?
    Good my friends, consider you are my guests:
    Do me no foul play, friends.

35 CORNWALL   Bind him, I say.   *Servants bind him*

REGAN   Hard, hard. O, filthy traitor!

GLOUCESTER   Unmerciful lady as you are, I'm none.

CORNWALL   To this chair bind him.— Villain, thou shalt find—

                    Regan plucks his beard

---

17 questrists seekers   **18 the lord's** i.e. Gloucester's   **25 Pinion him** bind his arms
26 pass . . . justice issue a death sentence without a formal trial   **28 do a court'sy** bow, yield
31 corky withered, dry   *plucks his beard* a highly insulting gesture

GLOUCESTER By the kind gods, 'tis most ignobly done
40   To pluck me by the beard.
REGAN   So white, and such a traitor?
GLOUCESTER Naughty lady,
    These hairs which thou dost ravish from my chin
    Will quicken and accuse thee. I am your host:
45 With robbers' hands my hospitable favours
    You should not ruffle thus. What will you do?
CORNWALL   Come, sir, what letters had you late from
        France?
REGAN   Be simple answered, for we know the truth.
CORNWALL   And what confederacy have you with the traitors
50 Late footed in the kingdom?
REGAN   To whose hands you have sent the lunatic king?
        Speak.
GLOUCESTER I have a letter guessingly set down,
    Which came from one that's of a neutral heart,
    And not from one opposed.
55 CORNWALL   Cunning.
REGAN   And false.
CORNWALL   Where hast thou sent the king?
GLOUCESTER To Dover.
REGAN   Wherefore to Dover? Wast thou not charged at
        peril—
60 CORNWALL   Wherefore to Dover? Let him answer that.
GLOUCESTER I am tied to th'stake and I must stand the
        course.
REGAN   Wherefore to Dover?
GLOUCESTER Because I would not see thy cruel nails
    Pluck out his poor old eyes, nor thy fierce sister

---

41 white i.e. old, dignified   **42 Naughty** wicked   **43 ravish** seize forcibly, pluck   **44 quicken**
come to life   **45 hospitable favours** welcoming (facial) features   **46 ruffle** treat roughly/
snatch   **48 Be simple answered** answer straightforwardly   **50 Late footed** recently landed
52 guessingly without certain knowledge   **54 opposed** i.e. to the dukes   **59 charged at peril**
commanded on peril of your life   **61 tied to th'stake** like a bear in the popular sport of bear-
baiting   **stand** endure   **course** designated bout, during which the bear was attacked by dogs

65   In his anointed flesh stick boarish fangs.
      The sea, with such a storm as his bare head
      In hell-black night endured, would have buoyed up
      And quenched the stellèd fires:
      Yet, poor old heart, he holp the heavens to rain.
70   If wolves had at thy gate howled that stern time,
      Thou shouldst have said 'Good porter, turn the key.'
      All cruels else subscribe: but I shall see
      The wingèd vengeance overtake such children.

CORNWALL   See't shalt thou never. Fellows, hold the
      chair.—
75   Upon these eyes of thine I'll set my foot.

GLOUCESTER   He that will think to live till he be old,
      Give me some help! O cruel! O you gods!   *Cornwall grinds out his eye*

REGAN   One side will mock another: th'other too.

CORNWALL   If you see vengeance—

80   SERVANT   Hold your hand, my lord:
      I have served you ever since I was a child,
      But better service have I never done you
      Than now to bid you hold.

REGAN   How now, you dog?

85   SERVANT   If you did wear a beard upon your chin,   *To Regan*
      I'd shake it on this quarrel.— What do you mean?

CORNWALL   My villain?   *They draw and fight*

SERVANT   Nay, then, come on, and take the chance of anger.

REGAN   Give me thy sword. A peasant stand up   *To a Servant*
      thus?
      Kills him

90   SERVANT   O, I am slain! My lord, you have one eye left
      To see some mischief on him. O!   *Dies*

---

65 anointed i.e. holy (having been anointed with holy oil at the coronation)   **67 buoyed**
swelled, risen   **68 stellèd** starry   **69 holp . . . rain** i.e. by weeping   **holp** helped   **70 stern**
cruel, unyielding   **71 turn the key** i.e. to let them in   **72 All . . . subscribe** i.e. in such
circumstances, all other cruel people would sanction a kind action   **73 wingèd vengeance** i.e.
vengeance of the gods   **74 Fellows** servants   **86 shake . . . quarrel** i.e. defy you (or
"challenge you to a fight") over this cause   **What . . . mean?** What do you think you are
doing?   **87 villain** servant   **88 chance of anger** risk of what anger may bring (in a fight)
91 mischief on him injury done to him

CORNWALL   Lest it see more, prevent it. Out, vile jelly!   *Puts out*

Where is thy lustre now?   *Gloucester's other eye*

GLOUCESTER All dark and comfortless. Where's my son
Edmund?

95   Edmund, enkindle all the sparks of nature
To quit this horrid act.

REGAN   Out, treacherous villain!
Thou call'st on him that hates thee: it was he
That made the overture of thy treasons to us,

100   Who is too good to pity thee.

GLOUCESTER O, my follies! Then Edgar was abused.
Kind gods, forgive me that, and prosper him!

REGAN   Go thrust him out at gates, and let him smell
His way to Dover.   *Exit [a Servant] with Gloucester*

105   How is't, my lord? How look you?

CORNWALL   I have received a hurt: follow me, lady.—
Turn out that eyeless villain: throw this slave
Upon the dunghill.— Regan, I bleed apace:
Untimely comes this hurt. Give me your arm.   *Exeunt*

Act 4 Scene 1   *running scene 12*

Enter Edgar   *Disguised as Poor Tom*

EDGAR   Yet better thus, and known to be contemned,
Than still contemned and flattered. To be worst,
The lowest and most dejected thing of fortune,
Stands still in esperance, lives not in fear:

---

95 **sparks of nature** warmth of natural filial affection   96 **quit** requite, avenge   97 **Out**
expression of impatience and disgust   99 **overture** disclosure   101 **abused** wronged,
maligned   105 **How look you?** How are you?   108 **apace** rapidly   109 **Untimely** at the
wrong time (with war imminent)   *Exeunt* here the Quarto text has an additional sequence in
which loyal servants apply a palliative to Gloucester's eye sockets (see "Quarto Passages That
Do Not Appear in the Folio," p. 134)   **4.1   *Location: somewhere out in the open, not far
from the Earl of Gloucester's residence*   1 **thus** i.e. a beggar   **contemned** despised
2 **contemned and flattered** despised secretly though flattered to your face   4 **esperance** hope

5   The lamentable change is from the best,
       The worst returns to laughter. Welcome, then,
       Thou unsubstantial air that I embrace!
       The wretch that thou hast blown unto the worst
       Owes nothing to thy blasts.

Enter Gloucester and an Old Man

10   But who comes here? My father, poorly led?
       World, world, O world!
       But that thy strange mutations make us hate thee,
       Life would not yield to age.

OLD MAN   O, my good lord, I have been your tenant and your
15   father's tenant these fourscore years.

GLOUCESTER Away, get thee away! Good friend, be
       gone:
       Thy comforts can do me no good at all,
       Thee they may hurt.

OLD MAN   You cannot see your way.

20 GLOUCESTER I have no way and therefore want no eyes:
       I stumbled when I saw. Full oft 'tis seen
       Our means secure us, and our mere defects
       Prove our commodities. O dear son Edgar,
       The food of thy abusèd father's wrath!

25   Might I but live to see thee in my touch,
       I'd say I had eyes again!

OLD MAN   How now? Who's there?

EDGAR   O gods! Who is't can say, 'I am at the worst'?   *Aside*
       I am worse than e'er I was.

30 OLD MAN   'Tis poor mad Tom.

EDGAR   And worse I may be yet: the worst is not   *Aside*
       So long as we can say 'This is the worst.'

---

5 The . . . laughter the most miserable kind of change is a decline in fortunes; when things are
at their worst they can only get better   **10 poorly led** led by a poor man/led in a way
unsuitable to his status   **12 But** were it not   **mutations** changes/fickleness   **13 Life . . . age**
we would not accept old age   **15 fourscore** eighty   **18 Thee . . . hurt** i.e. you may be
punished for helping me   **22 means secure us** wealth gives us false security, overconfidence
mere defects sheer deficiencies   **23 Prove our commodities** turn out to be benefits
24 abusèd deceived   **31 is not** has not yet arrived

OLD MAN   Fellow, where goest?

GLOUCESTER Is it a beggar-man?

35 OLD MAN   Madman and beggar too.

GLOUCESTER He has some reason, else he could not beg.
　　I'th'last night's storm I such a fellow saw,
　　Which made me think a man a worm: my son
　　Came then into my mind and yet my mind
40　Was then scarce friends with him. I have heard more
　　　since.
　　As flies to wanton boys are we to th'gods:
　　They kill us for their sport.

EDGAR   How should this be?   *Aside*
　　Bad is the trade that must play fool to sorrow,
45　Ang'ring itself and others.— Bless thee, master!

GLOUCESTER Is that the naked fellow?

OLD MAN   Ay, my lord.

GLOUCESTER Get thee away: if for my sake
　　Thou wilt o'ertake us hence a mile or twain
50　I'th'way toward Dover, do it for ancient love,
　　And bring some covering for this naked soul,
　　Which I'll entreat to lead me.

OLD MAN   Alack, sir, he is mad.

GLOUCESTER 'Tis the time's plague, when madmen lead the
　　blind.
55　Do as I bid thee, or rather do thy pleasure:
　　Above the rest, be gone.

OLD MAN   I'll bring him the best 'pparel that I have,
　　Come on't what will.   *Exit*

GLOUCESTER Sirrah, naked fellow—

60 EDGAR   Poor Tom's a-cold.— I cannot daub it further.   *Aside*

GLOUCESTER Come hither, fellow.

---

36 reason rationality, sanity   **41 wanton** unruly/cruelly mischievous   **44 trade** course of
action/practice   **50 ancient love** old affection   **54 plague** affliction   **56 the rest** all
57 'pparel apparel, clothing   **58 Come . . . will** whatever may come of it   **60 daub it** put on a
false face, pretend

EDGAR   And yet I must.— Bless thy sweet eyes, they   *Aside*
    bleed.
GLOUCESTER Know'st thou the way to Dover?
EDGAR   Both stile and gate, horseway and footpath. Poor
65   Tom hath been scared out of his good wits: bless thee, good
    man's son, from the foul fiend!
GLOUCESTER Here, take this purse, thou whom the heav'ns'
    plagues   *Gives a purse*
    Have humbled to all strokes: that I am wretched
    Makes thee the happier: heavens, deal so still.
70   Let the superfluous and lust-dieted man,
    That slaves your ordinance, that will not see
    Because he does not feel, feel your pow'r quickly,
    So distribution should undo excess,
    And each man have enough. Dost thou know Dover?
75   EDGAR   Ay, master.
GLOUCESTER There is a cliff, whose high and bending
    head
    Looks fearfully in the confinèd deep:
    Bring me but to the very brim of it
    And I'll repair the misery thou dost bear
80   With something rich about me: from that place
    I shall no leading need.
EDGAR   Give me thy arm:
    Poor Tom shall lead thee.   *Exeunt*

68 strokes blows, afflictions   **69 happier** more fortunate   **70 superfluous** immoderate,
extravagant, overindulgent   **lust-dieted** fed solely by pleasure   **71 slaves your ordinance**
subjects your laws to his desires   **72 feel** empathize, feel compassion (sense then shifts to
"experience")   **quickly** soon/while he is alive/sharply   **76 bending** overhanging
77 confinèd channeled (between England and France)   **78 brim** edge   **80 about me** that I
have on my person

Act 4 Scene 2

Enter Goneril, Bastard [Edmund] and Steward [Oswald]

GONERIL   Welcome, my lord: I marvel our mild husband
Not met us on the way.— Now, where's your
master?

OSWALD   Madam, within, but never man so changed.
I told him of the army that was landed,

5   He smiled at it: I told him you were coming,
His answer was 'The worse': of Gloucester's
treachery
And of the loyal service of his son
When I informed him, then he called me 'sot'
And told me I had turned the wrong side out.

10   What most he should dislike seems pleasant to him;
What like, offensive.

GONERIL   Then shall you go no further.   *To Edmund*
It is the cowish terror of his spirit,
That dares not undertake: he'll not feel wrongs

15   Which tie him to an answer. Our wishes on the way
May prove effects. Back, Edmund, to my brother:
Hasten his musters and conduct his powers.
I must change names at home and give the distaff
Into my husband's hands. This trusty servant

20   Shall pass between us: ere long you are like to
hear —
If you dare venture in your own behalf —
A mistress's command. Wear this; spare speech.   *Gives a favor*
Decline your head: this kiss, if it durst speak,   *Kisses him*

4.2   *Location: outside Goneril and the Duke of Albany's residence*   **1 my lord** i.e.
Edmund   **4 army** i.e. French army   **8 'sot'** fool   **9 turned . . . out** turned inside out, got
things the wrong way round (clothing metaphor)   **13 cowish** cowardly   **14 undertake** take
action   **15 tie . . . answer** oblige him to respond   **on the way** i.e. that we expressed during
the journey here   **16 prove effects** be fulfilled   **brother** brother-in-law, i.e. Cornwall
17 musters gathering of troops   **conduct his powers** escort his forces   **18 change** exchange
distaff spindle for weaving, common symbol of womanhood or wifeliness   **20 like** likely
22 mistress ruler/lover   *favor* love token

Would stretch thy spirits up into the air.

25   Conceive, and fare thee well.

EDMUND   Yours in the ranks of death.   *Exit*

GONERIL   My most dear Gloucester!

O, the difference of man and man!

To thee a woman's services are due:

30   My fool usurps my body.

OSWALD   Madam, here comes my lord.   *Exit*

Enter Albany

GONERIL   I have been worth the whistle.

ALBANY   O Goneril,

You are not worth the dust which the rude wind

35   Blows in your face.

GONERIL   Milk-livered man,

That bear'st a cheek for blows, a head for wrongs,

Who hast not in thy brows an eye discerning

Thine honour from thy suffering.

40   ALBANY   See thyself, devil!

Proper deformity seems not in the fiend

So horrid as in woman.

GONERIL   O vain fool!

Enter a Messenger

MESSENGER   O, my good lord, the Duke of Cornwall's

dead,

45   Slain by his servant, going to put out

The other eye of Gloucester.

ALBANY   Gloucester's eyes?

---

24 thy Goneril starts to use the more intimate pronoun to Edmund   **spirits** plays on sense of "penis"   **25 conceive** understand/imagine (with procreative connotations)   **26 death** plays on sense of "orgasm"   **29 services** sexual services   **30 fool** i.e. Albany   **usurps** wrongfully possesses   **32 worth the whistle** worth looking for (from the proverb "it is a poor dog that is not worth the whistling")   **33 Goneril . . . face** the Quarto text has a longer dialogue in which Albany berates Goneril (see "Quarto Passages That Do Not Appear in the Folio," p. 135) **34 rude** rough   **36 Milk-livered** pale-livered, cowardly (cowardice was associated with lack of blood in the liver and milk with women)   **38 discerning . . . suffering** that can distinguish between what may be honorably tolerated from what must not be endured   **41 Proper . . . woman** deformity does not seem as abhorrent in a devil (to whom it is appropriate) as it does in a woman   **43 vain** stupid/worthless

MESSENGER   A servant that he bred, thrilled with
    remorse,
    Opposed against the act, bending his sword
50   To his great master, who, threat-enraged,
    Flew on him and amongst them felled him dead,
    But not without that harmful stroke which since
    Hath plucked him after.
ALBANY   This shows you are above,
55   You justices, that these our nether crimes
    So speedily can venge. But, O, poor Gloucester!
    Lost he his other eye?
MESSENGER   Both, both, my lord.—
    This letter, madam, craves a speedy answer: *Gives a letter*
60   'Tis from your sister.
GONERIL   One way I like this well: *Aside*
    But being widow, and my Gloucester with her,
    May all the building in my fancy pluck
    Upon my hateful life: another way,
65   The news is not so tart.— I'll read, and answer.   [*Exit*]
ALBANY   Where was his son when they did take his eyes?
MESSENGER   Come with my lady hither.
ALBANY   He is not here.
MESSENGER   No, my good lord, I met him back again.
70 ALBANY   Knows he the wickedness?
MESSENGER   Ay, my good lord: 'twas he informed against
    him,
    And quit the house on purpose that their punishment
    Might have the freer course.
ALBANY   Gloucester, I live
75   To thank thee for the love thou showed'st the king

---

48 bred brought up in his household   **thrilled** pierced, moved   **remorse** pity (for Gloucester)
49 Opposed opposed himself   **bending** aiming, directing   **50 threat-enraged** enraged by the
threat   **53 after** i.e. to death   **55 justices** (divine) judges   **nether** earthly   **56 venge**
avenge, punish   **63 all . . . life** demolish the dream (of having Edmund) that I have
constructed, leaving me with the life I hate   **65 tart** sour   **69 back** going back

And to revenge thine eyes.— Come hither, friend:
Tell me what more thou know'st.   *Exeunt*

Act 4 Scene 3   *running scene 14*

Enter with Drum and Colours Cordelia, Gentleman and Soldiers

CORDELIA   Alack, 'tis he: why, he was met even now
As mad as the vexed sea, singing aloud,
Crowned with rank fumiter and furrow weeds,
With burdocks, hemlock, nettles, cuckoo-flowers,

5   Darnel, and all the idle weeds that grow
In our sustaining corn. A sentry send forth;
Search every acre in the high-grown field
And bring him to our eye.—   [*Exit a Soldier*]
                    What can man's wisdom
In the restoring his bereavèd sense?

10   He that helps him take all my outward worth.
GENTLEMAN   There is means, madam:
Our foster-nurse of nature is repose,
The which he lacks: that to provoke in him
Are many simples operative, whose power

15   Will close the eye of anguish.
CORDELIA   All blest secrets,
All you unpublished virtues of the earth,
Spring with my tears! Be aidant and remediate

4.3   *Location: the French camp, near Dover. The Quarto text precedes this scene
with another one in which Kent and a Gentleman discuss the French king's return to
France and Cordelia's concern for her father (see "Quarto Passages That Do Not
Appear in the Folio," pp. 137–39)   Colours* military banners   *Gentleman* perhaps the
same man that Kent gave instructions to in Act 3 Scene 1   2 *vexed* angry, turbulent   3 *rank
fumiter* abundant fumitory (a vigorously growing weed)   *furrow weeds* weeds that grow in
the furrows of plowed fields   4 *burdocks* weeds with prickly flower heads or burs   *hemlock*
plant producing a potentially lethal sedative   *cuckoo-flowers* name given to various
wildflowers growing when the cuckoo calls (i.e. May/June)   5 *Darnel* type of grass that grows
as a weed among corn   *idle* useless   8 *What . . . wisdom* what can human knowledge do
9 *bereavèd* stolen, lost   10 *outward worth* worldly goods   12 *repose* rest, sleep   13 *that . . .
operative* there are many effective medicinal herbs that can induce that in him
17 *unpublished virtues* secret powers (of herbs)   18 *aidant* helpful   *remediate* remedial,
healing

In the good man's distress! Seek, seek for him,
20 Lest his ungoverned rage dissolve the life
That wants the means to lead it.

Enter Messenger

MESSENGER   News, madam:
The British powers are marching hitherward.

CORDELIA   'Tis known before: our preparation stands
25 In expectation of them. O dear father,
It is thy business that I go about:
Therefore great France
My mourning and importuned tears hath pitied.
No blown ambition doth our arms incite,
30 But love, dear love, and our aged father's right:
Soon may I hear and see him!   *Exeunt*

Act 4 Scene 4

Enter Regan and Steward [Oswald]

REGAN   But are my brother's powers set forth?
OSWALD   Ay, madam.
REGAN   Himself in person there?
OSWALD   Madam, with much ado:
5   Your sister is the better soldier.
REGAN   Lord Edmund spake not with your lord at home?
OSWALD   No, madam.
REGAN   What might import my sister's letter to him?
OSWALD   I know not, lady.
10 REGAN   Faith, he is posted hence on serious matter.
It was great ignorance, Gloucester's eyes being out,
To let him live: where he arrives he moves
All hearts against us. Edmund, I think, is gone,

---

20 rage frenzy   **21 wants the means** i.e. lacks the sanity   **24 preparation** equipped military force   **27 France** i.e. the King of France   **28 importuned** importunate, pressing   **29 blown** swollen with pride/corrupt   **4.4   *Location: the Earl of Gloucester's residence*   **4 ado** fuss   **8 import** mean, contain   **10 posted** hurried   **11 ignorance** folly

In pity of his misery, to dispatch
15   His nighted life: moreover, to descry
The strength o'th'enemy.

OSWALD   I must needs after him, madam, with my letter.

REGAN   Our troops set forth tomorrow. Stay with us:
The ways are dangerous.

20   OSWALD   I may not, madam:
My lady charged my duty in this business.

REGAN   Why should she write to Edmund? Might not you
Transport her purposes by word? Belike,
Some things I know not what. I'll love thee much,
25   Let me unseal the letter.

OSWALD   Madam, I had rather—

REGAN   I know your lady does not love her husband,
I am sure of that: and at her late being here
She gave strange oeillades and most speaking looks
30   To noble Edmund. I know you are of her bosom.

OSWALD   I, madam?

REGAN   I speak in understanding. Y'are, I know't.
Therefore I do advise you, take this note.
My lord is dead: Edmund and I have talked,
35   And more convenient is he for my hand
Than for your lady's: you may gather more.
If you do find him, pray you give him this,   *Gives a token or a letter*
And when your mistress hears thus much from you,
I pray desire her call her wisdom to her.
40   So, fare you well.
If you do chance to hear of that blind traitor,
Preferment falls on him that cuts him off.

---

15 nighted darkened (literally, and in terms of his fortunes)   **descry** discover   **17 after** go
after   **19 ways** roads   **21 charged my duty** swore me to obedience   **23 Belike** perhaps/
probably   **24 I'll love thee** Regan switches to the familiar **thee** to cajole him—**love** implies the
promise of favors, sexual or otherwise   **29 oeillades** amorous glances   **speaking** eloquent
30 of her bosom in her confidence/sexually intimate   **32 Y'are** ye (you) are   **33 take this
note** note this well   **35 convenient** fitting   **36 gather more** infer the rest   **39 call . . . her**
have more sense

OSWALD   Would I could meet, madam, I should show
What party I do follow.

45 REGAN   Fare thee well.   *Exeunt*

Act 4 Scene 5

Enter Gloucester and Edgar   *Edgar dressed like a peasant*

GLOUCESTER When shall I come to th'top of that same
hill?

EDGAR   You do climb up it now: look how we labour.

GLOUCESTER Methinks the ground is even.

EDGAR   Horrible steep.

5 Hark, do you hear the sea?

GLOUCESTER No, truly.

EDGAR   Why, then, your other senses grow imperfect
By your eyes' anguish.

GLOUCESTER So may it be, indeed:

10 Methinks thy voice is altered and thou speak'st
In better phrase and matter than thou didst.

EDGAR   You're much deceived: in nothing am I changed
But in my garments.

GLOUCESTER Methinks you're better spoken.

15 EDGAR   Come on, sir, here's the place: stand still. How
fearful
And dizzy 'tis to cast one's eyes so low!
The crows and choughs that wing the midway air
Show scarce so gross as beetles: halfway down
Hangs one that gathers samphire, dreadful trade!

20 Methinks he seems no bigger than his head.
The fishermen that walk upon the beach

---

43 **meet** i.e. meet him   **4.5** *Location: somewhere out in the open, near Dover*   1 **that**
same hill the hill I mentioned (i.e. the cliff Gloucester described at the end of Act 4 Scene 1)
11 **phrase and matter** style and sense   17 **choughs** jackdaws or other birds of the crow family
wing fly across   **midway** i.e. middle regions of   18 **gross** large   19 **samphire** aromatic plant
used in pickling; it was picked from cliffs by men suspended on ropes

Appear like mice, and yond tall anchoring bark
Diminished to her cock, her cock, a buoy
Almost too small for sight. The murmuring surge,
25 That on th'unnumbered idle pebble chafes,
Cannot be heard so high. I'll look no more,
Lest my brain turn and the deficient sight
Topple down headlong.

GLOUCESTER Set me where you stand.

30 EDGAR   Give me your hand: you are now within a foot
Of th'extreme verge: for all beneath the moon
Would I not leap upright.

GLOUCESTER Let go my hand.

Here, friend's another purse: in it a jewel   *Gives a purse*
35 Well worth a poor man's taking: fairies and gods
Prosper it with thee! Go thou further off:
Bid me farewell, and let me hear thee going.

EDGAR   Now fare ye well, good sir.

GLOUCESTER With all my heart.

40 EDGAR   Why I do trifle thus with his despair   *Aside*
Is done to cure it.

GLOUCESTER O you mighty gods!   *Kneels*
This world I do renounce, and in your sights
Shake patiently my great affliction off:
45 If I could bear it longer, and not fall
To quarrel with your great opposeless wills,
My snuff and loathèd part of nature should
Burn itself out. If Edgar live, O, bless him!—
Now, fellow, fare thee well.   *He falls forward*

50 EDGAR   Gone, sir: farewell.—
And yet I know not how conceit may rob   *Aside*
The treasury of life, when life itself

---

22 yond yonder, that   **bark** small ship   **23 her cock** (the size of) her cock boat, a small boat
towed behind a ship   **25 th'unnumbered idle pebble** countless insignificant pebbles   **27 the
deficient** my defective   **28 Topple** topple me   **32 leap upright** jump up in the air   **34 Here,
friend's** here, friend, is   **36 Prosper it** cause it to prosper   **40 trifle** play   **46 opposeless**
irresistible   **47 My . . . nature** the smoldering wick and hated remains of my life
51 conceit imagination

Yields to the theft: had he been where he thought,
By this had thought been past. Alive or dead?—

55 Ho, you sir! Friend! Hear you, sir! Speak!—
Thus might he pass indeed: yet he revives.—   *Aside*
What are you, sir?

GLOUCESTER Away, and let me die.

EDGAR   Hadst thou been aught but gossamer, feathers,
air —

60 So many fathom down precipitating —
Thou'dst shivered like an egg: but thou dost breathe,
Hast heavy substance, bleed'st not, speak'st, art
sound.
Ten masts at each make not the altitude
Which thou hast perpendicularly fell:

65 Thy life's a miracle. Speak yet again.

GLOUCESTER But have I fall'n or no?

EDGAR   From the dread summit of this chalky bourn.
Look up a-height: the shrill-gorged lark so far
Cannot be seen or heard: do but look up.

70 GLOUCESTER Alack, I have no eyes.
Is wretchedness deprived that benefit,
To end itself by death? 'Twas yet some comfort
When misery could beguile the tyrant's rage
And frustrate his proud will.

75 EDGAR   Give me your arm.   *Helps him up*
Up, so. How is't? Feel you your legs? You stand.

GLOUCESTER Too well, too well.

EDGAR   This is above all strangeness.
Upon the crown o'th'cliff what thing was that

80 Which parted from you?

GLOUCESTER A poor unfortunate beggar.

---

53 **Yields** submits willingly   54 **this** this time, now   56 **pass** die   57 **What** who (Edgar
adopts another persona)   59 **aught** anything   60 **precipitating** falling headlong
61 **shivered** shattered   63 **at each** end to end   67 **bourn** boundary (between land and sea)
68 **a-height** on high   **shrill-gorged** shrill-throated   73 **beguile** cheat

EDGAR   As I stood here below, methought his eyes
               Were two full moons: he had a thousand noses,
               Horns whelked and waved like the enragèd sea.
85   It was some fiend: therefore, thou happy father,
               Think that the clearest gods, who make them
                   honours
               Of men's impossibilities, have preserved thee.
GLOUCESTER I do remember now: henceforth I'll bear
               Affliction till it do cry out itself
90   'Enough, enough' and die. That thing you speak of,
               I took it for a man: often 'twould say
               'The fiend, the fiend': he led me to that place.
EDGAR   Bear free and patient thoughts.

Enter Lear   *Dressed with weeds*
                                But who comes here?

               The safer sense will ne'er accommodate
95   His master thus.
LEAR   No, they cannot touch me for crying: I am the king
               himself.
EDGAR   O thou side-piercing sight!
LEAR   Nature's above art in that respect. There's your
100   press-money. That fellow handles his bow like a crow-keeper.
               Draw me a clothier's yard. Look, look, a mouse! Peace, peace,
               this piece of toasted cheese will do't. There's my gauntlet: I'll

---

84 whelked twisted   85 fiend i.e. tempting him to the sin of suicide   happy father fortunate
old man (father was a form of address for an elderly man, though Edgar plays with the literal
sense)   86 clearest brightest, purest   make . . . impossibilities acquire honor for themselves
by performing things that are impossible in the human world   93 free untroubled
94 The . . . thus were he (Lear) in his right mind, he would never permit himself to dress like
this (or possibly "Gloucester's senses will not be able to withstand seeing his master like this")
96 touch accuse, blame/lay hands on   100 press-money money paid to military recruits
when they were conscripted (Lear seems to imagine he is recruiting an army)   crow-keeper
scarecrow/person employed to scare crows from the crops   101 Draw . . . yard draw your bow
to its fullest extent (the length of a longbow's arrow, which, at about thirty-six inches, was the
same as the length of a cloth-seller's measuring rod)   102 gauntlet armored glove thrown
down as a challenge to a duel

prove it on a giant. Bring up the brown bills. O, well flown,
bird! I'th'clout, i'th'clout: hewgh! Give the word.

105 EDGAR   Sweet marjoram.

LEAR   Pass.

GLOUCESTER   I know that voice.

LEAR   Ha? Goneril with a white beard? They flattered me
like a dog and told me I had the white hairs in my beard ere
110 the black ones were there. To say 'Ay' and 'No' to everything
that I said 'Ay' and 'No' to was no good divinity. When the
rain came to wet me once and the wind to make me chatter,
when the thunder would not peace at my bidding, there I
found 'em, there I smelt 'em out. Go to, they are not men
115 o'their words: they told me I was everything: 'tis a lie, I am
not ague-proof.

GLOUCESTER   The trick of that voice I do well remember:
Is't not the king?

LEAR   Ay, every inch a king.
120 When I do stare, see how the subject quakes.
I pardon that man's life. What was thy cause?
Adultery?
Thou shalt not die: die for adultery? No.
The wren goes to't and the small gilded fly
125 Does lecher in my sight. Let copulation thrive,
For Gloucester's bastard son was kinder to his father
Than were my daughters got 'tween the lawful
        sheets.

---

103 prove it on make good my cause against   **brown bills** long-handled weapons, painted or
varnished brown and topped with axe-like blades; or soldiers carrying such weapons   **well
flown, bird** the language of falconry, here used to describe an arrow's flight   **104 I'th'clout**
cloth at the center of an archer's target   **hewgh** perhaps Lear imitates the sound of the arrow
as it flies through the air or hits the target   **word** password (continues Lear's military fantasy)
105 Sweet marjoram Edgar invents a password that relates to Lear's headgear and to the
plant's alleged medicinal properties in treating brain disorders   **109 like a dog** i.e. as if they
were fawning dogs   **had . . . there** i.e. was wise even while I was still a child   **111 divinity**
theology   **112 me** i.e. my teeth   **113 peace** be still   **116 ague-proof** immune to fever and
shivering   **117 trick** characteristic, individual quality   **121 cause** charge, offense
124 goes to't does it, has sex   **125 lecher** fornicate   **127 got** begot, conceived

To't, luxury, pell-mell, for I lack soldiers.
Behold yond simp'ring dame,
130   Whose face between her forks presages snow,
That minces virtue and does shake the head
To hear of pleasure's name:
The fitchew nor the soilèd horse goes to't
With a more riotous appetite. Down from the waist
135   They are centaurs, though women all above:
But to the girdle do the gods inherit,
Beneath is all the fiends':
There's hell, there's darkness, there is the sulphurous pit:
burning, scalding, stench, consumption. Fie, fie, fie! Pah,
140   pah! Give me an ounce of civet, good apothecary, sweeten
my imagination: there's money for thee.

GLOUCESTER   O, let me kiss that hand!

LEAR   Let me wipe it first: it smells of mortality.

GLOUCESTER   O, ruined piece of nature! This great world
145   Shall so wear out to nought. Dost thou know me?

LEAR   I remember thine eyes well enough. Dost thou
squinny at me? No, do thy worst, blind Cupid: I'll not love.
Read thou this challenge, mark but the penning of it.

GLOUCESTER   Were all thy letters suns, I could not see.

150   EDGAR   I would not take this from report: it is,   *Aside*
And my heart breaks at it.

LEAR   Read.

GLOUCESTER   What, with the case of eyes?

---

128 luxury lechery, lust   **for . . . soldiers** i.e. more sex means more children to man his army
130 between . . . snow forecasts frigidity between her legs   **131 minces virtue** affects chastity
shake the head i.e. in disapproval   **133 fitchew** polecat/prostitute   **soilèd** fed with green
fodder, so lively, skittish   **134 riotous** unrestrained, lustful   **135 centaurs** mythical creatures
that were human above the waist and horse below; reputed to be lustful   **136 But . . . girdle**
only as far as the waist   **inherit** possess, have power over   **138 hell** slang term for the vagina
sulphurous suggests both hell and syphilis   **139 burning . . . consumption** alludes to painful
syphilitic burning, odor and decay (**consumption**)   **140 civet** perfume   **apothecary** person
who prepared and sold drugs, spices, perfumes etc.   **143 mortality** being human/death
145 so similarly   **147 squinny** squint   **Cupid** Roman god of **love**, traditionally depicted as
blind or blindfolded   **148 challenge** written challenge to a duel   **penning** style/handwriting
150 take . . . report believe it if I heard it reported   **153 case** sockets

LEAR   O, ho, are you there with me? No eyes in your head,
155   nor no money in your purse? Your eyes are in a heavy case,
       your purse in a light, yet you see how this world goes.

GLOUCESTER I see it feelingly.

LEAR   What, art mad? A man may see how this world goes
       with no eyes. Look with thine ears: see how yond justice rails
160   upon yond simple thief. Hark, in thine ear: change places,
       and handy-dandy, which is the justice, which is the thief?
       Thou hast seen a farmer's dog bark at a beggar?

GLOUCESTER Ay, sir.

LEAR   And the creature run from the cur? There thou
165   mightst behold the great image of authority: a dog's obeyed
       in office.
       Thou rascal beadle, hold thy bloody hand!
       Why dost thou lash that whore? Strip thy own back:
       Thou hotly lusts to use her in that kind
170   For which thou whip'st her. The usurer hangs the
           cozener.
       Through tattered clothes great vices do appear:
       Robes and furred gowns hide all. Place sins with gold,
       And the strong lance of justice hurtless breaks:
       Arm it in rags, a pigmy's straw does pierce it.
175   None does offend, none, I say, none: I'll able 'em.
       Take that of me, my friend, who have the power
       To seal th'accuser's lips. Get thee glass eyes,
       And like a scurvy politician seem
       To see the things thou dost not. Now, now, now,
           now.
180   Pull off my boots: harder, harder: so.

---

155 heavy case sorrowful predicament   **157 feelingly** literally, through touch/with great
emotion   **159 justice** judge   **160 simple** humble   **161 handy-dandy** take your pick (from
the child's game of guessing which clenched hand contains something)   **165 a . . . office**
given authority, even a dog will be obeyed   **167 beadle** parish officer, responsible for
punishing thieves, prostitutes, and vagabonds   **169 use** employ sexually   **kind** manner
170 usurer moneylender, notorious for charging excessively high interest   **cozener** cheat
172 Place . . . gold i.e. when sins are committed by the rich   **173 hurtless** harmlessly
174 it i.e. sin   **175 able 'em** authorize them   **178 scurvy politician** despicable schemer
179 Now . . . now perhaps comforting Gloucester, perhaps distracted by his boots

EDGAR   O, matter and impertinency mixed! Reason in   *Aside*
        madness!

LEAR   If thou wilt weep my fortunes, take my eyes.
        I know thee well enough: thy name is Gloucester.
        Thou must be patient; we came crying hither.
185   Thou know'st the first time that we smell the air
        We wail and cry. I will preach to thee: mark.

GLOUCESTER   Alack, alack the day!

LEAR   When we are born, we cry that we are come
        To this great stage of fools. This a good block:
190   It were a delicate stratagem to shoe
        A troop of horse with felt: I'll put't in proof,
        And when I have stol'n upon these son-in-laws,
        Then kill, kill, kill, kill, kill, kill!

Enter a Gentleman [with Attendants]

GENTLEMAN   O, here he is: lay hand upon him.— Sir,
195   Your most dear daughter—

LEAR   No rescue? What, a prisoner? I am even
        The natural fool of fortune. Use me well,
        You shall have ransom. Let me have surgeons:
        I am cut to th'brains.

200 GENTLEMAN   You shall have anything.

LEAR   No seconds? All myself?
        Why, this would make a man a man of salt
        To use his eyes for garden water-pots,
        I will die bravely, like a smug bridegroom. What?
205   I will be jovial. Come, come, I am a king,
        Masters, know you that?

GENTLEMAN   You are a royal one, and we obey you.

---

181 matter and impertinency sense and nonsense   184 hither i.e. into this world   189 block
style of hat or mold for hats (perhaps Lear removes his headgear)/block from which to mount a
horse/tree stump (stage may even give rise to a sense of "scaffold and executioner's block")
190 delicate ingenious   191 put't in proof try it out   197 natural fool born fool (as opposed
to a professional jester)   201 seconds supporters (as for a duel)   202 salt i.e. tears   204 die
plays on the sense of "orgasm"   bravely handsomely   205 jovial cheerful/majestic (like Jove,
king of the gods)   206 Masters sirs

LEAR   Then there's life in't. Come, an you get it, you shall
get it by running. Sa, sa, sa, sa.   *Exit Running,*

210 GENTLEMAN   A sight most pitiful in the meanest   *Attendants follow*
wretch,

Past speaking of in a king! Thou hast a daughter
Who redeems nature from the general curse
Which twain have brought her to.

EDGAR   Hail, gentle sir.

215 GENTLEMAN   Sir, speed you: what's your will?

EDGAR   Do you hear aught, sir, of a battle toward?

GENTLEMAN   Most sure and vulgar: everyone hears that
Which can distinguish sound.

EDGAR   But, by your favour,

220 How near's the other army?

GENTLEMAN   Near and on speedy foot: the main descry
Stands on the hourly thought.

EDGAR   I thank you, sir: that's all.

GENTLEMAN   Though that the queen on special cause is
here,

225 Her army is moved on.   *Exit*

EDGAR   I thank you, sir.

GLOUCESTER   You ever-gentle gods, take my breath from
me:

Let not my worser spirit tempt me again

230 To die before you please!

EDGAR   Well pray you, father.

GLOUCESTER   Now, good sir, what are you?

EDGAR   A most poor man, made tame to fortune's blows,
Who, by the art of known and feeling sorrows,

---

209 Sa . . . sa hunting cry, from French *ça* ("that's it," "it's there")   **212 nature** i.e. human
nature   **general curse** curse of original sin   **213 twain** Adam and Eve (but also suggests
Goneril and Regan)   **214 gentle** noble   **215 speed you** (may God) prosper you   **216 toward**
impending   **217 vulgar** widely known   **219 by your favour** if you would be so good
221 main . . . thought sight of the main army is expected hourly   **224 Though that** though
on special cause for a special reason (i.e. to find Lear)   **229 worser spirit** evil angel/bad side
of my nature   **234 known . . . sorrows** deeply felt sorrows I have experienced

235   Am pregnant to good pity. Give me your hand:
     I'll lead you to some biding.   *Takes his arm*
GLOUCESTER Hearty thanks:
     The bounty and the benison of heaven
     To boot, and boot.
Enter Steward [Oswald]
240 OSWALD   A proclaimed prize! Most happy!
     That eyeless head of thine was first framed flesh
     To raise my fortunes. Thou old unhappy traitor,   *Draws*
     Briefly thyself remember: the sword is out
     That must destroy thee.
245 GLOUCESTER Now let thy friendly hand
     Put strength enough to't.   *Edgar interposes*
     OSWALD   Wherefore, bold peasant,
     Darest thou support a published traitor? Hence,
     Lest that th'infection of his fortune take
250   Like hold on thee. Let go his arm.
     EDGAR   'Chill not let go, zir, without vurther 'casion.
     OSWALD   Let go, slave, or thou diest!
     EDGAR   Good gentleman, go your gait, and let poor volk
     pass. An 'chud ha' bin zwaggered out of my life, 'twould not
255   ha' bin zo long as 'tis by a vortnight. Nay, come not near
     th'old man: keep out, che vor ye, or I'se try whether your
     costard or my ballow be the harder. 'Chill be plain with you.
     OSWALD   Out, dunghill!
     EDGAR   'Chill pick your teeth, zir: come, no matter *They fight*
     vor your foins.
260 OSWALD   Slave, thou hast slain me. Villain, take my
     purse:

---

235 pregnant . . . pity disposed to compassion   **236 biding** dwelling   **238 benison** blessing
239 To . . . boot in addition, and may it benefit you   **240 proclaimed prize** i.e. a man with a
price on his head   **happy** fortunate   **241 framed flesh** conceived and born   **243 thyself
remember** recall your sins (i.e. prepare to die)   **248 published** proclaimed   **251 'Chill . . .
'casion** I shall not let go, sir, without further occasion (cause); for his new persona, Edgar
adopts a West Country accent in which he substitutes "v" for "f" and "z" for "s"   **'Chill** I shall
253 your gait on your way   **254 An . . . vortnight** if I could have been killed by boasting, I
would not have lasted a fortnight (or "it would have been shorter by a fortnight")   **256 che
vor ye** I warrant you, I promise you   **I'se** I shall   **257 costard** head (literally, a large apple)
ballow cudgel   **259 pick** knock out with the cudgel   **foins** sword thrusts

If ever thou wilt thrive, bury my body
And give the letters which thou find'st about me
To Edmund, Earl of Gloucester: seek him out
Upon the English party. O, untimely death! Death!   *He dies*

265 EDGAR   I know thee well: a serviceable villain,
As duteous to the vices of thy mistress
As badness would desire.

GLOUCESTER What, is he dead?

EDGAR   Sit you down, father: rest you.

270 Let's see these pockets: the letters that he speaks of
May be my friends. He's dead: I am only sorry
He had no other deathsman. Let us see.   *Opens the letter*
Leave, gentle wax, and manners, blame us not:
To know our enemies' minds we rip their hearts:

275 Their papers is more lawful.
Reads the letter
'Let our reciprocal vows be remembered. You have many
opportunities to cut him off: if your will want not, time and
place will be fruitfully offered. There is nothing done if he
return the conqueror: then am I the prisoner, and his bed my

280 jail, from the loathed warmth whereof deliver me, and
supply the place for your labour. Your — wife, so I would say
— affectionate servant, Goneril.'
O, undistinguished space of woman's will!
A plot upon her virtuous husband's life,

285 And the exchange my brother! Here in the sands
Thee I'll rake up, the post unsanctified
Of murderous lechers: and in the mature time
With this ungracious paper strike the sight
Of the death-practised duke: for him 'tis well

290 That of thy death and business I can tell.

---

264 party side   **265 serviceable** eager to serve, ready to do anything   **272 deathsman**
executioner   **273 Leave** give me leave, permit me   **277 will** desire/lust   **want not** is not
lacking   **278 done** achieved   **281 for your labour** as a reward for your efforts/as a place for
sexual activity   **282 servant** lover   **283 undistinguished space** limitless scope   **will** lust
286 Thee . . . up I will bury you (Oswald)   **post unsanctified** unholy messenger   **287 in . . .
time** when the time is ripe   **288 ungracious** wicked, sinful   **strike** blast/afflict   **289 death-
practised** whose death is plotted

GLOUCESTER The king is mad: how stiff is my vile sense,
That I stand up and have ingenious feeling
Of my huge sorrows. Better I were distract,
So should my thoughts be severed from my griefs,

Drum afar off

295   And woes by wrong imaginations lose
The knowledge of themselves.

EDGAR   Give me your hand:
Far off, methinks, I hear the beaten drum.
Come, father, I'll bestow you with a friend.   *Exeunt*

Act 4 Scene 6   *running scene 17*

Enter Cordelia, Kent and Gentleman   *Kent still disguised*

CORDELIA   O thou good Kent, how shall I live and work
To match thy goodness? My life will be too short,
And every measure fail me.

KENT   To be acknowledged, madam, is o'erpaid.

5   All my reports go with the modest truth,
Nor more nor clipped, but so.

CORDELIA   Be better suited:
These weeds are memories of those worser hours,
I prithee put them off.

10   KENT   Pardon, dear madam,
Yet to be known shortens my made intent:
My boon I make it, that you know me not
Till time and I think meet.

CORDELIA   Then be't so, my good lord.— How does the
king?

---

291 **stiff** stubborn   292 **ingenious** sensitive, intelligent   293 **distract** mad   295 **wrong
imaginations** illusions   **4.6   *Location: the French camp, near Dover***   3 **every . . . me**
all my efforts will be inadequate   4 **o'erpaid** i.e. already more than enough   5 **All . . . truth**
everything I have told you is the simple truth (or possibly "may all reports of me be
unexaggerated and accurate")   6 **Nor . . . clipped** neither overstated nor abbreviated
7 **suited** dressed   8 **weeds** clothes   11 **Yet . . . intent** to have my identity known now would
spoil the plan I have devised   12 **My . . . it** the favor I ask is   **know me not** do not
acknowledge me   13 **meet** suitable

15 GENTLEMAN   Madam, sleeps still.

CORDELIA   O you kind gods,
Cure this great breach in his abusèd nature!
Th'untuned and jarring senses, O, wind up
Of this child-changèd father!

20 GENTLEMAN   So please your majesty
That we may wake the king: he hath slept long.

CORDELIA   Be governed by your knowledge, and proceed
I'th'sway of your own will. Is he arrayed?

Enter Lear in a chair carried by Servants

GENTLEMAN   Ay, madam: in the heaviness of sleep
25 We put fresh garments on him.
Be by, good madam, when we do awake him:
I doubt of his temperance.

CORDELIA   O my dear father! Restoration hang   *Kisses him*
Thy medicine on my lips and let this kiss
30 Repair those violent harms that my two sisters
Have in thy reverence made!

KENT   Kind and dear princess!

CORDELIA   Had you not been their father, these white
flakes
Did challenge pity of them. Was this a face
35 To be opposed against the jarring winds?
Mine enemy's dog though he had bit me
Should have stood that night against my fire,
And wast thou fain, poor father,
To hovel thee with swine and rogues forlorn
40 In short and musty straw? Alack, alack!
'Tis wonder that thy life and wits at once
Had not concluded all.— He wakes: speak to him.

---

18 wind up put in tune (by tightening the pegs on a stringed instrument)   **19 child-changèd**
changed by his children   **23 I'th'sway . . . will** as you see fit, under your own authority
arrayed dressed (appropriately)   **27 doubt of** fear for   **temperance** self-control
31 reverence i.e. position deserving respect, venerable state   **33 Had you** even if you had
flakes locks of hair   **34 Did challenge** would have demanded   **of** from   **38 fain** obliged
39 rogues forlorn destitute vagabonds   **40 short** i.e. broken up (and hence less comfortable)
41 at once at the same time   **42 concluded all** come entirely to an end

GENTLEMAN   Madam, do you: 'tis fittest.

CORDELIA   How does my royal lord? How fares your
       majesty?

45   LEAR   You do me wrong to take me out o'th'grave:
       Thou art a soul in bliss, but I am bound
       Upon a wheel of fire, that mine own tears
       Do scald like molten lead.

CORDELIA   Sir, do you know me?

50   LEAR   You are a spirit, I know: where did you die?

CORDELIA   Still, still, far wide!

GENTLEMAN   He's scarce awake: let him alone awhile.

LEAR   Where have I been? Where am I? Fair daylight?
       I am mightily abused. I should ev'n die with pity
55   To see another thus. I know not what to say.
       I will not swear these are my hands. Let's see:
       I feel this pinprick. Would I were assured
       Of my condition!

CORDELIA   O, look upon me, sir,   *Kneels?*
60   And hold your hand in benediction o'er me:
       You must not kneel.   *Stops him from kneeling?*

LEAR   Pray, do not mock me:
       I am a very foolish fond old man,
       Fourscore and upward, not an hour more nor less,
65   And to deal plainly,
       I fear I am not in my perfect mind.
       Methinks I should know you and know this man,
       Yet I am doubtful, for I am mainly ignorant
       What place this is, and all the skill I have
70   Remembers not these garments, nor I know not
       Where I did lodge last night. Do not laugh at me,
       For, as I am a man, I think this lady
       To be my child Cordelia.

---

46 bliss i.e. heaven   **47 wheel of fire** i.e. one of hell's tortures of the damned; recalls Ixion, who, in Greek mythology, was bound to a wheel of fire for attempting to seduce the queen of the gods   **that** so that   **51 wide** wide of the mark, confused   **54 abused** wronged, ill-treated/deluded   **57 Would . . . condition!** I wish I could be sure of what state I am in!
63 fond silly

CORDELIA	And so I am, I am.	*Weeps*

75 LEAR   Be your tears wet? Yes, faith. I pray, weep not:
If you have poison for me, I will drink it.
I know you do not love me, for your sisters
Have, as I do remember, done me wrong:
You have some cause, they have not.

80 CORDELIA No cause, no cause.

LEAR   Am I in France?

KENT   In your own kingdom, sir.

LEAR   Do not abuse me.

GENTLEMAN Be comforted, good madam: the great rage,

85 You see, is killed in him. Desire him to go in:
Trouble him no more till further settling.

CORDELIA Will't please your highness walk?

LEAR   You must bear with me. Pray you now, forget and
forgive:
I am old and foolish.   *Exeunt*

Act 5 Scene 1

Enter with Drum and Colours Edmund, Regan, Gentlemen and Soldiers

EDMUND   Know of the duke if his last purpose hold,   *To a*
Or whether since he is advised by aught   *Gentleman*
To change the course: he's full of alteration
And self-reproving: bring his constant pleasure.

[*Exit Gentleman*]

5 REGAN   Our sister's man is certainly miscarried.

EDMUND   'Tis to be doubted, madam.

REGAN   Now, sweet lord,
You know the goodness I intend upon you:

---

84 **rage** frenzy   86 **further settling** his mind is more settled   **5.1** *Location: the British camp, near Dover   Drum and Colours* soldiers with military flags and a drum beating   1 **Know of** find out from   **last purpose** most recent intention   2 **since** subsequently   **advised** persuaded/warned   **aught** anything, i.e. any news   4 **self-reproving** self-reproach   **constant pleasure** fixed wishes   5 **miscarried** come to harm   6 **doubted** feared

Tell me but truly — but then speak the truth —
10   Do you not love my sister?

EDMUND   In honoured love.

REGAN   But have you never found my brother's way
To the forfended place?

EDMUND   No, by mine honour, madam.

15 REGAN   I never shall endure her: dear my lord,
Be not familiar with her.

EDMUND   Fear not. She and the duke her husband!

Enter with Drum and Colours Albany, Goneril, Soldiers

ALBANY   Our very loving sister, well be-met.
Sir, this I heard: the king is come to his daughter,
20   With others whom the rigour of our state
Forced to cry out.

REGAN   Why is this reasoned?

GONERIL   Combine together gainst the enemy,
For these domestic and particular broils
25   Are not the question here.

ALBANY   Let's then determine
With th'ancient of war on our proceeding.

REGAN   Sister, you'll go with us?

GONERIL   No.

30 REGAN   'Tis most convenient: pray, go with us.

GONERIL   O, ho, I know the riddle.— I will go.   *Aside*

                      Exeunt both the armies. [Albany remains]

Enter Edgar   *Disguised*

EDGAR   If e'er your grace had speech with man so poor,
Hear me one word.

ALBANY   I'll overtake you.— Speak.

---

11 honoured honorable   **13 forfended place** forbidden place, i.e. Goneril's vagina   **15 I . . . her** I cannot stand her   **16 familiar** too friendly/sexually intimate   **20 rigour . . . state** harshness of our government   **21 cry out** i.e. protest in pain   **22 Why . . . reasoned?** Why are we discussing this?   **23 Combine together** i.e. let us combine our two armies   **24 domestic . . . broils** private internal squabbles   **27 th'ancient of war** experienced senior officers   **30 convenient** suitable, seemly   **31 know the riddle** understand your enigmatic request, see your trick (Regan wants to keep a suspicious eye on Goneril)   **34 I'll overtake you** presumably Albany calls after those who have or are in the process of departing

| 35 | EDGAR | Before you fight the battle, ope this letter: *Gives a letter* |

35 EDGAR Before you fight the battle, ope this letter: *Gives a letter*
If you have victory, let the trumpet sound
For him that brought it. Wretched though I seem,
I can produce a champion that will prove
What is avouchèd there. If you miscarry,
40 Your business of the world hath so an end,
And machination ceases. Fortune loves you.

ALBANY Stay till I have read the letter.

EDGAR I was forbid it.
When time shall serve, let but the herald cry
45 And I'll appear again.   *Exit*

ALBANY Why, fare thee well: I will o'erlook thy paper.

Enter Edmund

EDMUND The enemy's in view: draw up your powers.
Here is the guess of their true strength and forces *Offers a paper*
By diligent discovery, but your haste
50 Is now urged on you.

ALBANY We will greet the time.   *Exit*

EDMUND To both these sisters have I sworn my love,
Each jealous of the other, as the stung
Are of the adder. Which of them shall I take?
55 Both? One? Or neither? Neither can be enjoyed
If both remain alive. To take the widow
Exasperates, makes mad her sister Goneril,
And hardly shall I carry out my side,
Her husband being alive. Now then, we'll use
60 His countenance for the battle, which being done,
Let her who would be rid of him devise
His speedy taking off. As for the mercy
Which he intends to Lear and to Cordelia,

---

35 **ope** open   **letter** i.e. the letter Oswald was carrying from Goneril to Edmund   **36 sound** i.e. sound a summons   **38 champion** one who fights in single combat   **39 avouchèd** declared, affirmed   **miscarry** lose the battle and die   **41 machination** plotting   **44 cry** make the proclamation   **46 o'erlook** read over   **47 powers** troops   **49 discovery** intelligence-gathering, reconnaissance   **51 greet the time** be ready when the time comes   **53 jealous** suspicious, mistrustful   **58 hardly** with difficulty   **carry . . . side** fulfill my side of the agreement (with Goneril)/achieve my own (power-seeking) ends   **60 countenance** authority   **62 taking off** murder

The battle done and they within our power,
65   Shall never see his pardon, for my state
Stands on me to defend, not to debate.   *Exit*

Act 5 Scene 2   *running scene 19*

Alarum within. Enter, with Drum and Colours, Lear, Cordelia and
Soldiers over the stage and exeunt. Enter Edgar and Gloucester

EDGAR   Here, father, take the shadow of this tree
For your good host. Pray that the right may thrive.
If ever I return to you again,
I'll bring you comfort.
5   GLOUCESTER Grace go with you, sir!   *Exit [Edgar]*
Alarum and retreat within
Enter Edgar
EDGAR   Away, old man! Give me thy hand, away!
King Lear hath lost, he and his daughter ta'en:
Give me thy hand, come on.
GLOUCESTER No further, sir: a man may rot even here.
10   EDGAR   What, in ill thoughts again? Men must endure
Their going hence, even as their coming hither:
Ripeness is all: come on.
GLOUCESTER And that's true too.   *Exeunt*

Act 5 Scene 3   *running scene 20*

Enter in conquest, with Drum and Colours, Edmund, Lear and Cordelia
as prisoners, Soldiers, Captain

EDMUND   Some officers take them away: good guard,
Until their greater pleasures first be known
That are to censure them.

65 Shall i.e. they shall   my . . . debate my position relies on action not discussion
5.2 *Location: not far from the battlefield, near Dover*   *Alarum* trumpet call to arms
1 father form of address for an old man   2 host i.e. shelter   *retreat* trumpet call signaling
retreat   7 ta'en (are) captured   12 Ripeness readiness/the right time   5.3 *Location:*
the British camp, near Dover   1 good guard guard them carefully   2 greater pleasures
the wishes of more important people (i.e. Goneril, Regan, Albany)   3 censure judge, sentence

CORDELIA   We are not the first   *To Lear*
5   Who with best meaning have incurred the worst.
       For thee, oppressèd king, I am cast down:
       Myself could else out-frown false fortune's frown.
       Shall we not see these daughters and these sisters?
LEAR   No, no, no, no! Come, let's away to prison.
10   We two alone will sing like birds i'th'cage:
       When thou dost ask me blessing, I'll kneel down
       And ask of thee forgiveness: so we'll live,
       And pray, and sing, and tell old tales, and laugh
       At gilded butterflies, and hear poor rogues
15   Talk of court news, and we'll talk with them too —
       Who loses and who wins, who's in, who's out —
       And take upon's the mystery of things,
       As if we were God's spies: and we'll wear out
       In a walled prison packs and sects of great ones
20   That ebb and flow by th'moon.
EDMUND   Take them away.
LEAR   Upon such sacrifices, my Cordelia,
       The gods themselves throw incense. Have I caught
          thee?
       He that parts us shall bring a brand from heaven
25   And fire us hence like foxes. Wipe thine eyes:
       The good years shall devour them, flesh and fell,
       Ere they shall make us weep: We'll see 'em starved
          first. Come.
                          Exeunt [Lear and Cordelia, guarded]
EDMUND   Come hither, captain, hark.
       Take thou this note, go follow them to prison.   *Gives a paper*

---

5 meaning intentions   **6 cast down** humbled by fortune/defeated in battle/dejected
14 gilded butterflies actual butterflies/lavishly dressed courtiers   **poor rogues** wretched
fellows   **17 take . . . things** understand the secret inner workings of the world   **18 God's
spies** spying on the world on God's behalf/looking at the world from a lofty vantage point, like
God   **wear out** outlive   **19 packs and sects** cliques and factions   **20 That . . . th'moon** i.e.
whose fortunes ebb and flow like the tides   **22 sacrifices** refers to either Cordelia's sacrifice for
Lear or their joint loss of freedom   **23 throw incense** i.e. like priests performing the sacrifice
24 brand . . . foxes alludes to the practice of smoking foxes out of their holes   **26 flesh and
fell** flesh and skin (i.e. entirely)   **27 starved** dead

30   One step I have advanced thee: if thou dost
        As this instructs thee, thou dost make thy way
        To noble fortunes. Know thou this: that men
        Are as the time is; to be tender-minded
        Does not become a sword. Thy great employment
35   Will not bear question: either say thou'lt do't
        Or thrive by other means.

CAPTAIN   I'll do't, my lord.

EDMUND   About it, and write happy when th'hast done.
        Mark, I say, instantly, and carry it so
40   As I have set it down.   *Exit Captain*

Flourish. Enter Albany, Goneril, Regan, Soldiers

ALBANY   Sir, you have showed today your valiant strain,
        And fortune led you well. You have the captives
        Who were the opposites of this day's strife:
        I do require them of you, so to use them
45   As we shall find their merits and our safety
        May equally determine.

EDMUND   Sir, I thought it fit
        To send the old and miserable king to some retention
        Whose age had charms in it, whose title more,
50   To pluck the common bosom on his side
        And turn our impressed lances in our eyes
        Which do command them. With him I sent the
            queen,
        My reason all the same, and they are ready
        Tomorrow, or at further space, t'appear
55   Where you shall hold your session.

---

33 **tender-minded** sensitive, soft-hearted   34 **become** befit, suit   35 **bear question** permit
discussion   38 **write happy** count yourself fortunate   39 **carry** manage   41 **strain** lineage
43 **opposites** opponents   44 **use** treat   48 **retention** detention, confinement   49 **Whose**
refers to the **king   charms** bewitching spells   **title** name of king/legal entitlement (to land
and power)   50 **pluck . . . bosom** draw the sympathies of the common people   51 **turn . . .
them** i.e. turn our conscripted soldiers' weapons against ourselves   52 **queen** i.e. Cordelia
55 **session** hearing in a court of justice

ALBANY   Sir, by your patience,
I hold you but a subject of this war,
Not as a brother.

REGAN   That's as we list to grace him.

60 Methinks our pleasure might have been demanded
Ere you had spoke so far. He led our powers,
Bore the commission of my place and person,
The which immediacy may well stand up
And call itself your brother.

65 GONERIL   Not so hot:
In his own grace he doth exalt himself
More than in your addition.

REGAN   In my rights,
By me invested, he compeers the best.

70 ALBANY   That were the most if he should husband you.

REGAN   Jesters do oft prove prophets.

GONERIL   Holla, holla!
That eye that told you so looked but asquint.

REGAN   Lady, I am not well, else I should answer
75 From a full-flowing stomach.— General,   *To Edmund*
Take thou my soldiers, prisoners, patrimony:
Dispose of them, of me: the walls is thine:
Witness the world that I create thee here
My lord and master.

80 GONERIL   Mean you to enjoy him?

ALBANY   The let-alone lies not in your good will.

EDMUND   Nor in thine, lord.

ALBANY   Half-blooded fellow, yes.

---

56 **by your patience** if you'll excuse me   57 **subject of** subordinate in   59 **list** please
60 **pleasure . . . demanded** wishes might have been asked   62 **commission** authority
63 **immediacy** closeness, connection   66 **grace** merit   67 **your addition** the honors or titles
you bestow on him   69 **compeers** equals   70 **That . . . most** i.e. he would be most fully
invested with your rights   72 **Holla** whoa, stop   73 **asquint** crookedly, distortedly
75 **full-flowing stomach** a stomach full of anger (where **stomach** is used like "heart" for the
seat of the passions)   76 **patrimony** inheritance   77 **Dispose of** use, deal with   **walls** Regan
images herself as a fortress surrendering   78 **Witness the world** let the world witness
80 **enjoy** i.e. have sex with him as your husband   81 **let-alone** permission or refusal to give it
83 **Half-blooded** illegitimate (**fellow** is contemptuous)

REGAN   Let the drum strike and prove my title thine. *To Edmund*

85 ALBANY   Stay yet, hear reason. Edmund, I arrest thee
On capital treason, and, in thy arrest,
This gilded serpent. For your claim, fair sister,
I bar it in the interest of my wife:
'Tis she is subcontracted to this lord,
90 And I, her husband, contradict your banns.
If you will marry, make your loves to me,
My lady is bespoke.

GONERIL   An interlude!

ALBANY   Thou art armed, Gloucester: let the trumpet sound:
95 If none appear to prove upon thy person
Thy heinous, manifest, and many treasons,
There is my pledge: I'll make it on thy heart,   *Throws down a glove*
Ere I taste bread, thou art in nothing less
Than I have here proclaimed thee.

100 REGAN   Sick, O, sick!

GONERIL   If not, I'll ne'er trust medicine.   *Aside*

EDMUND   There's my exchange: what in the world he's
That names me traitor, villain-like he lies.   *Throws down a glove*
Call by the trumpet: he that dares approach,
105 On him, on you — who not? — I will maintain
My truth and honour firmly.

Enter a Herald

ALBANY   A herald, ho!
Trust to thy single virtue, for thy soldiers,   *To Edmund*
All levied in my name, have in my name
110 Took their discharge.

REGAN   My sickness grows upon me.

---

86 **in** i.e. along with   87 **gilded serpent** i.e. Goneril   **For** as for   88 **bar it** prevent its
advancement (legal term)   89 **subcontracted** engaged for a second time, entered into a
contract that is subsidiary to her marriage contract with Albany   90 **banns** proclamation of
marriage (spelled "banes" in Folio, perhaps playing on "evil-doings")   91 **make . . . to** woo,
make advances to   92 **bespoke** spoken for   93 **interlude** brief comic play (i.e. "What a
farce!")   97 **pledge** challenge/pledge to fight   **make it** i.e. make it good   98 **nothing** no way
101 **medicine** drugs (i.e. poison)   102 **what** whoever   108 **single virtue** unaided courage or
strength

ALBANY   She is not well: convey her to my tent.—

[*Exit Regan, led*]

Come hither, herald. Let the trumpet sound
And read out this.

A trumpet sounds

115 HERALD   *Reads* 'If any man of quality or degree within the
lists of the army will maintain upon Edmund, supposed Earl
of Gloucester, that he is a manifold traitor, let him appear by
the third sound of the trumpet: he is bold in his defence.'

First trumpet

HERALD   Again!

Second trumpet

120 HERALD   Again!

Third trumpet

Trumpet answers within

Enter Edgar armed   *His helmet visor down*

ALBANY   Ask him his purposes, why he appears
Upon this call o'th'trumpet.

HERALD   What are you?
Your name, your quality, and why you answer
125 This present summons?

EDGAR   Know, my name is lost
By treason's tooth bare-gnawn and canker-bit:
Yet am I noble as the adversary
I come to cope.

130 ALBANY   Which is that adversary?

EDGAR   What's he that speaks for Edmund Earl of
Gloucester?

EDMUND   Himself: what say'st thou to him?

EDGAR   Draw thy sword,
That, if my speech offend a noble heart,
135 Thy arm may do thee justice: here is mine.   *Draws*

115 **quality or degree** noble birth or high rank   116 **lists** catalog of soldiers
127 **canker-bit** eaten away by canker-worms (grubs that feed on plants)   129 **cope** encounter, fight with

Behold, it is my privilege —
The privilege of mine honours —
My oath and my profession. I protest,
Maugre thy strength, place, youth and eminence,
140   Despise thy victor sword and fire-new fortune,
Thy valour and thy heart, thou art a traitor:
False to thy gods, thy brother and thy father,
Conspirant gainst this high illustrious prince,
And from th'extremest upward of thy head
145   To the descent and dust below thy foot
A most toad-spotted traitor. Say thou no,
This sword, this arm and my best spirits are bent
To prove upon thy heart whereto I speak,
Thou liest.
150   EDMUND   In wisdom I should ask thy name,
But since thy outside looks so fair and warlike,
And that thy tongue some say of breeding breathes,
What safe and nicely I might well delay
By rule of knighthood, I disdain and spurn.
155   Back do I toss these treasons to thy head,
With the hell-hated lie o'erwhelm thy heart,
Which, for they yet glance by and scarcely bruise,
This sword of mine shall give them instant way,
Where they shall rest forever. Trumpets, speak!   *Draws*
Alarums. Fights   *Edmund falls*
160   ALBANY   Save him, save him!
GONERIL   This is practice, Gloucester:
By th'law of war thou wast not bound to answer

---

137 honours . . . profession i.e. as a knight   138 protest declare   139 Maugre despite
place position, rank   140 fire-new i.e. brand new, freshly minted   143 Conspirant a
conspirator   144 upward top, crown   145 descent lowest part, sole   146 toad-spotted
toads' spots were believed to contain venom   147 bent resolved/tensed for action   152 say
assay, evidence   153 nicely in strict keeping with the rules   156 hell-hated lie the lie I hate
as much as hell   157 for they since they (the **treasons**)   by off   158 instant way an
immediate passage (to your heart)   160 him probably a call to Edgar to spare Edmund's life so
that a confession can be obtained from him   161 practice trickery

An unknown opposite: thou art not vanquished,
But cozened and beguiled.

ALBANY   Shut your mouth, dame,
Or with this paper shall I stop it.— Hold, sir.—
Thou worse than any name, read thine own evil.   *To Goneril*
No tearing, lady: I perceive you know it.   *Shows her the letter*

GONERIL   Say, if I do, the laws are mine, not thine:
Who can arraign me for't.   *Exit*

ALBANY   Most monstrous! O, know'st thou this paper?

EDMUND   Ask me not what I know.

ALBANY   Go after her: she's desperate: govern her.

[Exit a soldier]

EDMUND   What you have charged me with, that have I
done,
And more, much more: the time will bring it out:
'Tis past and so am I.— But what art thou   *To Edgar*
That hast this fortune on me? If thou'rt noble,
I do forgive thee.

EDGAR   Let's exchange charity.
I am no less in blood than thou art, Edmund:
If more, the more th'hast wronged me.
My name is Edgar, and thy father's son.   *Removes his helmet*
The gods are just, and of our pleasant vices
Make instruments to plague us:
The dark and vicious place where thee he got
Cost him his eyes.

EDMUND   Th'hast spoken right: 'tis true,
The wheel is come full circle: I am here.

ALBANY   Methought thy very gait did prophesy   *To Edgar*
A royal nobleness: I must embrace thee.
Let sorrow split my heart if ever I
Did hate thee or thy father!

---

164 cozened and beguiled cheated and deceived   **165 dame** woman   **168 know** recognize
170 arraign indict, bring to trial   **173 govern** restrain   **177 fortune on** good fortune to defeat
179 charity forgiveness   **181 th'hast** thou hast (i.e. you have)   **183 pleasant** pleasurable
(sexually so in this case)   **185 dark** literally and metaphorically   **vicious** immoral   **got**
begot, conceived   **188 wheel** wheel of fortune   **189 prophesy** suggest, foretell

EDGAR   Worthy prince, I know't.

ALBANY   Where have you hid yourself?

195   How have you known the miseries of your father?

EDGAR   By nursing them, my lord. List a brief tale,
And when 'tis told, O, that my heart would burst!
The bloody proclamation to escape
That followed me so near — O, our lives' sweetness!
200   That we the pain of death would hourly die
Rather than die at once! — taught me to shift
Into a madman's rags, t'assume a semblance
That very dogs disdained: and in this habit
Met I my father with his bleeding rings,
205   Their precious stones new lost, became his guide,
Led him, begged for him, saved him from despair,
Never — O, fault! — revealed myself unto him
Until some half-hour past, when I was armed.
Not sure, though hoping, of this good success,
210   I asked his blessing, and from first to last
Told him our pilgrimage: but his flawed heart —
Alack, too weak the conflict to support —
'Twixt two extremes of passion, joy and grief,
Burst smilingly.

215   EDMUND   This speech of yours hath moved me,
And shall perchance do good: but speak you on:
You look as you had something more to say.

ALBANY   If there be more, more woeful, hold it in,
For I am almost ready to dissolve,
220   Hearing of this.

Enter a Gentleman   *With a bloody knife*

GENTLEMAN   Help, help, O, help!

EDGAR   What kind of help?

---

196 List listen (to)   **198 bloody proclamation** i.e. the sentence of death pronounced on him
200 the . . . die would repeatedly suffer pain as bad as death   **202 semblance** outward
appearance   **203 habit** clothing/guise, appearance   **204 rings** i.e. eye sockets   **206 despair**
the spiritual hopelessness that precedes suicide   **209 success** outcome (in the duel with
Edmund)   **211 pilgrimage** course of events/period of exile/spiritual journey   **flawed** cracked
219 dissolve i.e. in tears

ALBANY   Speak, man.

EDGAR   What means this bloody knife?

225 GENTLEMAN   'Tis hot, it smokes:

It came even from the heart of — O, she's dead!

ALBANY   Who dead? Speak, man.

GENTLEMAN   Your lady, sir, your lady; and her sister

By her is poisoned: she confesses it.

230 EDMUND   I was contracted to them both: all three

Now marry in an instant.

EDGAR   Here comes Kent.

Enter Kent

ALBANY   Produce the bodies, be they alive or dead:

Goneril and Regan's bodies brought out

This judgement of the heavens, that makes us tremble,

235   Touches us not with pity.— O, is this he?—   *Sees Kent*

The time will not allow the compliment   *To Kent*

Which very manners urges.

KENT   I am come

To bid my king and master aye goodnight:

240   Is he not here?

ALBANY   Great thing of us forgot!

Speak, Edmund, where's the king? And where's

Cordelia?—

See'st thou this object, Kent?   *Points to the bodies*

KENT   Alack, why thus?

245 EDMUND   Yet Edmund was beloved:

The one the other poisoned for my sake

And after slew herself.

ALBANY   Even so. Cover their faces.

EDMUND   I pant for life: some good I mean to do,

250   Despite of mine own nature. Quickly send —

Be brief in it — to th'castle, for my writ

---

225 smokes i.e. steams with hot blood   236 compliment etiquette (of greeting)   239 aye
forever (Kent is aware he is dying)   241 Great thing vital matter   243 object sight
248 Even exactly   251 writ written order (for execution; a legal term)

Is on the life of Lear and on Cordelia:
Nay, send in time.

255 ALBANY   Run, run, O, run!

EDGAR   To who, my lord? Who has the office?
Send thy token of reprieve.   *To Edmund*

EDMUND   Well thought on: take my sword,
Give it the captain.

EDGAR   Haste thee, for thy life.   *To a Gentleman*

[*Exit Gentleman*]

260 EDMUND   He hath commission from thy wife and me
To hang Cordelia in the prison and
To lay the blame upon her own despair,
That she fordid herself.

ALBANY   The gods defend her! Bear him   *Edmund is borne off*
hence awhile.

Enter Lear with Cordelia in his arms   *Gentleman and others following*

265 LEAR   Howl, howl, howl! O, you are men of stones:
Had I your tongues and eyes, I'd use them so
That heaven's vault should crack. She's gone for
ever!
I know when one is dead and when one lives:
She's dead as earth. Lend me a looking-glass:
270 If that her breath will mist or stain the stone,
Why, then she lives.

KENT   Is this the promised end?

EDGAR   Or image of that horror?

ALBANY   Fall and cease!

275 LEAR   This feather stirs: she lives! If it be so,
It is a chance which does redeem all sorrows
That ever I have felt.

KENT   O my good master!   *Kneels*

LEAR   Prithee, away.

---

255 office task, responsibility   **263 fordid** killed   **270 stone** specular stone, a crystalline
substance used to make mirrors   **272 promised end** the death Lear expected (when he
divided the kingdom)/Judgment Day, the end of the world (the sense that Edgar understands)
274 Fall and cease! either Albany calls for the end of the world, or he wishes for Lear to die
and be put out of his anguish

280 EDGAR   'Tis noble Kent, your friend.

LEAR   A plague upon you, murderers, traitors all!
I might have saved her: now she's gone for ever!—
Cordelia, Cordelia! Stay a little. Ha?
What is't thou say'st?— Her voice was ever soft,
285 Gentle and low, an excellent thing in woman.—
I killed the slave that was a-hanging thee.

GENTLEMAN   'Tis true, my lords, he did.

LEAR   Did I not, fellow?
I have seen the day, with my good biting falchion
290 I would have made him skip: I am old now,
And these same crosses spoil me.— Who are you?
Mine eyes are not o'th'best: I'll tell you straight.

KENT   If fortune brag of two she loved and hated,
One of them we behold.

295 LEAR   This is a dull sight. Are you not Kent?

KENT   The same,
Your servant Kent: where is your servant Caius?

LEAR   He's a good fellow, I can tell you that:
He'll strike, and quickly too. He's dead and rotten.

300 KENT   No, my good lord, I am the very man—

LEAR   I'll see that straight.

KENT   That from your first of difference and decay
Have followed your sad steps.

LEAR   You are welcome hither.

305 KENT   Nor no man else: all's cheerless, dark and deadly.
Your eldest daughters have fordone themselves,
And desperately are dead.

---

286 slave villain/wretched servant   **289 falchion** curved sword   **291 crosses** troubles, frustrations   **292 Mine . . . o'th'best** failing sight was believed to be a sign of approaching death   **straight** in a moment   **293 two . . . hated** perhaps "two people she first loved and then hated"; it is not entirely clear who the **one** Kent refers to is   **295 dull sight** refers either to Lear's dim eyesight or to the motionless Cordelia   **297 Caius** the only mention of the name Kent assumed when he was in disguise   **301 I'll . . . straight** I'll attend to that in a moment   **302 your . . . decay** the beginning of the change and decline in your fortunes (may also suggest mental decay)   **305 Nor . . . else** completes Kent's previous, unfinished sentence with "and no one else" as well as beginning his current one with "neither I nor anyone else (is welcome)"   **306 fordone** killed   **307 desperately** as a result of the spiritual despair that precedes suicide

LEAR   Ay, so I think.

ALBANY   He knows not what he says, and vain is it

310   That we present us to him.

Enter a Messenger

EDGAR   Very bootless.

MESSENGER   Edmund is dead, my lord.

ALBANY   That's but a trifle here.

You lords and noble friends, know our intent:

315   What comfort to this great decay may come

Shall be applied. For us, we will resign,

During the life of this old majesty,

To him our absolute power:— you, to your rights   *To Edgar*

With boot and such addition as your honours   *and Kent*

320   Have more than merited. All friends shall taste

The wages of their virtue, and all foes

The cup of their deservings.— O, see, see!

LEAR   And my poor fool is hanged! No, no, no life?

Why should a dog, a horse, a rat have life,

325   And thou no breath at all? Thou'lt come no more,

Never, never, never, never, never!

Pray you undo this button: thank you, sir.

Do you see this? Look on her, look, her lips,

Look there, look there!   *He dies*

330   EDGAR   He faints! My lord, my lord!

KENT   Break, heart, I prithee, break.

EDGAR   Look up, my lord.

KENT   Vex not his ghost: O, let him pass! He hates him

That would upon the rack of this tough world

335   Stretch him out longer.

---

309 vain . . . him it is useless for us to tell him who we are   **311 bootless** pointless
315 this great decay noble ruin, i.e. Lear   **316 For** as for   **resign** hand over   **319 boot**
advantage, additions   **addition** titles, honors   **322 cup** painful experience (plays on the
related sense of "drinking vessel")   **see, see** something attracts Albany's attention,
presumably to Lear   **323 fool** i.e. Cordelia (**fool** was a term of endearment), but recalls Lear's
Fool as well   **327 this button** may refer to Cordelia's (hoping to help her breathe) or Lear's
own (if he is once again afflicted by "the mother," the hysteria that causes one to struggle for
breath)   **sir** it is unclear whom Lear addresses here   **333 ghost** spirit   **334 rack** torture
instrument that stretched the limbs   **335 longer** for a longer period of time/to longer physical
dimensions

EDGAR   He is gone, indeed.

KENT   The wonder is he hath endured so long:
He but usurped his life.

ALBANY   Bear them from hence. Our present business
340 Is general woe.—
Friends of my soul, you twain   *To Kent and Edgar*
Rule in this realm, and the gored state sustain.

KENT   I have a journey, sir, shortly to go:
My master calls me, I must not say no.

345 EDGAR   The weight of this sad time we must obey:
Speak what we feel, not what we ought to say.
The oldest hath borne most: we that are young
Shall never see so much nor live so long.

Exeunt with a dead march

---

338 usurped stole, made illegal use of (beyond its rightful length)   **342 gored** wounded, bleeding   **sustain** support/keep alive   **343 journey** i.e. to death

TEXTUAL NOTES

Q = First Quarto text of 1608
F = First Folio text of 1623
F2 = a correction introduced in the Second Folio text of 1632
Ed = a correction introduced by a later editor
SD = stage direction
SH = speech heading (i.e. speaker's name)

List of parts = Ed

EDMUND *sometimes spelled* Edmond, *often referred to in directions and speech headings as* Bastard

1.1.30 SD *one . . . then* = Q. *Not in* F **33 lord** = F. Q = Liege **36 fast** = F. Q = first **37 age** = F. Q = state **38 Conferring** = F. Q = Confirming **strengths** = F. Q = yeares **38–43** *while . . . now* = F. *Not in* Q **47–48** *Since . . . state* = F. *Not in* Q **57 found** = F. Q = friend **62–63** *and . . . rivers* = F. *Not in* Q **66 of Cornwall** = F. Q = to *Cornwell*, speake **77 ponderous** = F. Q = richer **81 conferred** = F. Q = confirm'd **82 our . . . love** = F. Q = the last, not least in our deere loue **84 interessed** = Ed. F = interest **draw** = F. Q = win **87 SH LEAR Nothing? . . . Nothing.** = F. *Not in* Q **103 sisters** = F. Q = sisters, to loue my father all. **110 mysteries** = F2. F = miseries. Q = mistresse **night** = F. Q = might **118 shall . . . bosom** = F. Q = Shall **136 shall** = F. Q = still **151 falls** = F. Q = stoops **Reserve thy state** = F. Q = Reuerse thy doome **158 pawn** = F. Q = a pawne **159 ne'er** = F. Q = nor **164 SH LEAR** = Q. F = *Kear.* **165 SH KENT** = Q. F = *Lent.* **167 Miscreant** = F. Q = recreant **168 SH ALBANY . . . forbear.** = F. *Not in* Q **SH CORDELIA** *some editors expand* F*'s Cor. to* Cornwall **170 gift** = F. Q = doome **175 strained** = F. Q = straied **176 sentences** = F *corrected.* F *uncorrected,* Q = sentence **179 Five** = F. Q = Foure **180 disasters** = F. Q = diseases **181 sixth** = F. Q = fift **182 next** = Ed. F, Q = tenth **187 Freedom** = F. Q = Friendship **194 SH CORDELIA** = F *(corrected). Some editors expand to* Cornwall. Q = *Glost.* **213 Dowered** = F. Q = Couered **225 object** = F. Q = best obiect **234 Should** = F. Q = Could **237 will** = F. Q = well **238 make known** = F. Q = may know **248 but** = F. Q = no more but **252 regards** = F. Q = respects **255 king** = F. Q = *Leir* **263 respect and fortunes** = F. Q = respects / Of fourtune **270 my** = F. Q = thy **286 Love** = F. Q = vse **291 SH REGAN** = F *(Regn).* Q = *Gonorill* **292 SH GONERIL** = F. Q = *Regan* **295 want** = F. Q = worth **296 plighted** = F. Q = pleated **297 with shame derides** = F. Q = shame them derides **306 not been** = Q. F = beene **319 sit** = F. Q = hit

1.2.1 SH EDMUND = Ed. F, Q = *Bast. (throughout)* **13 tirèd** = F. Q = lyed **18 fine word, 'legitimate'** = F. *Not in* Q **21 to th'legitimate** = F. *Sometimes emended to* top the legitimate **24 Prescribed** = F. Q = subscribd **38 o'erlooking** = F. Q = liking **53 wake** = F. Q = wakt **55 you to this** = F. Q = this to you **67 declined** = F. Q = declining **80 that . . . writ** = F. Q = he hath wrote **81 other** = F. Q = further **99–104 This . . . graves** = F. *Not in* Q **106–7 honesty! 'Tis strange** = F. Q = honest, strange strange **111 stars** = F. Q = the starres **113 spherical** = F. Q = spirituall **117 a star** = F. Q = Starres **119 I should** = F. Q = Fut, I should. **120 maidenliest** *spelled* maidenlest *in* F *and* Q **121 bastardizing** = F. Q = bastardy **122 Pat** = F. Q = *Edgar*; and out **123 sigh . . . o'Bedlam** = F. Q = sith like them of Bedlam **124 Fa . . . mi.** = F. *Not in* Q **130 writes** = F. Q = writ **146–49 I . . . brother?** = F. *Not in* Q **150 I am** = F. Q = go arm'd, I am
1.3.0 SD *Steward* = F. Q = *Gentleman* **3 SH OSWALD** = Ed. F = *Ste.* Q = *Gent. (throughout)* **14 I'd** = F. *Sometimes emended to* I'll **15 distaste** = F. Q = dislike **17 have said** = F. Q = tell you **20 so.** = F. Q = so. I would breed from hence occasions, and I shall, That I may speak: **21 course. Prepare** = F. Q = very course, goe prepare
1.4.1 will = F. Q = well **6 So . . . thy** = F. Q = thy **7 SD *Horns . . . Attendants*** = F. Q = *Enter Lear* **43 SD *Enter Steward*** *appears one line later in* F **49 SH KNIGHT** = F *(spelled* Knigh *here and on two other occasions in Act 1 scene 4).* Q = *Kent* **daughter** = Q. F = Daughters **51 SH KNIGHT** = F. Q = *seruant (throughout)* **57 of kindness appears** = F. Q = apeer's **66 purpose** = F. Q = purport **73 SD *Enter Steward*** *placed one line later in* F **78 these** = F. Q = this **your pardon** = F. Q = you pardon me **80 strucken** = F. Q = struck **86 Have . . . So** = F. Q = you haue wisedome **93 SH LEAR Why, my boy?** = F. Q = *Kent.* Why Fool? **102 all my** = F. Q = any **106 the Lady Brach** = F. Q = Ladie oth'e brach **107 gall** = F. Q = gull **110 nuncle** = F. Q = vncle **121 SH KENT** = F. Q = *Lear* **130 one** = F. Q = foole **141 grace** = F. Q = wit **143 And** = F. Q = They **to** = F. Q = doe **152 fool** = F. Q = fooles **164 You** = F. Q = Methinks you **166 frowning** = F. Q = frowne **171 nor crust** = F. Q = neither crust **nor crumb** = Q. F = not crum **173 shelled** *spelled* sheal'd *in* F, sheald *in* Q **188 know** = F. Q = trow **193 I** = F. Q = Come sir, I **your** = F. Q = that **195 transport** = F. Q = transforme **199 This** = F. Q = why this **201 weakens, his** = F. Q = weaknes, or his **202 Ha! Waking?** = F. Q = sleeping or wakeing; ha! sure **204 SH FOOL Lear's shadow.** = F. *Assigned to Lear in* Q **206 This admiration, sir** = F. Q = Come sir, this admiration **215 graced** = F. Q = great **227 SD *Albany*** = F. Q = *Duke (throughout)* **228 Woe** = F. Q = We **229 Speak . . . my** = F. Q = that wee prepare any **233 SH ALBANY Pray . . . patient.** = F. *Not in* Q **234 liest** = F. Q = list **235 My** = F. Q = list my **are** = F. Q = and **246 Of . . . you.** = F. *Not in* Q **258 cadent** = F. Q = accent **262 Away, away!** = F. Q = goe, goe, my people? **264 more of it** = F. Q = the cause **273 thee worth them** = F.

Q = the worst 274 Th'untented = F. Q *uncorrected* = the vntender
275 Pierce = F. Q *uncorrected* = peruse thee! Old = F. Q = the old
277 loose = F. Q = make 278–79 Ha? . . . daughter = F. Q = yea, i'st
come to this? yet haue I left a daughter 282 flay *spelled* flea *in* F *and* Q
285 that = F. Q = that my Lord 288–89 Pray . . . sir = F. Q = Come sir no
more, you 297–309 SH GONERIL This . . . SD *Enter Steward* = F. Q =
Gon. What *Oswald*, ho. 309 How now, Oswald? = F. Q = *Oswald.* Here
Madam. 310 What = F. Q = *Gon.* What 318 condemn = F. Q = dislike
319 at task = F. Q *uncorrected* = alapt. Q *corrected* = attaskt 322 better,
oft = F. Q = better ought
1.5.0 SD *Enter . . . Fool* = F. Q = *Enter Lear.* 18 tell = F. Q = not tell
42–43 Keep . . . now, = F. Q = I would not be mad, keepe me in temper, I
would not be mad, 44 SH GENTLEMAN = F. Q = *Seruant.*
2.1.2 you = Q. F = your 8–9 ear-kissing = F. Q = eare-bussing 18 act . . .
work = F. Q = aske breefnes . . . helpe 29–30 pardon . . . I = F. Q = pardon me in crauing, I 37 SD *Enter . . . torches* = F. Q = *Enter Glost.*
40 Mumbling = F. Q = warbling 41 stand = F. Q = stand's 49 revenging
= F. Q = reuengiue 50 the thunder = F. Q = their thunders 56 latched =
F. Q = lancht 57 And = F. Q = but 60 Full = F. Q = but 67 coward = F. Q
= caytife 73 would the reposal = F. Q = could the reposure 75 should I
= F. Q = I should 78 practice = F. Q = pretence 81 spirits = F. Q =
spurres 83 O, strange = F. Q = Strong 84 said he? = F. Q = I neuer got
him, 85 where = F. Q = why 91 SD *Enter . . . Attendants* = F. Q = *Enter
the Duke of Cornwall* 93 strangeness = F. Q = strange newes
101 tended = F. Q = tends 106 th'expense . . . of = F. Q *uncorrected* =
these—and wast of this. Q *corrected* = the wast and spoyle of
115 bewray = F. Q = betray 129 threading = F. Q = threatning
130 prize = F. Q *corrected* = poyse 133 differences = F. Q *uncorrected* =
defences best = F. Q *corrected* = lest thought = Q. F = though
134 home = F. Q *uncorrected* = hand 137 businesses = F. Q = busines
2.2.1 dawning = F. Q *corrected* = euen. Q *uncorrected* = deuen 15 worsted-
stocking = Q *corrected.* F = woosted-stocking. Q *uncorrected* = wosted
stocken 16 whoreson = F. Q = knaue, a whorson super-serviceable
finical = F. Q = supersinicall 20 clamorous *spelled* clamours *in* F
25 since = F. Q = ago since 27 you = F. Q = draw, you 39 if = F. Q = and
51 they = F. Q = hee 51–52 years o'th'trade = F. Q = houres at the trade
53 SH CORNWALL = F. Q = *Glost.* 61 know you = F. Q = you haue
66 the holy = F. Q = those 67 too intrinse = Ed. F = t'intrince 69 fire =
F. Q = stir the = F. Q = their 70 Revenge = F. Ed = Reneage 71 gall = F.
Q = gale 72 dogs = F. Q = dayes 74 Smile *spelled* Smoile *in* F, *smoyle in*
Q 77 What = F. Ed = Why 81 fault = F. Q = offence 92 An . . . plain = F.
Q = he must be plaine 98 faith, in = F. Q = sooth, or in 101 flickering =
Q (flitkering). F = flicking 111 compact = F. Q = coniunct 116 flesh-
ment = F. Q = flechuent dread = Q. F = dead 121 ancient = F. Q *cor-*

rected = miscreant. Q *uncorrected* = ausrent **129 Stocking** = F. Q *corrected* = stopping. Q *uncorrected* = stobing. **139 he** = F. Q = hee's **145 duke's** = Q. F = Duke **148 travelled** *spelled* trauail'd *in* F *and* Q **153 saw** = F. Q *uncorrected* = say **158 miracles** = F. Q *corrected* = my wracke. Q *uncorrected* = my rackles **160 most** = F. Q *uncorrected* = not **164 Take** = F. Q *uncorrected* = Late **heavy** *spelled* heanie *in* F **170 unusual** *spelled* vnusall *in* F **176 hairs** = F. Q = haire **181 arms** = F. Q = bare arms **180 Pins** = F. Q *uncorrected* = Pies **183 farms** = F. Q = seruice **185 Sometimes** = F. Q = Sometime **187 SD** *Enter . . .* **Gentleman** = F. Q = *Enter King* **190 SH GENTLEMAN** = F. Q = *Knight (throughout)* **192 this** = F. Q = his **194 thy** = Q. F = ahy **197 heads** = F. Q = heeles **198 man's** = Q. F = man **208–9 By . . . ay** = F. Q = No no, they would not./ *Kent.* Yes they haue **214 impose** = F. Q = purpose **220 panting** = Q. F = painting **223 those** = F. Q = whose **224 meiny** = F. Q = men **235–43 SH FOOL Winter's . : . a year.** = F. *Not in* Q **245** *Hysterica spelled Historica in* F *and* Q **250 the** = Q. F = the the **251 number** = F. Q = traine **258 twenty** = F. Q = a I00 **260 upward** = F. Q = vp the hill **262 have** = Q. F = hause **264 serves and seeks** = F. Q = serues **275 have . . . the** = F. Q = traueled hard to; **travelled** *spelled* travail'd *in* F **fetches** = F. Q = Iustice **285–86 SH GLOUCESTER Well . . . man?** = F. *Not in* Q **288 father** = F. Q *uncorrected* = fate **289 commands, tends,** = F. Q *corrected* = commands her. Q *uncorrected* = come and tends **290–91 Are . . . Fiery?** = F. *Not in* Q **310 knapped** = F. Q = rapt **316 you** = Q. F = your **318 mother's tomb** = Q *corrected.* F = Mother Tombe. Q *uncorrected* = mothers fruit **328–33 SH LEAR Say? . . . blame.** = F. *Not in* Q **337 her** = Q. F = his **360 blister** = F. Q = blast her pride **384 SH LEAR** = F. Q = *Gon.* **stocked** = F. Q = struck **410 hotblooded** = F *uncorrected.* F *corrected* = hot-bloodied. Q = hot bloud in **422 boil** *spelled* Byle *in* F **468 need** = F. Q = deed **471 is** = F. Q = as. *Sometimes emended to* is as **480 tamely** = F. Q = lamely **488 flaws** = F. Q = flowes **497 SH GONERIL** = F. Q = *Duke* **499 SH CORNWALL** = F. Q = *Reg.* **501–2 SH CORNWALL Whither . . . horse** = F. *Not in* Q **503 SH CORNWALL** = F. Q = *Re.* **505 high** = F. Q = bleak

3.1.1 Who's there, besides = F. Q = Whats here beside **12 note** = F. Q = Arte **16–23 Who . . . furnishings** = F. *See "Quarto passages that do not appear in the Folio," p. 134, for alternative lines in* Q **30 that** = F. Q = your **35–6 in . . . this** = F. Q = Ile this way, you that

3.2.8 all = F. Ed = an **germens** *spelled* germaines *in* F **12 wise . . . fools** = F. Q = wise man nor foole **16 tax** = F. Q = taske **22 will . . . join** = F. Q = haue . . . ioin'd **42 are** = F. Q = sit **49 fear** = F. Q = force **55 of** = F. Q = man of **59 concealing continents** = F. Q = concealed centers **67 you** = F. Q = me **76 That's sorry** = F. Q = That sorrowes **77 little tiny** = Ed. F = little-tyne. Q = little tine **80 Though** = F. Q = for **81 True, boy** = F. Q = True my good boy **82–98 SH FOOL This . . . time.** = F. *Not in* Q

3.3.0 SD *Edmund* = F. Q = *the Bastard with lights.* **4 perpetual** = F. Q = their
12 footed = F. Q = landed **15 if** = F. Q = though **17 strange things** = F.
Q = some strange thing

3.4.8 contentious = F. Q *corrected* = tempestious. Q *uncorrected* = crulen-
tious **9 skin so:** = F *corrected.* F *uncorrected* = skin: so: **12 thy** = Q. F =
they **roaring** = F. Q *uncorrected* = raging **18 home** = F. Q = sure
19–20 In . . . endure = F. *Not in* Q **22 all** = F. Q = you all **29–30 In . . .
sleep** = F. *Not in* Q **32 storm** = F. Q = night **34 lopped** = F. Q = loopt
40 SH EDGAR Fathom . . . Tom! = F. *Not in* Q **48 blow the winds** = F. Q
= blowes the cold wind **Hum! . . . bed** = F. Q = goe to thy cold bed
50 Did'st . . . thy = F. Q = Hast thou giuen all to thy two **53 through fire**
= Q. F = though Fire **and through flame** = F. *Not in* Q **ford** = Q. F =
Sword **58 Bless** = Q. F = Blisse **58–59 O . . . de.** = F. *Not in* Q **59 Bless**
= Q. F = blisse **63 Has** = F. Q = What. Ed = What, have **64 Wouldst** = F.
Q = didst **68 light** = F. Q = fall **79 word's justice** = F. Q = words justly
87 I dearly = F. Q = I deeply **94 says . . . nonny** = F. Q = hay no on ny
95 boy, boy = F. Q = boy, my boy, **sessa** = Ed. F = *Sesey.* Q = cease
96 a = F. Q = thy **101–2 lendings! . . . here** = F. Q *corrected* = lendings,
come on. Q *uncorrected* = leadings, come on bee true **106 on's** = F.
Q = in **108 foul** = F. Q = foul fiend **109 till the** = Q. F = at **110 squints** =
F. Q *corrected* = squemes. Q *uncorrected* = queues **114 alight** = F. Q = O
light **126 stocked, punished** = F. Q = stock-punisht **127 hath had
three** = Q. F = hath three **131 Smulkin** = F. Q = snulbug **135 my . . . vile**
= F. Q = is growne so vild my Lord **147 same** = F. Q = most **163 you** = F.
Ed = your **176 tower came** = F. Q = towne come

3.5.10 were not = F. Q = were

3.6.12–14 SH FOOL No . . . him. = F. *Not in* Q **21 They** = F. Q = Theile
27 mongrel grim, 28 Hound = Ed. F = Mongrill,Grim, / Hound. Q =
mungril, grim-hound **him** = F *(Hym). Sometimes emended to* lym
29 tyke = Q (tike). F = tight **33 Do . . . Sessa!** = F. Q = loudla doodla
37 these hard hearts = F. Q = this hardnes **39 Persian** = F. Q = Persian
attire **40 and rest awhile** = F. Q = awhile **42 So, so, we'll** = F. Q = so,
so, so, / Weele **i'th'morning** = F. Q = i'th'morning so, so, so **43 SH
FOOL And . . . noon** = F. *Not in* Q **53 Take up, take up** = F. Q *corrected* =
Take vp the King. Q *uncorrected* = Take vp to keepe

3.7.3 traitor = F. Q = vilaine **8 Advise** = Q. F = Aduice **9 festinate** *spelled*
festiuate *in* F *and* festuant *in* Q **37 none** = F. Q = true **48 answered** = F.
Q = answerer **60 answer** = F. Q = first answere **62 Dover?** = F. Q =
Dover, sir? **65 stick** = F. Q = rash **66 as his bare** = F. Q *corrected* = on his
lowd. Q *uncorrected* = of his lou'd **67 buoyed** = F. Q *corrected* = bod. Q
uncorrected = layd **69 rain** = F. Q = rage **70 howled that stern** = F. Q =
heard that dearne **95 enkindle** = F. Q = vnbridle

4.1.6–10 Welcome . . . comes = F. Q = Who's **10 poorly led** = F. Q *corrected*
= parti,eyd **15 these fourscore years** = F. Q = this forescore **19 You** = F.

Q = Alack sir, you **42 kill** = F. Q = bitt **48 Get thee away** = F. Q = Then, prethee, get thee gon **49 hence** = F. Q = here **60 daub** = F. Q = dance **62 And . . . Bless** = F. Q = Blesse **65–6 thee . . . son** = F. Q = the good man **71 slaves** = F. Q = stands **73 undo** = F. Q = under **77 fearfully** = F. Q = firmely

4.2.10 most . . . dislike = F. Q = hee should most desire **13 terror** = F. Q *uncorrected* = curre **16 Edmund** = F. Q = *Edgar* **18 names** = F. Q = armes **28 O . . . man!** = F. *Not in* Q **30 My fool** = F. Q *corrected* = A Foole. Q *uncorrected* = My foote **body** = F. Q *corrected* = bed **32 whistle** = F. Q *corrected* = whistling **41 seems** = F. Q *corrected* = shewes **44 SH MESSENGER** = F. Q = *Gent.* **48 thrilled** = F. Q = thrald **50 threat-enraged** = F. Q = thereat inraged **55 justices** = F. Q *corrected* = Iustisers. Q *uncorrected* = your Iustices **65 tart** = F. Q = tooke

4.3.0 SD Gentleman = Ed. F = *Gentlemen.* Q = *Doctor* **2 vexed** = F. Q = vent **3 fumiter** = Ed. F = Fenitar. Q = femiter **4 burdocks** = Ed. F = Hardokes. Q = hor-docks **6 sentry** *spelled* Centery *in* F, centurie *in* Q **send** = F. Q = sent **10 helps** = F. Q = can help **19 distress** = Q. F = desires **28 importuned** = F. Q = important **29 incite** = F. Q = in sight

4.4.6 lord = F. Q = lady **13 Edmund** = F. Q = and now **16 o'th'enemy** = F. Q = at'h army **17 madam . . . letter** = F. Q = with my letters **18 troops set** = F. Q = troope sets **24 Some things** = F. Q = Some thing **29 oeillades** *spelled* Eliads *in* F, aliads *in* Q **43 meet** = F. Q = meet him **should** = F. Q = would

4.5.0 SD Edgar = F. Q = *Edmund* **1 I** = F. Q = we **21 walk** = Q. F = walk'd **48 bless him** = F. Q = blesse **67 summit** = F. Q = summons **76 How is't? Feel** = F. Q = how feele **84 whelked** *spelled* wealk'd *in* F **enragèd** = F. Q = enridged **86 make them** = F. Q = made their **96 crying** = F. Q = coyning **102 piece of toasted** = F. Q = tosted **104 I'th'clout, i'th'clout: hewgh** = F. Q = in the ayre, hagh **108 Goneril . . . beard?** = F. Q = *Gonorill*, ha *Regan*, **116 ague-proof** = F. Q = argue-proofe **127 were** = Ed. *Not in* F, Q **139 consumption** = F. Q = consumation **140 civet . . . sweeten** = F. Q = Ciuet, good Apothocarie, to sweeten **143 Let me** = F. Q = Here **148 this** = F. Q = that **149 thy** = F. Q = the **see** = F. Q = see one **160 change places, and** = F. *Not in* Q **165 dog's obeyed** = F. Q = dogge, so bade **171 tattered clothes great** = F. Q = tottered raggs, smal **172–77 Place . . . lips** = F. *Not in* Q; **Place sins** = F. Ed. = Plate sin **179 Now . . . now.** = F. Q = no now **186 wail** *spelled* wawle *in* F, wayl *in* Q **190 shoe** = F. Q = shoot **191 felt** = F. Q = fell **I'll . . . proof** = F. *Not in* Q **194 hand . . . Sir** = F. Q = hands upon him sirs **198 surgeons** = F. Q = a churgion **203 water-pots** = F. Q = water-pots, Ay, and laying autumn's dust. / *Gent.* Good sir— / *Lear.* **204 smug bridegroom** = F. Q = bridegroome **206 Masters** = F. Q = my maisters **208 Come** = F. Q = nay **209 Sa . . . sa.** = F. *Not in* Q **211 a daughter** = F. Q = one daughter **218 sound** = F. Q = sence **221 speedy foot** = F. Q = speed fort **233 tame**

to = F. Q = lame by **238 bounty . . . benison** = F. Q *uncorrected* = bornet and beniz **239 To . . . boot** = F. Q *corrected* = to boot, to boot. Q *uncorrected* = to saue thee **242 old** = F. Q = most **256 I'se** *spelled* ice *in* F **257 ballow** = F. Q *corrected* = bat. Q *uncorrected* = battero **264 English** = F. Q = *British* **270 these** = F. Q = his **the** = F. Q = These **271 sorry** = F. Q = sorrow **282 affectionate servant, Goneril** = F. Q = your affectionate seruant and for your own *Venter, Gonorill* **283 will** = F. Q = wit **294 severed** = F. Q = fenced

Act 4 Scene 6 = Ed. F = *Scna Septima*

4.6.0 SD *Gentleman* = F. Q = *Doctor* **18 jarring** = F. Q = hurrying **24 SH GENTLEMAN** = F. Q *assigns this and the next line to the Doctor, and the following two lines to a Gentleman* **27 of** = F. Q = not of **temperance.** = F. Q = temperance. / *Cord.* Very well. / *Doct.* Please you draw neere, louder the musicke there, **35 opposed** = F. Q = exposd **jarring** = F. Q = warring **36 enemy's** = F. Q = iniurious **49 do . . . me?** = F. Q = know me. **64 not . . . less** = F. *Not in* Q **85 killed** = F. Q = cured **him.** = F. Q = him and yet it is danger to make him euen ore the time hee has lost

5.1.3 alteration = F. Q *uncorrected* = abdication **11 In** = F. Q = I, **17 not** = F. Q = me not **19 Sir . . . heard** = F. Q = For . . . heare **24 and particular broils** = F. Q = dore particulars **27 proceeding.** = F. Q = proceeding. / *Bast.* I shall attend you presently at your tent. **41 And machination ceases** = F. *Not in* Q **loves** = F. Q = loue **48 Here** = F. Q = Hard **guess** = F. Q = quesse **true** = F. Q = great

5.2.1 tree = F. Q = bush **14 SH GLOUCESTER And . . . too.** = F. *Not in* Q.

5.3.2 first = F. Q = best **26 good years** = F. Q = goode **40 down.** = F. Q = down. / *Cap.* I cannot draw a cart, nor eate dride oats, / If it bee mans worke ile do't. **48 send** = F. Q *uncorrected* = saue **retention** = F. Q *uncorrected* = retention and appointed guard **49 had** = F. Q = has **60 might** = F. Q = should **63 immediacy** = F. Q = imediate **67 addition** = F. Q = aduancement **70 SH ALBANY** = F. Q = *Gon.* **77 Dispose . . . thine:** = F. *Not in* Q **84 SH REGAN** = F. Q = *Bast.* **thine** = F. Q = good **86 thy arrest** = F. Q = thine attaint **87 sister** = Q. F = sister **88 bar** = Ed. F = bare **91 loves** = F. Q = loue **94 let . . . sound:** = F. *Not in* Q **95 person** = F. Q = head **97 make** = F. Q = proue **101 medicine** = F. Q = poyson **116 lists** = F. Q = hoast **117 by** = F. Q = at **120 SH HERALD** = F. Q = *Edmund* **128–29 Yet . . . cope** = F. Q = yet are I mou't / Where is the aduersarie I come to cope with all **136–37 my . . . honours —** = F. Q = the priuiledge of my tongue, **140 Despise** = F. Q = Despite **143 Conspirant** = F. Q = Conspicuate **145 below thy foot** = F. Q = beneath thy feet **147 are** = F. Q = As **152 tongue** = F. Q = being **153 What . . . delay** = F. *Not in* Q **154 rule** = F. Q = right **155 Back** = F. Q = Heere **156 hell-hated lie o'erwhelm** = F. Q = hell hatedly, oreturnd **157 scarcely** = Q. F = scarely **162 war** = F. Q = armes **wast** = F. Q = art **166 stop . . . sir** = F. Q = stople it **167 name** = F. Q = thing **172 SH EDMUND** = F. Q = *Gon.*

183 vices = F. Q = vertues **184 plague** = F. Q = scourge **200 we** = F. Q = with **207 fault** = F. Q = Father **211 our** = F. Q = my **222 SH EDGAR** = F. Q = *Alb.* **223 SH ALBANY Speak, man.** = F. *Not in* Q **224 SH EDGAR** = F. Q *assigns line to Albany* **226 O, she's dead!** = F. *Not in* Q **227 Who . . . man.** = F. Q = Who man, speake? **229 confesses** = F. Q = hath confest **234 judgement** = F. Q = Iustice **235 is this** = F. Q = tis **265 you** = Q. F = your **281 you, murderers, traitors** = F. Q = your murderous traytors **287 SH GENTLEMAN** = F. Q = *Cap.* **290 him** = F. Q = them **295 This . . . sight.** = F. *Not in* Q **298 you that** = F. Q = that **302 first** = F. Q = life **309 says** = F. Q = sees **327 sir.** = F. Q = sir, O, o, o, o. **328–29 Do . . . there!** = F. *Not in* Q **331 SH KENT** = F. Q = *Lear* **342 realm** = F. Q = kingdome **345 SH EDGAR** = F. Q = *Duke*

QUARTO PASSAGES THAT DO NOT APPEAR IN THE FOLIO

Lines are numbered continuously, for ease of reference.

Following 1.2.88:

EDMUND   Nor is not, sure.

GLOUCESTER To his father, that so tenderly and entirely loves him.
Heaven and earth!

Following 1.2.130:

as of unnaturalness between the child and the parent,
5   death, dearth, dissolutions of ancient amities, divisions in
state, menaces and maledictions against king and nobles,
needless diffidences, banishment of friends, dissipation of
cohorts, nuptial breaches, and I know not what.

EDGAR   How long have you been a sectary astronomical?

10 EDMUND   Come, come,

Following 1.3.16:

Not to be overruled. Idle old man,
That still would manage those authorities
That he hath given away! Now by my life
Old fools are babes again, and must be used
15   With checks as flatteries, when they are seen abused.

Following 1.4.131:

FOOL   That lord that counselled thee to give away thy land,
Come place him here by me, do thou for him stand,

---

1 Nor . . . sure and I am sure he is not   4 unnaturalness lack of natural family feeling
5 dearth famine   ancient amities long-standing friendships   divisions breaches,
disagreements   6 maledictions curses   7 diffidences doubts, mistrust   dissipation of
cohorts dispersal of troops   8 nuptial breaches breaking of marriage vows   9 sectary
astronomical devotee of astrology (in the period, astronomy and astrology were often
indistinguishable from one another)   11 Not i.e. we are not   Idle foolish/useless   14 used
handled, dealt with   15 checks as flatteries rebukes instead of flattery   seen abused seen
to be misguided   17 stand i.e. stand in

The sweet and bitter fool will presently appear:
The one in motley here, the other found out there.

20 LEAR   Dost thou call me fool, boy?

FOOL   All thy other titles thou hast given away, that thou
was born with.

KENT   This is not altogether fool my lord.

FOOL   No, faith, lords and great men will not let me, if I
25 had a monopoly out, they would have part on't: and ladies
too, they will not let me have all the fool to myself, they'll be
snatching.

Following 1.4.204:
I would learn that, for by the marks of sovereignty,
knowledge, and reason, I should be false persuaded I had
30 daughters.

FOOL   Which they will make an obedient father.

Following 2.2.137:
His fault is much, and the good king, his master,
Will check him for't: your purposed low correction
Is such as basest and 'temnest wretches
35 For pilf'rings and most common trespasses
Are punished with.

Following 3.1.7:
                                        tears his white hair,
Which the impetuous blasts with eyeless rage
Catch in their fury, and make nothing of,
40 Strives in his little world of man to out-scorn,
The to-and-fro-conflicting wind and rain:
This night wherein the cubdrawn bear would couch,
The lion and the belly-pinchèd wolf

18 **presently** immediately   19 **motley** the traditional multicolored costume of the fool
23 **altogether fool** entirely foolish (the Fool replies to the sense of "the only fool")   25 **on't** of it
27 **snatching** may imply snatching at the Fool's genitals or phallic baton (picking up on and
shifting the sense of **part**; fools were proverbially well-endowed)   28 **marks** outward signs
29 **false** falsely   33 **check** rebuke   **low correction** base punishment   34 **'temnest** most
despised (contemnest)   35 **pilf'rings** petty thefts   **trespasses** crimes   38 **eyeless** blind
39 **Catch** seize   42 **cubdrawn** drained of milk by her cubs, ravenous   **couch** take cover, lie in
its lair   43 **belly-pinchèd** starving

Keep their fur dry, unbonneted he runs,
45   And bids what will take all.

Replaces 3.1.16–23:

But true it is, from France there comes a power
Into this scattered kingdom, who already
Wise in our negligence, have secret feet
In some of our best ports, and are at point
50   To show their open banner.
Now to you:
If on my credit you dare build so far
To make your speed to Dover, you shall find
Some that will thank you, making just report
55   Of how unnatural and bemadding sorrow
The king hath cause to 'plain.
I am a gentleman of blood and breeding,
And from some knowledge and assurance,
Offer this office to you.

Following 3.6.16:

60   EDGAR   The foul fiend bites my back.

FOOL   He's mad that trusts in the tameness of a wolf, a
horse's health, a boy's love, or a whore's oath.

LEAR   It shall be done, I will arraign them straight,
Come sit thou here most learnèd justice.—   *To Edgar*
65   Thou, sapient sir sit here.   *To the Fool*
No, you she foxes—

EDGAR   Look where he stands and glares. Want'st thou eyes
at trial, madam?
Come o'er the bourn, Bessy, to me—

---

44 **unbonneted** bare-headed   45 **bids . . . all** invites anyone who wishes to do so to take
everything   46 **power** army   47 **scattered** divided   48 **Wise in** aware of/taking advantage
of   **feet** footholds   49 **at . . . show** on the point of displaying   52 **on . . . far** i.e. if you trust
me so far as   **credit** trustworthiness   54 **making just report** for making an accurate report
55 **bemadding** madness-provoking   56 **'plain** complain, lament   57 **blood** noble family
58 **assurance** certainty   59 **office** task   63 **arraign** indict, put on trial   **straight** straight
away   64 **justice** judge   65 **sapient** wise   67 **Want'st thou** do you lack   **eyes** may signify
"spectators"   69 **Come . . . me** a snatch of popular song   **bourn** stream

| 70 | FOOL | Her boat hath a leak, | *Sings* |

70   FOOL   Her boat hath a leak,   *Sings*
                  And she must not speak
                  Why she dares not come over to thee.

EDGAR   The foul fiend haunts poor Tom in the voice of a
nightingale, Hopdance cries in Tom's belly for two white
75 herring,
                  Croak not black angel, I have no food for thee.

KENT   How do you sir? Stand you not so amazed,
                  Will you lie down and rest upon the cushings?

LEAR   I'll see their trial first, bring in their evidence.—
80   Thou robèd man of justice, take thy place—   *To Edgar*
                  And thou, his yoke-fellow of equity,   *To the Fool*
                  Bench by his side:— you are o'th'commission,   *To Kent*
                  Sit you too.

EDGAR   Let us deal justly.
85   Sleepest or wakest thou, jolly shepherd?
                  Thy sheep be in the corn,
                  And for one blast of thy minikin mouth,
                  Thy sheep shall take no harm.
                  Purr, the cat is grey.

90 LEAR   Arraign her first, 'tis Goneril. I here take my oath
before this honourable assembly, she kicked the poor king
her father.

FOOL   Come hither, mistress. Is your name Goneril?

LEAR   She cannot deny it.

95 FOOL   Cry you mercy, I took you for a joint-stool.

LEAR   And here's another whose warped looks proclaim
                  What store her heart is made on: stop her there!

---

70 Her . . . leak i.e. she is menstruating (or possibly "she has gonorrhea")   **71 speak** say
72 come over i.e. for sex   **73 foul** possible pun on "fool"   **74 Hopdance** a devil associated
with music (like all of the fiends Edgar mentions, taken from Samuel Harsnett's 1603
Declaration of Egregious Popish Impostures)   **76 black angel** i.e. the fiend in Tom's belly, which
is causing it to rumble   **77 do** are   **amazed** stunned, overwhelmed   **78 cushings** cushions
81 yoke-fellow of equity partner in fairness   **82 Bench** sit on the bench   **o'th'commission** of
the panel of judges   **87 for . . . mouth** i.e. if the shepherd summons his sheep back by playing
his pipe   **minikin** dainty/shrill   **89 Purr** Harsnett mentions a devil called Purr, though devils
were popularly thought to assume the shape of cats   **95 Cry you mercy** I beg your pardon
joint-stool a well-made stool   **96 another** i.e. Regan   **warped looks** contorted facial
expression/warped wood   **97 store** material/tradesman's stock   **on** of

Arms, arms, sword, fire! Corruption in the place!
False justicer, why hast thou let her scape?

Following 3.6.55:

100   KENT   Oppressed nature sleeps:
This rest might yet have balmed thy broken sinews,
Which, if convenience will not allow,
Stand in hard cure.— Come help to bear thy master: *To Fool*
Thou must not stay behind.   *Exeunt. [Edgar remains]*

105   EDGAR   When we our betters see bearing our woes,
We scarcely think our miseries our foes.
Who alone suffers, suffers most i'th'mind,
Leaving free things and happy shows behind,
But then the mind much sufferance doth o'erskip,
110   When grief hath mates, and bearing fellowship:
How light and portable my pain seems now,
When that which makes me bend, makes the king bow:
He childed as I fathered. Tom away!
Mark the high noises and thyself bewray
115   When false opinion, whose wrong thoughts defile thee,
In thy just proof repeals and reconciles thee.
What will hap more tonight, safe scape the king:
Lurk, lurk.   *Exit*

Following 3.7.109:

SERVANT   I'll never care what wickedness I do,
120   If this man come to good.

---

99 **False justicer** corrupt judge   **scape** escape   100 **Oppressed** overwhelmed/afflicted
101 **balmed . . . sinews** soothed your shattered nerves   102 **convenience** opportunity
103 **Stand . . . cure** will be hard to heal   105 **bearing our woes** enduring the same suffering
as us   107 **Who . . . i'th'mind** mental anguish is worst for those who suffer alone   108 **free**
carefree   **happy shows** displays of happiness/visions of good fortune   109 **sufferance**
suffering   **o'erskip** pass over, not notice   110 **bearing** endurance (of affliction)
111 **portable** bearable   112 **bow** i.e. bow down under a truly heavy weight (with suggestion
of servile bowing, inappropriate to a king)   113 **He . . . fathered** his children have treated him
as my father has treated me   114 **high noises** important rumors/what is being said among
the powerful   **bewray** reveal   116 **In . . . proof** in proving you to be just   117 **What . . . king**
whatever else happens tonight, may the king escape safely   118 **Lurk** i.e. stay out of sight

SECOND SERVANT If she live long,
>And in the end meet the old course of death,
>Women will all turn monsters.

FIRST SERVANT Let's follow the old earl, and get the Bedlam
125 >To lead him where he would: his madness
>Allows itself to anything.

SECOND SERVANT   Go thou: I'll fetch some flax and whites of eggs
>To apply to his bleeding face. Now heaven help him!

Following 4.1.66:
>Five fiends have been in poor Tom at once: of lust, as
130 >Obidicut, Hobbididence, prince of dumbness, Mahu of
>stealing, Modo of murder, Flibbertigibbet of mopping and
>mowing, who since possesses chambermaids and waiting-
>women. So, bless thee, master.

Following 4.2.35:
>I fear your disposition:
135 >That nature, which contemns i'th'origin
>Cannot be bordered certain in itself.
>She that herself will sliver and disbranch
>From her material sap perforce must wither
>And come to deadly use.

140 GONERIL   No more, the text is foolish.

ALBANY   Wisdom and goodness to the vile seem vile:
>Filths savour but themselves. What have you done?
>Tigers, not daughters, what have you performed?
>A father, and a gracious agèd man,

---

122 old . . . death i.e. die naturally, in old age   **124 Bedlam** Bedlam beggar, i.e. Poor Tom
125 where he would wherever he wants to go   **126 Allows itself to** enables him to do
127 flax . . . eggs both were conventionally used to soothe damaged eyes   **129 Obidicut . . .
Flibbertigibbet** more fiends mentioned by Samuel Harsnett; "flibbertigibbet" can also mean "a
gossip" or "a flighty, frivolous woman"   **131 mopping and mowing** grimacing, making faces
135 contemns i'th'origin despises its originator (father)   **136 bordered certain** safely
contained   **137 sliver and disbranch** split and break off (like a branch from a tree)
138 material essential, substantial   **perforce** necessarily   **139 come . . . use** be destroyed
(like firewood)   **140 text** sermon   **142 savour but** only enjoy, appreciate   **144 gracious**
generous/good/(as a king) possessed of divine grace

145   Whose reverence even the head-lugged bear would lick,
       Most barbarous, most degenerate, have you madded. Could
       my good brother suffer you to do it?
       A man, a prince, by him so benefited!
       If that the heavens do not their visible spirits
150   Send quickly down to tame the vile offences, it will come,
       Humanity must perforce prey on itself,
       Like monsters of the deep.

Following 4.2.39:

                              that not know'st
       Fools do those villains pity who are punished
155   Ere they have done their mischief. Where's thy drum?
       France spreads his banners in our noiseless land,
       With plumèd helm, thy state begins threat,
       Whilst thou, a moral fool, sits still and cries
       'Alack, why does he so?'

Following 4.2.43:

160   ALBANY   Thou changèd and self-covered thing, for shame
       Bemonster not thy feature. Were't my fitness
       To let these hands obey my blood,
       They are apt enough to dislocate and tear
       Thy flesh and bones: howe'er thou art a fiend,
165   A woman's shape doth shield thee.
       GONERIL   Marry, your manhood mew—
       Enter a Gentleman
       ALBANY   What news?

---

145 reverence position deserving respect, venerable condition   **head-lugged** that has been
pulled about by its head, i.e. enraged   **146 madded** sent mad   **147 brother** brother-in-law,
i.e. Cornwall   **suffer** allow   **149 visible spirits** spirits in visible form, avenging angels
150 tame crush   **154 Fools . . . mischief** i.e. only fools pity villains (like Lear) who are
punished as a preventative measure before they have done wrong   **156 France** the King of
France   **noiseless** silent, inactive   **157 plumèd helm** (soldiers') helmets adorned with
feathers   **thy . . . threat** begins to threaten the state   **158 moral** moralizing   **160 self-
covered** self-concealing   **161 Bemonster . . . feature** do not make your beauty hideous by
revealing your true fiend's face   **Were't my fitness** if it were proper for me   **162 blood** anger
164 howe'er however much, although   **166 Marry** by the Virgin Mary   **mew** a
contemptuous and belittling cat's meow

Following 4.2.77:

Enter Kent and a Gentleman

KENT   Why the King of France is so suddenly gone back,
know you no reason?

170 GENTLEMAN Something he left imperfect in the state, which
since his coming forth is thought of, which imports to the
kingdom so much fear and danger that his personal return
was most required and necessary.

KENT   Who hath he left behind him general?

175 GENTLEMAN The Marshal of France, Monsieur La Far.

KENT   Did your letters pierce the queen to any
demonstration of grief?

GENTLEMAN   Ay, sir, she took them, read them in my presence,
And now and then an ample tear trilled down

180 Her delicate cheek: it seemed she was a queen over
Her passion, who, most rebel-like,
Sought to be king o'er her.

KENT   O, then it moved her.

GENTLEMAN   Not to a rage: patience and sorrow strove

185 Who should express her goodliest. You have seen
Sunshine and rain at once: her smiles and tears
Were like a better way: those happy smilets,
That played on her ripe lip seem not to know
What guests were in her eyes, which, parted thence,

190 As pearls from diamonds dropped. In brief,
Sorrow would be a rarity most beloved,
If all could so become it.

KENT   Made she no verbal question?

GENTLEMAN   Faith, once or twice she heaved the name of 'father'

195 Pantingly forth, as if it pressed her heart:
Cried 'Sisters, sisters! Shame of ladies, sisters!
Kent, father, sisters! What, i'th'storm, i'th'night?

---

168 back i.e. to France   **170 imperfect** unfinished   **171 imports** signifies, brings with it
179 trilled trickled   **181 passion** strong emotion/grief   **185 goodliest** best, most effectively
187 smilets little smiles, half-smiles   **192 so become it** grace it so well, make it seem so
attractive

Let pity not be believed!' There she shook
The holy water from her heavenly eyes,

200 And clamour moistened her: then away she started
To deal with grief alone.

KENT   It is the stars,
The stars above us, govern our conditions,
Else one self mate and make could not beget

205 Such different issues. You spoke not with her since?

GENTLEMAN No.

KENT   Was this before the king returned?

GENTLEMAN No, since.

KENT   Well, sir, the poor distressèd Lear's i'th'town;

210 Who sometime, in his better tune, remembers
What we are come about, and by no means
Will yield to see his daughter.

GENTLEMAN Why, good sir?

KENT   A sovereign shame so elbows him: his own
unkindness,

215 That stripped her from his benediction, turned her
To foreign casualties, gave her dear rights
To his dog-hearted daughters: these things sting
His mind so venomously, that burning shame
Detains him from Cordelia.

220 GENTLEMAN Alack, poor gentleman!

KENT   Of Albany's and Cornwall's powers you heard not?

GENTLEMAN 'Tis so, they are afoot.

KENT   Well, sir, I'll bring you to our master Lear,
And leave you to attend him: some dear cause

225 Will in concealment wrap me up awhile.
When I am known aright, you shall not grieve

---

198 Let . . . believed! Put no trust in pity!   200 clamour moistened her the expression of her
grief moistened her with tears   started hastened, went abruptly   204 mate and make
husband and wife   205 issues children   210 sometime sometimes   tune i.e. frame of mind
214 sovereign overpowering (plays on the related literal sense of "kingly")   elbows pushes,
jostles   216 casualties chance, uncertainties   222 afoot on the move   224 attend wait on,
look after   dear cause important reason   226 aright rightly, as myself   grieve regret

Lending me this acquaintance. I pray you go
Along with me.   *Exeunt*

Following 4.6.27:

CORDELIA   Very well.
230 DOCTOR   Please you, draw near.— Louder the music there!

Following 4.6.35:

To stand against the deep dread-bolted thunder,
In the most terrible and nimble stroke
Of quick cross lightning? To watch — poor *perdu!* —
With this thin helm?

Following 4.6.89:

235 GENTLEMAN   Holds it true, sir, that the Duke of Cornwall was so
slain?

KENT   Most certain, sir.

GENTLEMAN   Who is conductor of his people?

KENT   As 'tis said, the bastard son of Gloucester.

240 GENTLEMAN   They say Edgar, his banished son, is with the Earl of
Kent in Germany.

KENT   Report is changeable. 'Tis time to look about: the
powers of the kingdom approach apace.

GENTLEMAN   The arbitrament is like to be bloody. Fare you well,
245 sir.

KENT   My point and period will be throughly wrought,
Or well or ill, as this day's battle's fought.

Exit

---

231 deep rumbling, deep-voiced   **dread-bolted** hurling terrifying thunderbolts   **233 cross**
forked   **watch** remain awake/be on guard   ***perdu*** "lost one" (French), the name given to a
guard placed in an extremely open, dangerous position   **234 helm** helmet/covering of hair
238 conductor . . . people commander of his forces   **242 Report** rumor   **243 powers . . .**
kingdom British forces   **apace** rapidly   **245 arbitrament** deciding of the dispute
246 point . . . wrought the conclusion of my aims will be throughly brought about   **247 Or**
either

Following 5.1.13:

EDMUND   That thought abuses you.

REGAN   I am doubtful that you have been conjunct

250   And bosomed with her, as far as we call hers

Following 5.1.17:

GONERIL   I had rather lose the battle than that sister
Should loosen him and me.

Following 5.1.21:

Where I could not be honest,
I never yet was valiant. For this business,
255   It touches us as France invades our land,
Not bolds the king, with others whom I fear,
Most just and heavy causes make oppose.

EDMUND   Sir, you speak nobly.

Following 5.3.55:

At this time
260   We sweat and bleed: the friend hath lost his friend;
And the best quarrels, in the heat, are cursed
By those that feel their sharpness:
The question of Cordelia and her father
Requires a fitter place.

Following 5.3.220:

265   EDGAR   This would have seemed a period
To such as love not sorrow, but another,
To amplify too much, would make much more,
And top extremity.

---

248 abuses dishonors, wrongs   **249 doubtful** fearful   **249–50 conjunct And bosomed**
sexually intimate   **250 as . . . hers** to the fullest extent   **253 honest** honorable   **254 For** as
for   **255 touches us as** i.e. affects our honor insofar as   **256 bolds** insofar as it emboldens
with (who) along with   **257 Most . . . oppose** has most just and weighty grounds for hostility
261–62 the . . . sharpness i.e. in the heat of emotion even the best grounds for hostility are
cursed by those who have suffered the losses and afflictions of battle (Edmund pretends to be
anxious that Lear and Cordelia receive a fair trial)   **265 period** limit, extreme point
266 such . . . not those who do not love   **266–68 another . . . extremity** to enlarge upon
another sorrowful tale (that of Kent) would increase sorrow even further and exceed all limits

Whilst I was big in clamour, came there in a man,
270 Who, having seen me in my worst estate,
Shunned my abhorred society, but then finding
Who 'twas that so endured, with his strong arms
He fastened on my neck and bellowed out
As he'd burst heaven, threw me on my father,
275 Told the most piteous tale of Lear and him
That ever ear received, which in recounting
His grief grew puissant and the strings of life
Began to crack: twice then the trumpets sounded,
And there I left him 'tranced.
280 **ALBANY**   But who was this?
EDGAR   Kent, sir, the banished Kent, who in disguise
Followed his enemy king and did him service
Improper for a slave.

TEXTUAL NOTES

Q = First Quarto text of 1608
Q2 = a correction introduced in the Second Quarto text of 1619
Ed = a correction introduced by a later editor
SH = Speech heading (i.e. speaker's name)

1 SH EDMUND = Ed. Q = *Bast. (throughout)* **25 on't** = Q. Q2 = an't **ladies** = Q *(corrected)*. Q *(uncorrected)* = lodes **34 basest and 'temnest** = Q *(corrected)*. Q *(uncorrected)* = belest and contaned **67 Want'st** = Q2. Q = wanst **69 bourn** = Ed. Q = broome **91 she kicked** = Ed. Q = kickt **95 joint-stool** = Q2. Q = ioyne stoole **97 on** = Ed. Q = an **125 madness** = Q *(corrected)*. Q *(uncorrected)* = rogish madnes **131 Flibbertigibbet** *spelled Stiberdigebit in* Q **131–32 mopping and mowing** = Ed. Q = Mobing, & *Mohing* **151 Humanity** = Q *(corrected)*. Q *(uncorrected)* = Humanly **157 threat** *spelled* threat *in* Q *(corrected)* **state begins threat** = Q (corrected). Q *(uncorrected)* = slayer begin threats **166 mew** = Q *(corrected)*. Q *(uncorrected)* = now **178 Ay, sir,** = Ed. Q = I say **184 strove** = Ed. Q = streme

269 big in clamour loud in lamentation   **270 estate** condition   **273 fastened . . . neck** i.e. embraced me   **274 As** as if   **277 puissant** powerful   **strings of life** i.e. heartstrings **279 'tranced** absorbed by grief/in a faint, unconscious   **282 enemy king** i.e. the king who had treated him as an enemy   **283 Improper** for unfitting even for

SCENE-BY-SCENE ANALYSIS

ACT 1 SCENE 1

Relationships between key characters are established. Several themes are introduced: power/authority, deception, nature, kinship, sanity, and sight.

Lines 1–33: Kent and Gloucester discuss Lear. Edmund is introduced. Gloucester insists that Edmund is as dear to him as his older, legitimate, son, Edgar, and claims that "the whoreson must be acknowledged." The bawdy language used to describe Edmund's conception undermines the good intentions behind this.

Lines 34–193: A trumpet flourish emphasizes the ceremonial, public nature of events from this point. Instructing Gloucester to fetch France and Burgundy, Lear reveals his "darker purpose"—to allocate a piece of kingdom to each of his three daughters, intending the "largest bounty" to whoever "doth love [him] most." This reveals Lear's inability to separate public and domestic and highlights his perception of emotions as subject to pecuniary measurement. Tensions exist between his love of power and his portrayal of himself as an old man who wishes to "Unburdened crawl toward death."

Goneril's speech is effusive but ambiguous, as she declares that she loves her father "more than word can wield the matter." Regan is similarly flattering but ambiguous, telling Lear to "prize" her at Goneril's "worth," as she is "made of that self-mettle" as her sister. Cordelia's asides show her dilemma—she is torn between genuine love for her father and reluctance or inability to voice this before the court. She is offered "a third more opulent" than her sisters—unlike Gloucester, Lear does not even suggest he values his daughters equally. In contrast to her sisters, Cordelia's response is simply "Nothing." Lear encourages her to say more, because "Nothing will come of nothing," a concept that is explored throughout the play. Lear disinherits Cordelia, and Kent's attempts to speak up for her fuel his anger.

Retaining a hundred knights, Lear divides his kingdom between Goneril and Regan, intending to live with each of them for alternate months. Kent intervenes, showing respect for Lear, but suggesting that he is not thinking clearly and urging him to "check / This hideous rashness." Lear banishes Kent.

Lines 194–281: Lear explains to the King of France and Duke of Burgundy that Cordelia's "price is fallen." She is no longer "dear" to him, a word that highlights his belief that love is quantifiable. Burgundy cannot decide, so Lear offers his daughter to France but says he would not want him to marry a "wretch" that "Nature is ashamed" of. France asks what Cordelia's "monstrous" offense is and she asks Lear to make it clear that it is lack of the "glib and oily art" of false speech. Burgundy says that he will take her with her original dowry. Echoing Cordelia, Lear declares that this is "Nothing," so Burgundy declines. France sees Cordelia's virtues and comments that "unprized precious" Cordelia is "most rich, being poor," highlighting France and Lear's differing perceptions of "worth," and challenging Lear's assertion that "Nothing will come of nothing."

Lines 282–299: Leaving with France, Cordelia says goodbye "with washèd eyes," suggesting tears but also clear perception of her sisters' characters.

Lines 300–323: Goneril and Regan discuss Lear's "poor judgement" and the "changes" and "infirmity" of his old age, but Regan observes that "he hath ever but slenderly known himself." Goneril expresses concern about Lear's desire for authority. Regan agrees that they must "think" about this, but Goneril says that they "must do something," highlighting a subtle difference between them.

ACT 1 SCENE 2

Lines 1–22: Edmund is angry that he will not inherit. He protests about the label "base" and argues that he is as good as "honest madam's issue"—better, even, because there was passion in his conception. He reveals his designs on Edgar's inheritance.

Lines 23–107: Edmund conceals a letter from Gloucester in a way that draws attention to it. He tells Gloucester it is "Nothing," but then pretends that it is from Edgar. Gloucester reads its contents, which suggest that Edgar and Edmund should murder Gloucester and split the inheritance. Edmund manipulates Gloucester, who is easily persuaded that Edgar is an "unnatural" villain. Edmund pretends to plead on Edgar's behalf and arranges that Gloucester will overhear a conversation between them. Gloucester exits, blaming all the problems in family and state on "These late eclipses in the sun and moon."

Lines 108–161: Edmund is scornful of those who believe that destiny is decided by the stars and blame their "evil" on "a divine thrusting on," thus raising a debate between free will and fate, as he claims that the stars have no influence on his personality or fortune. Edgar interrupts and Edmund changes behavior on "cue," suggesting his directorial role in the action. He persuades Edgar that Gloucester is angry with him and suggests that they avoid meeting. Giving Edgar the key to his lodging, he promises to help.

ACT 1 SCENE 3

Goneril and her steward Oswald discuss Lear's irrational temper. She gives instructions to say that she is ill and cannot see Lear and that the servants are to ignore him.

ACT 1 SCENE 4

Lines 1–89: Kent is disguised, but while his appearance has changed, his nature has not—he is still an "honest-hearted fellow." Not recognizing him, Lear employs Kent and asks Oswald for Goneril, but is ignored. One of Lear's knights says that Oswald refuses to come back, that Goneril is unwell, and points out that Lear has been neglected recently. When Oswald reappears, he is disrespectful and Lear loses his temper. Kent trips Oswald up and insults him, earning Lear's thanks.

Lines 90–174: Lear's Fool delivers a series of jokes, riddles, nonsense, and rhymes. These have comic effect, but they are also ambiguous, providing perceptive comment on Lear's circumstances and reinforcing some key themes such as cruelty, division, and folly. In the Quarto text, Kent comments that "This is not altogether fool my lord."

Lines 175–297: Goneril lists her grievances. Lear's temper and language become wilder, suggesting the growing disquiet of his mind. The interjections of the Fool, combining nonsense and wisdom, contribute to the growing disorder. Albany ineffectually attempts to calm Lear, who curses Goneril with either sterility or the future birth of a "child of spleen." He leaves. Goneril ignores Albany, showing where the power lies in their relationship. Lear returns, having discovered that Goneril has reduced his train of knights by fifty. Despite uncontrollable anger, his tears suggest weakness. He decides to go to Regan, saying she will "flay" Goneril's "wolfish visage"—an example of the animal imagery associated with the two sisters.

Lines 298–325: Goneril claims it is unwise to allow Lear to enforce the whims of his old age, and calls Oswald to take a letter to Regan. She criticizes Albany for his "milky gentleness."

ACT 1 SCENE 5

Lear sends letters to Gloucester with Kent, then struggles against madness as he talks to his Fool.

ACT 2 SCENE 1

Lines 1–91: Edmund urges Edgar to escape, suggesting that Cornwall believes Edgar is plotting against him, and that Gloucester is in pursuit. Edmund directs Edgar's flight, pretending that he is helping, but convincing Gloucester's party that he is trying to stop him. He wounds his own arm and tells Gloucester that Edgar stabbed him when he refused to help Edgar. Gloucester tells "Loyal and natural" Edmund that he will make him his heir.

Lines 92–140: Gloucester confirms Cornwall and Regan's queries about Edgar. Cornwall praises Edmund, takes him into his service, then begins to explain their arrival. Regan interrupts, showing her dominance, and claims that she wanted Gloucester's advice on letters from Lear and Goneril.

ACT 2 SCENE 2

Lines 1–144: Outside Gloucester's castle, Oswald claims not to know the disguised Kent, who insults and beats him. While Cornwall attempts to establish how the quarrel started, Kent continues to insult Oswald, who explains that Kent (who calls himself "Caius") is in Lear's service. Cornwall comments on Kent's plain-spoken nature, but ironically assumes that his "plainness / Harbour[s] more craft and more corrupter ends" and places him in the stocks. In the Quarto text, Gloucester argues stocks are for "basest and "temnest wretches" and it is insulting to Lear to punish his messenger in them.

Lines 145–166: Gloucester apologizes and says that he will plead for Kent's release, but Kent says not to. Kent's soliloquy reveals that he has a letter from Cordelia.

Lines 167–187: Edgar intends to disguise himself as a mad beggar from Bedlam. Edgar's soliloquy and the following sequence are sometimes edited and played as separate scenes, but the action continues uninterrupted in that Kent remains onstage asleep in the stocks.

Lines 188–271: Lear will not believe that Regan and Cornwall have put Kent in the stocks—it is an "outrage" "upon respect." Fighting his rising anger, Lear goes to confront them. The Fool comments on Kent's folly in continuing to serve Lear.

Lines 272–383: Enraged that Regan and Cornwall will not speak with him, Lear sends Gloucester to summon them. His language reflects his growing disturbance, which he fights to suppress—"my rising heart! But, down!" When they arrive, Lear pours out his grievances against Goneril. Regan responds in a reasoned but insulting manner, saying that Lear is old and needs to be "ruled and led," and suggests that he ask Goneril's forgiveness. Lear's pride and anger rise, but he thinks Regan will acknowledge the "dues of gratitude" that he has bought with "half o'th'kingdom."

Lines 384–515: Goneril and Regan unite against Lear, gradually reducing his number of knights—a symbol of his power—until he has nothing. He reminds them of what they owe him—"I gave you all." When Regan asks whether Lear needs even one follower, he replies "O, reason not the need! Our basest beggars / Are in the poorest thing superfluous: / Allow not nature more than nature needs, / Man's life is cheap as beast's." The encounter of king and beggar, the question of "superfluity," and the stripping down from courtly accoutrements to raw nature are at the core of the play. Lear asks the heavens for patience, but the growing storm reflects his turbulent mind and he leaves in "high rage" to go out onto the heath. Goneril, Regan, and Cornwall tell Gloucester to shut his doors against Lear and the storm.

ACT 3 SCENE 1

In this act, the relatively brief and fast-paced scenes move between different locations and characters. This, combined with the evocation of the storm, creates a sense of chaos that mirrors the breakdown of Lear's reason and kingdom.

Kent learns that Lear is on the heath in the storm with the Fool. He reveals that the French have spies in the courts of Cornwall and Albany, between whom dissension is growing. Kent gives the Gentleman a ring to show to Cordelia as confirmation of his true identity.

ACT 3 SCENE 2

Lear's disordered speech reflects his mental state as he invokes nature to destroy mankind and "Strike flat the thick rotundity o'th'world." In his chaotic speeches there are recurrent references to children, ingratitude, and justice as he blames his daughters for his situation. The Fool encourages Lear to shelter, commenting that the "night pities neither wise men nor fools," drawing attention to the blurred distinctions between wisdom and folly, sanity and insanity.

Lear rages about justice, still denying any responsibility and asserting that he is "a man / More sinned against than sinning." Kent persuades him to take shelter in a nearby hovel while he begs Goneril and Regan for shelter. Alone, the Fool speaks a rhymed "prophecy" that perhaps transcends the context of the play, warning against the injustices and corruption of "Albion" (Britain).

ACT 3 SCENE 3

Gloucester has been refused permission to help Lear and has lost control of his castle. He reveals that Edmund has a letter concerning Cornwall and Albany locked in his closet, and that he intends to help Lear. He asks Edmund to tell Cornwall that he is ill, to prevent his assistance of Lear being discovered. Once alone, Edmund reveals his intention to betray Gloucester.

ACT 3 SCENE 4

Lines 1–103: Kent tries to persuade Lear to enter the hovel out of the storm, but Lear is more concerned with the "tempest" in his mind and remains outside, dwelling on "Poor naked wretches" who, "houseless" and "unfed," have no defense against the elements. In a moment of brief self-awareness he declares: "O, I have ta'en / Too little care of this!" The Fool is frightened out of the hovel by Edgar, in disguise as the near-naked "Poor Tom." In a pitiful and ironic contrast to the genuine insanity of Lear, "Tom" feigns madness through fragmented speech. Like the Fool's nonsense, however, there are recognizable themes, pertinent to the play, such as lust, devilishness, and nakedness. Lear continues to dwell on his troubles, insisting that "Nothing" but "unkind daughters" could have "subdued nature / To such a lowness" in Tom. Asking "Is man no more than this?," Lear removes his clothes, approaching the raw condition of "the thing itself: unaccommodated man."

Lines 104–178: In a confused conversation that evokes the external storm and the "tempest" inside Lear's head, Gloucester and Kent attempt to persuade Lear to enter Gloucester's castle. Tom interjects with "insane" comments that focus on demons and witchcraft, but are taken by Lear to be the words of a "philosopher" and "learnèd Theban." Ironically, Gloucester talks of Edgar and "poor banished" Kent.

ACT 3 SCENE 5

Edmund has betrayed Gloucester. Cornwall swears that he will have revenge and rewards Edmund by giving him his father's title. Edmund pretends to be distressed at having to betray Gloucester, but plans to make it worse by discovering him "comforting the king."

ACT 3 SCENE 6

Gloucester shows Kent, Lear, Tom, and the Fool into a farmhouse adjoining his castle. The dialogue is fragmented as Lear continues to focus on injustice, the Fool continues to produce sense in nonsense, and Edgar acts his part as madman. Kent's voice of reason is unable to prevail. In a Quarto-only sequence, Lear insists on holding a "trial" of Goneril and Regan, seeing them before him in his madness. With Tom and the Fool as judges, this episode highlights the distorted nature of justice so far in the play. Edgar's pity for Lear makes it hard to sustain his "counterfeiting," and after Gloucester leads the others away, he rejects his disguise.

ACT 3 SCENE 7

Cornwall sends Goneril to tell Albany that France has landed, instructing Edmund to accompany her. Oswald informs Cornwall that Lear has gone to Dover. Gloucester is brought for questioning. Regan cruelly encourages the servant to bind Gloucester "hard" and disrespectfully plucks his beard. He admits that he sent Lear to Dover to protect him from Regan's "cruel nails" and Goneril's "boarish fangs." Cornwall puts out one of Gloucester's eyes. A servant tries to help Gloucester, but as Cornwall fights him, Regan seizes a sword— a symbol of her "unwomanly" power—and stabs the servant. Cornwall takes Gloucester's other eye as Regan reveals that it was

Edmund who betrayed him. Gloucester thus gains metaphorical "sight" as he is literally blinded. Regan orders Gloucester to be put out onto the heath to "smell / His way to Dover." She leads the mortally injured Cornwall away. In the Quarto text, the remaining servants discuss Regan's lack of womanly feeling, offer first aid to Gloucester and vow to get "the Bedlam" (Tom) to lead him to Dover.

ACT 4 SCENE 1

Edgar argues that even the "most dejected thing of fortune" can still have hope, but then he sees his blinded father and realizes he is "worse than e'er." Gloucester shows self-awareness when he says that he "stumbled" when he saw, and ironically talks of his "dear son Edgar." Gloucester blames the gods, to whom men are "As flies," and who "kill us for their sport." The old man leading Gloucester recognizes "Poor Tom" and Edgar realizes that he must remain disguised and "play fool to sorrow." Gloucester wishes Tom to lead him to Dover, despite the old man's protests, arguing that "'Tis the time's plague, when madmen lead the blind." Edgar's pity for Gloucester means that he struggles to maintain his deception. Gloucester asks to be taken to the edge of Dover's cliffs.

ACT 4 SCENE 2

Lines 1–31: Goneril wonders why Albany did not meet her. Oswald informs her that Albany has changed—he "smiled" to hear of the French army's arrival and said "The worse" at Goneril's return. He refuses to believe Gloucester's treachery or Edmund's loyalty. Goneril sends Edmund back, blaming Albany's change on his "cowish terror." She gives him a love token and kisses him, telling him to wait for "A mistress's command."

Lines 32–77: Albany and Goneril quarrel. In a Quarto-only sequence, Albany shows new strength as he berates Goneril for her treatment of her father, calling her and Regan "Tigers, not daughters"; she accuses him of cowardice, describing him as "a moral fool." In the Folio's edited version of their exchange, Goneril calls her husband a "Milk-livered man." A messenger brings news of Cornwall's death and Gloucester's blinding; he delivers Goneril a letter from Regan. Albany is horrified and swears revenge on Edmund for his betrayal of Gloucester. Goneril shows mixed feelings at Cornwall's death—Regan is less powerful as a widow, but she is also free to marry Edmund.

ACT 4 SCENE 3

In a Quarto-only scene, Kent and a Gentleman inform the audience that France has returned to his kingdom, leaving Cordelia in England. Kent asks for Cordelia's reaction to his letter. The natural imagery—"Sunshine and rain at once: her smiles and tears"—shows her goodness and contrasts with the darker images of nature associated with Goneril and Regan. Kent comments that the differences between the sisters can only be accounted for by "the stars above" who "govern our conditions," recalling the comments made about fate and free will by Gloucester and Edmund in Act 1 Scene 2. Lear is in Dover but refuses to see Cordelia because of his "burning shame" at his treatment of her.

The Folio text moves straight to a scene in which Cordelia marches onstage at the head of her army, informing the audience that Lear has been sighted, still mad, crowned with wildflowers and weeds. Cordelia sends soldiers to find him. A Gentleman (Doctor in Quarto) says that sleep will help Lear and that there are medicinal herbs that will achieve this—a benevolent image of nature that contrasts with the violent storm. A messenger brings news that the British are marching toward them and Cordelia makes it clear that France's armies are not fighting for "blown ambition"—unlike Goneril and Regan—but for love of Lear.

ACT 4 SCENE 4

Albany's army has set out, although Oswald says that it took "much ado" for Albany himself to join them and that Goneril "is the better soldier." Oswald has a letter from Goneril to Edmund that Regan wishes to read, but Oswald refuses. Regan expresses concern at

Goneril's interest in Edmund and argues that he is better suited to her, because she is a widow. She asks Oswald to remind Goneril of this and tells him there is a reward for whoever kills Gloucester.

ACT 4 SCENE 5

Lines 1–93: Edgar persuades Gloucester that they are at a cliff top. Gloucester comments that Edgar's "voice is altered." With truthful irony, Edgar responds that he is changed in nothing but his garments. Gloucester delivers a suicide speech and then throws himself forward. Edgar pretends to have found him at the bottom of the cliff, claiming that it is a miracle he survived the fall. He asks who was with Gloucester at the cliff's head, suggesting that "It was some fiend," but that he has been spared by the gods. Gloucester resolves to "bear / Affliction."

Lines 94–209: Lear appears dressed in flowers and talking nonsense, still fixated on his daughters. Gloucester recognizes his voice, but Lear does not recognize him, taking him for "Goneril with a white beard." In a pitifully ironic exchange Lear claims to remember Gloucester's eyes and demands that he read an imaginary challenge. Lear excoriates women for their sexual indulgence. He shows "reason in madness" as he talks of justice and how it is useless against sin that is plated "with gold." Lear runs away from Cordelia's attendants.

Lines 210–299: Edgar is leading Gloucester to safety, but Oswald finds them and tries to kill Gloucester. Under yet another persona, Edgar fatally wounds Oswald, who begs him to deliver a letter to Edmund. Edgar reads the letter from Goneril, urging Edmund to kill Albany so that she may marry him. Edgar buries Oswald, keeps the letter to show Albany, and leads Gloucester away.

ACT 4 SCENE 6

Cordelia thanks Kent and asks him to change out of his disguise. Kent replies that he has a reason to remain as he is. A Gentleman (Doctor in Quarto) asks Cordelia's permission to wake Lear. Cordelia kisses Lear and laments her sisters' treatment of him. When he wakes, she addresses him with respect fitting for a "royal lord." Lear is disorientated and humbled, in contrast to his earlier pride, and calls himself a "foolish fond old man." He recognizes Cordelia and assumes that she hates him, acknowledging that she has "some cause." She refutes this and leads him away. Kent reveals that Edmund is leading Cornwall's army.

ACT 5 SCENE 1

Lines 1–31: Edmund describes Albany's "alteration" and "self-reproving." Regan questions Edmund about Goneril and accuses him of adultery with her. Edmund denies this as Albany and Goneril arrive, bringing news that Lear and Cordelia are reunited. Albany is divided between his role as a leader who must defend his country and his personal reluctance to fight Lear. Goneril and Regan are both reluctant to leave Edmund alone with the other.

Lines 32–66: Disguised, Edgar hands Albany the letter and leaves. Edmund informs Albany that "The enemy's in view." Alone, Edmund contemplates the two sisters, coldly observing that "Neither can be enjoyed / If both remain alive." He resolves to let Goneril kill Albany if he survives the battle and swears that there will be no mercy for Lear and Cordelia.

ACT 5 SCENE 2

Edgar leaves Gloucester in safety and goes to fight for Lear. He returns to report that Lear and Cordelia have been defeated and captured. Gloucester wishes to remain where he is to be captured or to die, but Edgar says that men must "endure" until their appointed time.

ACT 5 SCENE 3

Lines 1–114: Cordelia thinks that they will see her sisters now they are captives, but Lear does not wish to, constructing a fantasy where he and Cordelia will live happily and safely in prison. Edmund orders them to be taken away and gives the captain instructions to kill them. Albany, Goneril, and Regan arrive, and Albany praises Edmund's "valiant strain," asking for the captives. Edmund says that he has sent Lear away so that he will not "pluck the common bosom on his side." Albany reproves Edmund for taking authority, but Regan claims that he has proved himself Albany's "brother" by leading her armies. Goneril and Regan begin to fight over Edmund and Regan claims him as her "lord and master." Albany arrests Edmund for treason and ironically bars Regan's claim on Edmund as he is "subcontracted" to Goneril. As Albany challenges Edmund, Regan is taken ill, poisoned by Goneril. The trumpet sounds to summon a champion for Albany who will maintain that Edmund, supposed Earl of Gloucester, is "a manifold traitor."

Lines 115–264: Edgar answers the summons but does not identify himself, except that he is "as noble" as Edmund. They fight and Edmund is mortally wounded, but Goneril argues that he is not defeated because he was not bound to fight "An unknown opposite." Albany demonstrates the shift in power between them as he tells her to "Shut [her] mouth" and produces her letter to Edmund. Goneril flees. Edmund admits the charges and wishes to know his killer, as he will forgive him if he is noble. Edgar reveals his identity and says that they should "exchange charity." He argues that "The gods are just," perhaps a response to Gloucester's lament in Act 4 Scene 1. Edgar relates how Gloucester died on being told of the true identity of the man who has led him in his blindness: his heart was too weak to support the extremes of "joy and grief" provoked by the knowledge. A messenger brings news that Goneril has poisoned Regan and stabbed herself. Their bodies are brought onstage as Kent arrives, seeking Lear. Edmund resolves to do "some good" before dying and reveals that Lear and Cordelia are condemned to death, and that Cordelia's hanging will be made to look like suicide. He sends his sword as a "token of reprieve" and is carried out.

Lines 265–348: Howling, Lear carries in Cordelia's body. He tries to revive her, ignoring Kent's attempts to speak to him, and reveals that he killed the executioner, remembering "the day" that he "would have made [them] skip," a brief return to his previous, regal self before he disintegrates once more. He dies believing that he sees Cordelia breathe, and Kent begs his own heart to break. Edmund's death is reported and Albany asks Kent and Edgar to rule and sustain "the gored state," but Kent refuses, feeling death is near. Despite Albany's assertion that "All friends shall taste / The wages of their virtue, and all foes / The cup of their deservings," any sense of justice, human or divine, seems scant, and the play's resolution is bleak.

KING LEAR IN PERFORMANCE: THE RSC AND BEYOND

The best way to understand a Shakespeare play is to see it or ideally to participate in it. By examining a range of productions, we may gain a sense of the extraordinary variety of approaches and interpretations that are possible—a variety that gives Shakespeare his unique capacity to be reinvented and made "our contemporary" four centuries after his death.

We begin with a brief overview of the play's theatrical and cinematic life, offering historical perspectives on how it has been performed. We then analyze in more detail a series of productions staged over the last half-century by the Royal Shakespeare Company. The sense of dialogue between productions that can only occur when a company is dedicated to the revival and investigation of the Shakespeare canon over a long period, together with the uniquely comprehensive archival resource of promptbooks, program notes, reviews, and interviews held on behalf of the RSC at the Shakespeare Birthplace Trust in Stratford-upon-Avon, allows an "RSC stage history" to become a crucible in which the chemistry of the play can be explored.

Finally, we go to the horse's mouth. Modern theater is dominated by the figure of the director. He or she must hold together the whole play, whereas the actor must concentrate on his or her part. The director's viewpoint is therefore especially valuable. Shakespeare's plasticity is wonderfully revealed when we hear directors of highly successful productions answering the same questions in very different ways.

FOUR CENTURIES OF *KING LEAR:* AN OVERVIEW

The first Lear was Richard Burbage, the leading actor with Shakespeare's company, the King's Men. He was described by an anonymous elegist listing his best-known roles as "Kind Lear."[1] Little is known otherwise of the earliest performances. The Fool is thought to have been played by Robert Armin, the company's leading comic actor after the departure of Will Kempe. A talented singer and musician, Armin was noted for his witty paradoxical fooling. Some scholars have, however, suggested that Armin may have played Edgar, since Tom o'Bedlam speaks a kind of fool's language and Armin was equally capable of the multiple role changes that the character puts himself through. This casting would have opened up the possibility for a boy actor to double the roles of Cordelia and the Fool, who never appear on stage together. Such doubling would give added poignancy to the line "And my poor fool is hanged," but it remains counterintuitive to suppose that Armin was cast in any role other than that of the Fool.

There is a record of a court performance at Whitehall on St. Stephen's night, 26 December 1606. It was a bold choice to play the mad king and the image of a "dog obeyed in office" before the court. A play of "king Lere" was performed at Gowthwaite Hall in Yorkshire in 1610. This was probably Shakespeare's version, not the old *Leir* play (which recently scholarship has ascribed to Thomas Kyd, author of the highly successful *Spanish Tragedy*). A company of English actors in Dresden in 1626 played the "Tragoedia von Lear, König in Engelandt," probably also Shakespeare's version.

The play was revived briefly after the Restoration of the monarchy in 1660 and subsequent reopening of the theaters, but in 1681 Nahum Tate staged a production using a text that he himself had adapted. In his dedicatory epistle Tate emphasized the idea of the rough and unfinished nature of Shakespeare's work. It was a "heap of jewels" that needed to have order, regularity, and polish applied to it for its true beauty to be revealed. Tate simplified language, plot, and character, eliminating the Fool and much of the play's complexity. He included a love story between Edgar and Cordelia, together with a confidante for Cordelia, Arante. The play's happy ending concludes with Lear restored, handing his throne over to Edgar and Cordelia. Tate's *Lear* and various revised forms of the adaptation, including one by David Garrick, replaced the original on stage, except possibly in Dublin, where the Smock Alley promptbooks are based on Shakespeare's printed text. The authentically Shakespearean original was

2. William Charles Macready as Lear in 1838, with the dead Cordelia: until this revival, the stage was dominated by Nahum Tate's reworking with a happy ending in which Cordelia survives and marries Edgar.

not performed on the London stage again, save for a handful of performances by Edmund Kean in the early nineteenth century, until Macready's restored (if heavily cut) production of 1838.

Thomas Betterton had been Tate's Lear. David Garrick, the most celebrated actor-manager of the eighteenth century, restored parts of Shakespeare's text in his own production at Drury Lane but retained Tate's ending. His performance was acclaimed for its pathos and humanity. In his diary James Boswell records: "I was fully moved, and I shed abundance of tears."[2] The Shakespearean editor George Steevens, after confessing his view that "Tate's alteration . . . had considerably improved the great original," went on to extol the virtues of Garrick's acting: "Were we to inquire in what particular scene Mr. Garrick is preeminently excellent it would be a difficult circumstance to point it out." He did, though, single out Garrick's "mode of speaking the curse at the end of the first act of the play." In his view Garrick "gives it additional energy, and it is impossible to hear him deliver it without an equal mixture of horror and admiration."[3] John Philip Kemble (Theatre Royal, Drury Lane, 1788) played Lear with his tragedian sister, Sarah Siddons, as Cordelia. The critic and poet Leigh Hunt was disappointed: "He personated the king's majesty perfectly well, but not the king's madness . . . he is always stiff, always precise, and he will never, as long as he lives, be able to act any thing mad unless it be a melancholy mad statue."[4]

During the Regency period, when old King George III was mad, the London theater managers tactfully abstained from staging the play. Soon after the king's death in 1820, the fiery Romantic actor Edmund Kean played the role at Drury Lane later to mixed reviews. The London *Times* objected that the storm scene "was less effective than many others" chiefly because it was "exhibited with so much accuracy that the performer could scarcely be heard amidst the confusion," but the reviewer was better pleased by the fifth act in which "there was scarcely a dry eye in the theatre."[5] William Hazlitt felt that "Mr. Kean chipped off a bit of the character here and there: but he did not pierce the solid substance, nor move the entire mass."[6] Hazlitt reviewed Junius Brutus Booth's production at Covent Garden in the same year more favorably: "There was no feebleness, and no vulgarity in any part of Mr. Booth's acting, but it was animated, vigorous, and pathetic throughout."[7]

When Macready, who had played Edmund to Booth's Lear, restored Shakespeare's text in his Covent Garden production of 1838, the Fool, reintroduced for the first time in more than a hundred and fifty years, was played by a young woman, Priscilla Horton.

Macready set the play in a pagan Saxon Britain replete with Druidic stone circles. Critics were generally enthusiastic:

> Mr. Macready's Lear, remarkable before for a masterly completeness of conception, is heightened by this introduction of the Fool to a surprising degree. It accords exactly with the view he seeks to present of Lear's character. . . . Mr. Macready's representation of the father at the end, broken down to his last despairing struggle, his heart swelling gradually upwards till it bursts in its closing sigh, completed the only perfect picture that we have of Lear since the age of Betterton.[8]

It may be asked how someone writing a century and a half after the event could have known that Betterton's was a "perfect picture" of Lear, but the point here is to stress how much the characterization of Lear gains from the restoration of his foil, the Fool.

Samuel Phelps produced the play at Sadler's Wells in 1845 using simpler staging and a fuller version of the text than that of Macready, which had remained heavily cut despite the rejection of Tate. The naturalism of Phelps' performance was praised but the storm was thought excessive: "It is not imitation, but realization."[9] Charles Kean staged a successful production at the Princess's Theater in 1858. Set in Anglo-Saxon Britain, it boasted a strong supporting cast including Kate Terry as Cordelia. Meanwhile in New York, Edwin Booth, son of Junius Brutus, revived the play using Shakespeare's text, giving a performance described by William Winter as "the fond father and the broken old man. It was the great heart, shattered by cruel unkindness, that he first, and most of all, displayed."[10] The great Italian actor Tommaso Salvini, also won praise for his performances at Boston's Globe Theatre in 1882 and London's Covent Garden in 1884, despite the fact that he spoke in Italian while the rest of the cast spoke in English, a proceeding that the novelist Henry James described as "grotesque, unpardonable, abominable."[11] Henry Irving's elaborately staged production at the Lyceum in 1892 was set in a Britain of Roman ruins with Druidic priests and Viking warriors. Using a heavily cut text that reduced the play's violence and sexuality, Irving emphasized Lear's age and paternalism in a performance that attracted mixed notices, although Ellen Terry's Cordelia was widely praised.

At the end of the nineteenth century directors such as William Poel and Harley Granville Barker promoted the simple staging of Shakespeare's plays, attempting to recreate the conditions of the Elizabethan playhouse, with its fast continuous action in contrast to the spectacular staging of the Victorians, which involved lengthy scene changes. In his *Prefaces to Shakespeare* (1927), Granville Barker argued vigorously against critical prejudice toward the play in performance and insisted on its theatrical viability, a judgment borne out by the many productions since. The twentieth and twenty-first centuries have produced a number of distinguished Lears but have also concentrated on more balanced productions that give greater weight and opportunity to lesser roles.

John Gielgud first played Lear in Harcourt Williams' production at the Old Vic in 1931 at the age of twenty-six. Despite his obvious talent, critics thought him too young for the part. In 1940 Gielgud had a second opportunity to play the part, again at the Old Vic, in a production set in early modern Europe, based on the ideas of Granville Barker, who oversaw the early rehearsals and personally coached Gielgud. In an essay of 1963 Gielgud claimed that the ten days in which Barker worked with the company "were the fullest in experience that I have ever had in all my years upon the stage."[12] The production was a success, although the noted critic James Agate concluded that Gielgud's performance was "a thing of great beauty, imagination, sensitiveness, understanding, executive virtuosity, and control. You would be wrong to say—this is not King Lear! You would be right to say that this is Lear every inch but one."[13]

In 1936 the director-designer Theodore Komisarjevsky staged a memorable and radical production at the Shakespeare Memorial Theatre in Stratford-upon-Avon. There was a simple but effective set, consisting mainly of a grand staircase, illuminated by a cyclorama that changed color to reflect the mood of the scene. As the London *Times* review put it:

3. Expressionist design in the 1930s: the opening scene of the Komisarjevsky production.

On this simple stage of steps and platforms, where every movement is sharp and significant and the light-borne colour keeps pace with the changing character of the scene, Mr. Randle Ayrton has complete freedom to act Lear.[14]

A decade later Laurence Olivier played Lear at the Old Vic as "a whimsical old tyrant who takes this way of dividing his kingdom simply as a jest, until the joke turns serious because Cordelia refuses to play."[15] His performance was not to all tastes but Alec Guinness as the Fool was widely praised. Sir Donald Wolfit, an old-style actor-manager, toured his own production between 1947 and 1953—Ronald Harwood's experience as Wolfit's backstage dresser inspired his play *The Dresser* (1980).

Gielgud played Lear for a third time in 1950, in a production which he co-directed with Anthony Quayle. Although his performance had developed in a number of ways, it was still largely influenced by his work with Granville Barker. He played the part again in 1955 in a production directed by George Devine and designed by

4. John Gielgud as Lear in the hovel (1950 production), with Fool and Poor Tom in the foreground, the disguised Kent behind.

Isamu Noguchi. This time Gielgud aimed for psychological realism in his performance but it was generally agreed that while the stylized set worked, the heavy costumes were problematic.

In 1956 Orson Welles directed and starred in a production at the New York City Center. Falling and breaking one ankle and spraining the other during rehearsals, Welles, undeterred, played the part in a wheelchair, pushed around by the Fool. In 1959 Charles Laughton played Lear in a production at the Shakespeare Memorial Theatre, directed by Glen Byam Shaw. Critics were divided, especially about Laughton's conception of the role. One of them, Alan Brien, complained that Laughton developed "from boyishness to senility without even an intervening glimpse of maturity."[16]

Three years later Peter Brook directed his groundbreaking production starring Paul Scofield (discussed in detail below). There have been numerous distinguished productions since: in 1968 Trevor Nunn directed with Eric Porter playing Lear; in 1974 Buzz Goodbody directed a pared-down version for the RSC's small studio theater, The Other Place; in 1976 Trevor Nunn directed Donald Sinden as Lear; in 1979 Peter Ustinov played Lear in a production directed by Robin Phillips at Stratford, Ontario; Adrian Noble's 1982 production with Michael Gambon is discussed below. In 1989 Jonathan Miller directed Eric Porter at the Old Vic; 1990 saw the Renaissance Theatre company's production, directed by Kenneth Branagh with Richard Briers as Lear and Emma Thompson as the Fool; in the same year Nicholas Hytner directed John Wood at Stratford; in 1993 Noble directed the play at Stratford again, this time with Robert Stephens as Lear (discussed below). In 1997 in the (London) National's intimate Cottesloe studio, Richard Eyre directed a production (his swansong as artistic director) with Ian Holm playing Lear—a highly acclaimed production that was later recorded for television; in the same year Peter Hall directed Alan Howard at the Old Vic; and in 1999 Yukio Ninagawa directed Nigel Hawthorne for the RSC; in 2001 Julian Glover played Lear in Barry Kyle's production at the Globe and the following year Jonathan Kent directed Oliver Ford-Davies at the Almeida, a performance much admired for its intelligence; Jonathan Miller again directed the play, this time for the 2002 Stratford Festival, Ontario, with Christopher Plummer in the lead; in 2004 Bill Alexander directed Corin Redgrave in a production that used a full conflated text and ran for nearly four hours; in 2007 the RSC's Complete Works Festival in which all Shakespeare's plays were performed closed with Trevor Nunn's production at the Courtyard

Theatre with Ian McKellen as King Lear (see interview with Nunn, below). Powerful small-scale productions include a touring one by Kaboodle Theatre Company (1991–94), which made very strong use of a mix of Oriental-imperial costumes and modernity (a feisty Cordelia in Doc Martens boots).

The tradition of adapting the play has been continued in the theater with versions such as Edward Bond's radical rewriting, *Lear* (1972) and the Women's Theatre Group and Elaine Feinstein's feminist *Lear's Daughters*, as well as Jane Smiley's novel, *A Thousand Acres* (1997). On film, there were early silent versions in America and Italy (1909–10). A number of stage productions have been filmed, including Peter Brook's, shot in a stark black-and-white style that intensified the existential bleakness of his stage version. Grigori Kozintsev (1970) produced a beautiful, deeply moving version featuring the sufferings of Russian peasants. It was based on a translation by Boris Pasternak and used haunting music by Dmitri Shostakovich. Akira Kurosawa's *Ran* (1985), set in feudal Japan, substantially reworked Shakespeare's play so as to eliminate Gloucester but incorporate the subplot material in a version in which Lear's daughters become his married sons. It played a major part in stimulating renewed western interest in epic eastern cinema.

AT THE RSC

Lears for Our Time

> Our own century seems better qualified to communicate and respond to the full range of experience in King Lear than any previous time, save possibly Shakespeare's own.[17]

In post–Second World War England, *King Lear* has been performed more times than in its entire prior performance history. The play speaks with special power to the contemporary psyche. In a violent age when atrocities, murders, poverty, and acts of self-destruction are commonly seen on television, the violence in the play, and its concerns about human rights, seem particularly apposite. However, *Lear* is so vast in its conception that, as well as societal concerns, it deals with very fundamental philosophical thoughts about what it is to be human in a godless world, or in a world where faith plays little part in the absurdity of human behavior.

Jan Kott's influential book entitled *Shakespeare Our Contemporary* (1964) was of great inspiration to late-twentieth-century directors. His thoughts about *King Lear* as a play about "the disintegration of the world" prompted a landmark production of the play by Peter Brook, which would alter the way the play was conceived and the characters performed to this day:

> In the 1950s it became apparent that the world might destroy itself through accidental nuclear warfare, and the plays of Samuel Beckett achieved international fame: *Waiting for Godot* (1953) showed a world of absurdity, *Endgame* (1957) a world without meaning at all. Soon afterward the Polish critic Jan Kott wrote an influential essay, "King Lear, or Endgame," which viewed Shakespeare through the spectacles or blinkers of Beckett and emphasized the element of grotesque tragicomedy in the play.[18]

Brook was also heavily influenced by the dramatic theories of Bertolt Brecht, with his desire to "alienate" the audience by breaking down the illusions of realism. Brecht's influence was especially evident in the bare staging of *Lear*. Two large flats at either side of the stage moved in and out at angles to create internal and external spaces. The storm was created by three large rusty thunder sheets with a vibrating motor behind creating a hint of rumbling thunder. The lighting was deliberately bright and constant, only dimming for the storm scene and Gloucester's blinding. Everything was seen with clarity, leaving no room for the dramatic signaling that darkness evokes. There was no background music. Brook firmly believed that *Lear* should be staged with no music at all. Music almost always controls our emotional reaction to a scene, and Brook was particularly keen to block any easy audience response.

J. C. Trewin described the set:

Visually we are taken to a terrifying world, a place of abstract symbols, a rust-flaking world, harsh and primitive. There are tall, coarse gray-white screens; metal shapes that might have been dredged from the sea-bed: things ancient, scaled with rust. As the night moves on, the stage grows barer and barer until nothing is left but the screens, and Lear and Gloucester play out their colloquy on a bleak infinity of stage; two voices at the world's end.[19]

Brook wanted this *Lear* to be a *Lear* of its time. He designed the production himself and wanted to create a totally believable society, both barbaric and sophisticated. It is notable that this production took place just after the Cuban missile crisis. He wished to create a nihilistic vision, to remove the sympathetic responses of the audience and blur the lines between good and evil in the play. As a result of this he was accused of distorting Shakespeare's tragedy to enhance his own directorial viewpoint.

Brook's interpretation meant that productions of *Lear* would never be the same after this point. Indeed, there have been very few productions since that have not followed his lead in some regard, whether their focus be political, metaphysical, or domestic.

Critics and directors of the Left have been quick to seize on Lear's demand that the ruling class expose themselves "to feel what wretches feel, / That thou mayst shake the superflux to them" and Gloucester's wish that "distribution should undo excess, / And each man have enough" as evidence of the play's critique of existing political structures, and much recent criticism has discussed *King Lear* as a political drama reflecting the ideological concerns that were to divide England during the seventeenth century.[20]

This trend in recent criticism has been reflected in performance. Set pre–First World War, the RSC's 1976 production made reference to

5. "What, art mad? A man may see how this world goes with no eyes": the bleakness of Peter Brook's 1962 production with Paul Scofield (left) as Lear and Alan Webb as the blinded Gloucester.

the conditions of those disenfranchised by war. One page of the program featured hundreds of faces of workhouse children; on another there was a bleak landscape with two figures in the distance, presumably working a land that yields little or nothing. In this production Donald Sinden's acclaimed performance as Lear chronicles the process by which suffering turns self-pity and self-love into outward versions of themselves. In practice this means that Lear learns to identify with the poor and down-trodden, classes never far from the drab, pockmarked, nine-teenth century face of this production. Indeed, the three-man directorate of Trevor Nunn, John Barton and Barry Kyle . . . do all they can to bring period penury to our attention, gratu-itously introducing a troupe of vagrants to trot round the stage between scenes, and transforming Michael Williams's Fool into a bald scrofulous relic, a seedily eccentric song-and-dance man who might have stumbled out of *Bleak House* . . . deter-mined to stress that *Lear* is a social as well as an elemental play.[21]

The setting for the 2004 production directed by Bill Alexander was of a postwar world in which the country was in a flux of inse-curity, distinctly modern in feel but without reference to a specific time:

This *Lear* appears at times to be set in a crumbling mental home, backed by the scaffolding and half-destroyed brick walls of Tom Piper's bleak setting. It suggests that a nuclear bomb has already fallen on Lear's kingdom and the survivors are left wandering about trying to work out—post-Apocalypse—who they are and what has happened and above all where the hell they are supposed to be going next. . . . There is a bizarre timelessness here—so that in a post-Victorian world, when the old King comes on dressed like a mad deserter from the First World War, there is no real surprise, just the feeling that Alexander and his cast have had yet another disturbing thought about the many insights into madness and identity-crisis offered in the play.[22]

Of the setting, designer Tom Piper explained:

Bill [Alexander] felt very strongly that you can't set this play in one particular place, it has to be an invented world, so we're aiming to create parallel worlds: the Victorian married with strange bits of technology. . . . I wanted to include a broken element, to convey a sense of a world that could be in decay or on the edge of industrialisation.[23]

Corin Redgrave, a noted left-wing campaigner as well as a member of a distinguished acting dynasty, played Lear in this production. He saw the play as "modern, topical and relevant because it so vividly portrays a country divided by an almost impassable fault-line between those who have enough and those who don't. Any attempt I make to build up an idea of Lear the man, Lear the ruler, is still very strongly influenced by that thinking."[24]

Again, although not overtly political in the actors' focus, Adrian Noble's 1993 production infused the political implication of Lear's decision into the setting:

This production turned the map into paper flooring whose divisions the Fool (a gag over his mouth emphasizing his obvious outrage) was made to mark with red paint. It was then gradually reduced to tatters until the ground beneath, which was covered with a great blood-red stain, was wholly revealed.[25]

There are numerous references in *King Lear* to the stars, gods, and the fates. Setting the play in a non-Christian era endows the play with an adaptable metaphysical stance that has international appeal. In 1999, Japanese director Yukio Ninagawa of the Sainokuni Shakespeare Company undertook a joint production with the RSC. This production focused on the elemental nature of the play, the dark forces of nature that emerge from the void created by Lear's misjudgments:

This is a hauntingly but savagely beautiful production. Yukio Horio's set is dominated by a huge black wooden walkway sloping gently toward you and widening into an immense platform. At the back the walkway seems to disappear into black darkness, whence the actors emerge like mythological figures, both real and remote. All this suggests the structure of the classical Noh stage, where the curtained entrance also leads somewhere indeterminate: a primeval darkness that holds no moral secrets . . . this reinforces the uncomfortable Shakespearian vision of a world where you are left without the consolation or guidance of a moral order.[26]

The handling of the storm scene was particularly controversial. Boulders of various sizes were choreographed to drop onto the stage as Lear raged against the storm. Most audience members and reviewers were more concerned about the safety of the actors than the director's vision, which "conjures a world in which Nature's moulds are cracked."[27]

The breakdown in family relationships is, of course, central to *King Lear* and modern directors have often used this as an accessible focal point in productions. Initially produced as a touring production for schools, Buzz Goodbody's small cast chamberpiece version of *Lear* in 1974

was performed by a cast of nine, with one musician playing gong, trumpet, snare and kettle drum. An all-purpose servant was added, while one sub-plot was cut (losing Albany, Cornwall, Oswald, and the French King). . . . The acting area was empty, except for a few props, like a rug and banners which unfurled when Lear appeared. . . . Scenes were set simply, using props and, as with the storm, music and lights, which at key moments in the production underscored the director's point. . . . *Lear* was not seen as epic in terms of great public scenes of wide-open spaces peopled with a huge cast. . . . Its focus was on two families, in which the personal as well as the age differences played a more important part than is usually recognised.[28]

In this powerful, intimate production, "the play as a whole became an intense study of private griefs of their two families, with Kent and the Fool both reduced to appalled outsiders, helplessly looking on."[29]

Described by critic Irving Wardle as "an all-too-familiar story of family life,"[30] Nicholas Hytner's 1990 production also turned *Lear* into a tale of dysfunctional family neurosis. He encoded his very cerebral reading in the set design of David Fielding, creating an enclosed space for the staging of *Lear* that took the form of a cube:

> Open on one side with its outer walls painted to look like heavy steel, the cube simply revolves and stops, to present a succession of interiors and exteriors. Sometimes it will stop with a corner pointing toward the audience so that actors can stand out of sight of each other while Shakespearian eavesdropping can take place. In the storm scene, it will revolve continuously—the idea being that, as a metaphor for the world of the play (as well as Lear's mental world), it is spinning out of control.[31]

The effect of the cube was to reduce the scale of the play—something apparently deliberate in the director's interpretation. Psychological and domestic, Lear's world became both a mental ward and the interior of his mind, a controlled civilized space allowed to go mad through neglect and misjudgment. John Wood's very human and neurotic Lear went on an inner and outer journey of physical suffering and mental awareness: "We are left with an interpretation which is as much medical as moral. The geriatric ward slugs it out with the psychiatric wing. There is little sense of hubris on the one hand, or of concentrated evil on the other."[32] The emphasis on Lear's genuine insanity stemming from the family reflected the wider world of the play and the state of Britain. Michael Billington described it as "an exploration of the insane contradictions of a world where the gods are seen as both just and wantonly cruel, where Nature is both purifying and destructive."[33]

Fools and Madmen

Real and assumed madness play an essential part in the plot of *King Lear*. In a program note by Michael MacDonald, author of a historical study called *Mystical Bedlam: Madness, Anxiety and Healing in Seventeenth Century England* (1983), Adrian Noble's 1993 production was contextualized by means of the suggestion that the audience

> is presented with three kinds of madness: real in Lear himself, assumed in Tom/Edgar, and professional in the Fool. To its original audience, in a population largely uneducated, unable to distinguish between epilepsy, demonic possession and a skilful beggar on the make, the spectacle of an old man and a half-naked creature railing at the weather and babbling about demons would not have been especially unusual: like the unemployed and other vagrants the countryside teemed with, they were a fact of life.[34]

Lear is very rarely played as being driven mad exclusively by the cruelty that is inflicted on him, but is often portrayed as being dangerously unhinged from the start. In Nicholas Hytner's production,

> the early household scenes are honeycombed with . . . micro-sequences, which take you inside Lear's head, showing his hunger for affection, his need to play the strong man, his short attention span, and his helpless descents into blind rage. These are an embarrassment to the court and they give the sisters every pretext for saying something to keep the old man happy. But it is only when they try to draw the line that you really see what they have had to put up with. At the suggestion that he should shed a few knights, all hell breaks loose in the Albany dining room, with Lear emptying his gun into the ceiling, crushing Goneril to the ground like a blubbering child, clearing the space for carnage by hanging the Fool on a coat-hook: and finally vanishing into the night leaving his shaken hosts facing each other down a long table for their solitary dinner.[35]

Very clearly a man with no control over his own emotions, John Wood's Lear was also an emotional vandal to his daughters, and his influence could be seen in their learned behavior.

In Buzz Goodbody's 1974 production, to be a sane man in a cruel world was to be part of that cruelty. Lear's madness became the transitional stage from cruelty to humanity:

> Tony Church did not play Lear as a virtuoso acting part, but as a down-to-earth king, a patriarch who got his pleasure from hunting. He is out in the cold because of who he is—not a mighty monarch fallen from grace, but an old man on the point of death, facing himself and his life. . . . When he is "sane," he represents the cruel world, arbitrary and aggressive, and only when he is "mad" does he embody human values.[36]

In the stunning visual sequence that started Adrian Noble's 1982 production, lunacy not only led to virtue but was linked to it through the characters of the Fool and Cordelia:

> On Lear's throne the Grock-like Fool and Cordelia sit facing each other, with their necks at opposite ends of a taut halter (resembling a noose), as if lunacy and virtue were inseparable. . . . What follows is a delirious descent into a world of barbarism in which farce and tragedy are umbilically linked.[37]

Antony Sher played the Fool as "Lear's alter-ego, the visible mark of his insanity. His Master's Voice as he perches on his lap like a ventriloquist's doll, the conscience of the King."[38] In the words of the reviewer in the *Jewish Chronicle*, "There is a strong sense in which, just as the great comic double acts are like watching a schizophrenic trying to pull himself together, Antony Sher's red-nosed clown and Michael Gambon's violent old man are two warring parts of one psyche."[39] The poet and critic James Fenton, writing in the London *Sunday Times*, pushed the point further:

> Michael Gambon's Lear was a man all too willing to cast off his role as king, and his relationship to the Fool pointed to this uneasiness.

Lear's foolishness and his love for his Fool are the points of departure for the interpretation. In all his madness, his anger and his suffering, we do not forget this. Indeed, I wonder if Lear has ever fooled around so enthusiastically.

Imagine a production in which the King, though condemned to kingship, would clearly love to have been a comedian, while the Fool, although unable to stop jesting, is transfixed by the horror of his true perception of the tragedy. This is the version which Adrian Noble has directed. . . . This is not the Fool of criticism, not an A-level "assess-the-significance-of-the-Fool" fool. This is your genuine professional fool. Inside whom is a man in a panic, the Cassandra of the play, whose raving prophesies terrify the prophet himself.[40]

Sher described how in rehearsals they came up with a solution to the disappearance of the Fool after the arrival of Tom o'Bedlam.[41] During the mock trial scene the Fool picked up a pillow to represent Regan. On the words "anatomize her," Lear stabbed the pillow in a frenzy of rage. In his insane and violent outburst he fatally stabbed the Fool accidentally. With all the attention on Lear leaving the hovel, the others did not realize what had happened. The Fool slumped down dead into a barrel in which he stood.

The emphasis put on the Fool in this production (the program cover featured a fool's face with a red nose that appeared to be an amalgam of Lear and the Fool), along with Sher's magnificent performance, led many critics to feel that the play became unbalanced, losing impetus in the final acts after the Fool was killed.

At the end of the hovel scene Edgar has replaced the Fool as Lear's spiritual mentor. Lear takes Edgar off in one direction as the Fool exits in another. According to director Adrian Noble,

That happens accidentally. He doesn't plan that. . . . For some reason he decides to take on the sins of others . . . in exactly the same way as a pilgrim, monk or nun . . . dedicate their lives in a particular way that enables other people to have a richer spiritual life. It is a gift of humanity to God. This is exactly the same thing with Edgar.[42]

Lear's journey into his own fooldom takes him from the enclosed mental space of the court out into the world and the secrets of humanity, to emotions denied and hidden from him by dint of his position in society. This awakening by the Fool and Poor Tom leads to a political and spiritual epiphany that is life-changing and possibly world-changing. Many directors have seen the following lines—often quoted in their program notes—as the core of the play:

> Poor naked wretches, wheresoe'er you are,
> That bide the pelting of this pitiless storm,
> How shall your houseless heads and unfed sides,
> Your lopped and windowed raggedness, defend you
> From seasons such as these? O, I have ta'en
> Too little care of this! Take physic, pomp,
> Expose thyself to feel what wretches feel,
> That thou mayst shake the superflux to them
> And show the heavens more just.

The political dimensions of *King Lear* are most clearly evidenced in the king's interaction with the mad beggar. Edgar, the abused son, and Poor Tom, the forgotten citizen of Lear's England, embody both familial and national neglect. Edgar's disguise as Bedlam beggar is also crucial to Lear's spiritual journey. In Noble's second production of the play for the RSC in 1993:

> [Lear's] growing obsession with this emblem of "unaccommo-dated man" causes the displacement of the Fool . . . was bril-liantly visualized in the image of Ian Hughes clinging forlornly to Poor Tom's hand at the end of a human chain that Glouces-ter led across the stage.[43]

Visually Edgar has variously appeared as a Caliban-type figure, the poor bare-forked animal spouting obscenities but in need of the world's pity, as Christ-like with a crown of thorns, bloodied and suf-fering for the world's sins, or alternatively as demonic, as in the RSC's 1982 production when "Jonathan Hyde's Edgar as a virtually naked Poor Tom [burst] through the splintering floor like some infernal demon born on to Lear's 'great stage of fools'."[44] "It was the modern equivalent of the entrance of a devil from the pit of Hell, and Tom's demonic side, which actors so often miss as they go for shivering pathos, was established at once."[45]

Thrown to the wilderness by his family, Edgar evolves from "worm" to potential king. His suffering appears as a barbaric initiation rite designed by the toughest of gods. It is a trial of cruelty fitting for the evil world that is unleashed in the play.

The Absence of Humanity

King Lear is a play rich with vicious bestial images, all symbolic of the barbaric capabilities of man and woman. Goneril, for instance, is described as having a "wolfish visage." Edward Topsell's *Historie of Foure-footed Beastes* (1607) mixed scientific fact, folklore, and classical allusions to animals and mythological creatures, giving them often exotic and fantastic attributes. It describes the customary attributes associated with the wolf in animal lore: treachery, deceit, hypocrisy, ravenousness, and cruelty. These associations gave Shakespeare's audience an accurate idea of Goneril's character and her subsequent behavior. However, for modern directors, "Another interpretative decision that must be faced . . . is whether to accept the moral polarity of Lear's daughters as a fact of the story or to suggest more naturalistic reasons for their behavior."[46]

In recent years patriarchal repression and child abuse of one form or another have often been regarded as the defining reasons for evil in children. Lear has accordingly been portrayed as physically and mentally abusive or neglectful, demanding, cantankerous, a bully who has created so much pent-up anger in his two elder daughters that it erupts when they are given the opportunity to release their feelings without recrimination; that is to say, when they are in power.

In the influential 1962 production, Peter Brook portrayed Lear's knights as rowdy and destructive, while Irene Worth's Goneril was self-contained and cool, remonstrating with Lear in measured tones, speaking as somebody with cause to complain. Some critics thought such a treatment a distortion of the text, but most modern directors have followed this interpretation to some degree. Though it helps to humanize Goneril, it does make the descent into evil very difficult to portray.

Janet Dale, who played the part in 1993, admitted that "I am trying to play her with a conscience, but I suspect the lines won't support it." Rather than an outright evil woman, she wished to portray her as a woman "of moral degeneration."[47]

By focusing on the psychology of these extremely dysfunctional families, the violence in Nicholas Hytner's 1990 production became rooted in explainable terms:

> The production is about confused people destroyed by their incomprehensible emotions or, as with Wood's massively erratic Lear, struggling through new ones. . . . The effects of long abuse are evident in his daughters. Alex Kingston's Cordelia has become rebellious, bloody-minded and rejects Lear almost more than he does her. Estelle Kohler's Goneril and Sally Dexter's Regan, seem still to want the love of this old, impossible man. . . . It is fashionable nowadays to allow us to see the "bad" daughters' point of view, but rarely as strongly as here. Both of them seem badly in need of Valium, psychoanalysis, or both. They are frustrated, exhausted, at the end of a tether which finally breaks, liberating all that suppressed anger and barely contained madness. Their evils proliferate, but they, like Goneril and Regan themselves, are ultimately Lear's fault.[48]

> Order opens up to reveal chaos. And the same pattern is visible in erratic human behaviour. Lear, having cursed Goneril with sterility, rushes back to embrace her. Astonishingly, Regan first conspires in the blinding of Gloucester and then tenderly asks him, rather than her wounded husband, "How dost my lord?" Mr. Hytner ushers us into a morally topsy-turvy universe in which good and evil frequently cohabit within the same person.[49]

One cannot escape the fact that what Regan and Goneril do is evil and unnatural. In Buzz Goodbody's 1974 production, which cut the role of Cornwall, "Regan put out Gloucester's eyes unaided, with a broach."[50] Modern stagings of the blinding scene nearly always show Regan's active participation in the mutilation of Gloucester.

Emily Raymond, who played Goneril in 2004, felt that Goneril and Regan "had a brutal upbringing—[with] smacks of physical violence and mental abuse. I think Lear probably took his daughters to hangings and taught them the brutal way to deal with traitors—you don't hang them, you pluck out their eyes and let them live, to serve as a deterrent to others."[51]

What impact does it have to turn the violence and evil in *Lear* into something psychological instead of metaphysical? Does the implication that it is somehow the "natural" result of a bad, neglected upbringing diminish the epic nature of the play and the horrific impact of the sisters' monstrous acts? Lear's world is thrown out of order by his inability to be an adequate father *and king*. James I, in his publication *The True Law of Free Monarchies*, underlined the divine right of kings and the duty of all monarchs to treat their subjects as a caring father would do his children. Lear's misunderstanding of his role as a fixed point in the natural order of things and his irresponsibility in relation to his position in society unleash unnatural chaos.

In 1993 Adrian Noble emphasized violent cosmic forces prevalent in the play by use of an abstract but symbolic set:

> When David Bradley's superlative Gloucester, his eyes gouged out, staggers away from the scene of atrocity and from Simon Dormandy's chillingly, psychopathic Cornwall, the focus clears at last. Noble used the Folio edition of the text, so cutting the aid of Gloucester's servants after the blinding. The sightless Bradley gazes in the direction of a blue and white model of the globe, fixed above the stage. As he stares, a crack runs across the globe's circumference and the sands of time begin to pour out of it. The society of King Lear, with family life collapsing in warfare and inhuman cruelty . . . is ominous of all civilized human life ruined and coming to an end.[52]

In this bleak vision,

> Noble's most original stroke is to suggest that the cruelty unleashed by Lear's folly spreads to even the conventionally

good characters. The chief beneficiary is Simon Russell Beale's extraordinary Edgar who starts as goody-two shoes and who is turned by the horrors he has witnessed into a symbol of revenge. In this production he doesn't just kill Oswald; he batters his face with a staff as if in retaliation for the blinding of his father. The most unplayable major role in Shakespeare suddenly acquires a specific identity: a man forever tainted by the contagion of violence.[53]

In his final battle with Edmund, Russell Beale as Edgar tried "to rip out the dying Edmund's eyes in reprisal."[54] Similarly, Bill Alexander's 2004 production included "chilling touches that alert you afresh to the barbarism of its world. For example, in the climactic duel between Edmund and Edgar, it's only chance that stops the virtuous brother from exacting primitive 'eye for an eye' justice"[55]—"In order to force Edmund to drop his arms, [Edgar] grabbed him by either side of his face and pushed his thumbs into his eyes. This reference to the blinding of Gloucester was eerily resonant."[56]

Our opinion of Edgar will determine how we consider the end of the play. His spiritual journey, which echoes Lear's, provides him with a unique understanding of humanity and the preciousness of life. But he is also a very human avenger who has to set the world right and provide hope for the future. To overbalance his character with deliberate malicious and violent action furthers a nihilistic vision of the play by removing the certainty of redemption for a lost and barbaric world. Adrian Noble in 1982 stressed this element of unredeemed cruelty. The *Guardian* critic Michael Billington explains:

> Edgar slays Oswald by breaking his back with a staff, and the fraternal duel between Edgar and Edmund is a bare-chested, bloody, unchivalric combat that ends with Edmund's head being dumped in water. Even at the last the characters look out into the future in a spirit of skeptical uncertainty.[57]

In Peter Brook's vision of the play chaos was part of the natural order. His production emphasized the inhumanity and disinterestedness of the forces that annihilate Lear. There was no moral structure beneath the surface of civilization: "Everywhere one looks, one sees only the facades and emblems of a world and, ironically, as characters acquire sight, it enables them to see only into a void."[58]

Brook removed key moments of redemption and humanity: the servants did not tend Gloucester after he has been blinded but callously bumped into him as they cleared away the stage. Edmund's attempt to redeem himself and stop the order that will see the death of Cordelia was cut. As Lear died, his final words "Look there" were spoken as he stared ahead into nothingness. We were not left with the usual tableau of survivors grieving over Lear and Cordelia. The cast left, carrying out their dead bodies, leaving Edgar and the dead Edmund on stage alone. Edgar moved center-stage, and then went to his brother. As he dragged his brother's corpse up toward the back of the stage a distant rumble of thunder sounded in the background, leaving the audience with the impression that worse was to follow. "[W]e that are young / Shall never see so much nor live so long" took on a genuinely apocalyptic meaning. This was an image of the horror of "the promised end" of the world.

Where Brook's production succeeded was in making the audience grieve for humanity, or more specifically for the absence of humanity. It seemed a fitting statement for its time, and it is one that still touches us today. Lear's speech in the hovel is central to Brook's vision—it is not by chance that he used this quote in the program for the production's world tour: "Expose thyself to feel what wretches feel." Corin Redgrave, who played King Lear in 2004, also took this line:

> The play investigates how, in a dying or decaying world, we can live better and be better toward one another. It can't produce any conclusions to that because the world as Shakespeare saw it at that time was dying, just as our world as we see it is dying. Shakespeare was writing in a world which he sees going to hell on wheels and writing a text book in case the world should ever recover. So it is the most bleak of plays, but it is a very salutary play, a very necessary play . . . you could not possibly lose *King Lear* without impoverishing ourselves terribly.[59]

THE DIRECTOR'S CUT: INTERVIEWS WITH ADRIAN NOBLE, DEBORAH WARNER, AND TREVOR NUNN

Adrian Noble, born in 1950, arrived at the RSC from the Bristol Old Vic, where he had directed several future stars in productions of classic plays. His first production on the main stage of the Royal Shakespeare Theatre in Stratford was the acclaimed 1982 *Lear*, discussed here, with Michael Gambon as the king and Antony Sher as an extraordinarily powerful Fool. Two years later his *Henry V* sowed the seed for Kenneth Branagh's film. Among his other major productions during his two decades at the RSC were *Hamlet*, again with Branagh in the title role, *The Plantagenets*, based on the *Henry VI/Richard III* tetralogy, and the two parts of *Henry IV*, with Robert Stephens as Falstaff. Stephens returned in 1993 to play Lear in a second production of the tragedy, also discussed here. Noble's 1994 *Midsummer Night's Dream* was made into a film. He was artistic director from 1991 to 2003, since when he has been a freelance director. His production style is characterized by strong use of colors and objects (such as umbrellas), and fluid scenic structure.

Deborah Warner, born in 1959, trained in stage management at the Central School of Speech and Drama. At the age of twenty-one she formed her own "fringe" company, Kick Theatre, imaginatively staging stripped-down productions of the classics, including *King Lear* (1985, discussed here), at the Edinburgh Festival. In 1987 she made her RSC debut with a rigorously simple but deeply moving *Titus Andronicus*, starring Brian Cox, on the intimate stages of the Swan at Stratford and The Pit at London's Barbican. A *King John* in a similar style followed the next year and in 1990 she directed *King Lear*, again with Brian Cox, on the proscenium Lyttelton stage of the National Theatre in London (also discussed here). She has subsequently specialized in Samuel Beckett and opera, but has returned to Shakespeare with a *Richard II* at the National, featuring her collaborator Fiona Shaw cross-dressed in the title role, and a large-scale *Julius Caesar* at the Barbican.

Sir Trevor Nunn is the most successful and one of the most highly regarded of modern British theater directors. Born in 1940, he was a brilliant student at Cambridge, strongly influenced by the literary close reading of Dr. F. R. Leavis. At the age of just twenty-eight he succeeded Peter Hall as artistic director of the RSC, where he remained until 1978. He greatly expanded the range of the company's work and its ambition in terms of venues and touring. He also achieved huge success in musical theater and subsequently became artistic director of the National Theatre in London. His productions are always full of textual insights, while being clean and elegant in design. Among his most admired Shakespearean work has been a series of tragedies with Ian McKellen in leading roles: *Macbeth* (1976, with Judi Dench, in the dark, intimate space of The Other Place), *Othello* (1989, with McKellen as Iago and Imogen Stubbs as Desdemona), and *King Lear* (2007, in the Stratford Complete Works Festival, on world tour, and then in London).

One of the first questions one always wonders about with *King Lear* is: What do you decide on as a setting for the play? We've seen everything from a Stonehenge-like world to contemporaneity by way of Samurai Japan. So what kind of a world did you and your designer seek to create?

Noble: There are two or three driving forces in relation to the setting. First of all there is the need to create a series of credible family units, because the dynamic of the play emanates from damaged families; in particular Lear's and Gloucester's two parallel families. So one needs to be able to create a domesticity and parallel familial worlds. The second thing one needs to be able to explore is an epic quality, by which I mean the fact that the reality we live in fractures and splinters as the reality inside Lear's head fractures and splinters. Shakespeare quite deliberately expresses the horrors and the madness that are happening inside the human being through the physicality of it.

In both productions I sought for a setting and a world that could fragment and start behaving in an almost independent way. With both productions the walls started splitting and almost exploded apart. In 1993 with Robert Stephens as Lear I found an image at the very end of the first act which I felt was rather telling: the moon started bleeding sand. That seemed to me an exquisitely painful image, with the moon's very strong connection with the eye. The milk of human kindness had completely disappeared.

I found myself eschewing a completely modern, contemporary world, because it seemed to me that would quite swiftly become a highway to nowhere. In a similar way I eschewed the old Stonehenge version which seemed to me as silly as setting it in Wapping. So we found a world that probably related to Europe a hundred and fifty years ago, with greatcoats, where people still hunted, where the motor vehicle hadn't taken over our world. Neither myself, Bob Crowley, who designed the first, or Anthony Ward, who designed the second, would I think be able to place it within fifty years of a particular date.

Warner: My interest in both my productions was to release the characters through their language and their relationships. What the play does is to take the audience into the interior of themselves. It is a mirror of the desolation of the human spirit, how lost it is, how far we fall in families and how hard sought are the conditions that prompt personal change. That's why the setting of any given production has little connection to the key that may unlock the scenes and acts. The play has to flow through our imaginations and then it has to lodge, and that is why I used such a pared-down aesthetic so that the space is clear for that to happen. All great plays do this but each must be met in their particular. With Kick Theatre in 1985 we were in a church hall in Edinburgh with three ladders and a bucket of water for the heath scene. With the NT [National Theatre] we were on the wide open stage of the Lyttelton Theatre where different aesthetic choices needed to be made before we began. Hildegard Bechtler's set was poetic and beautiful but bare, and the "world" was not precisely named by it. It was not the "Stone Age *Lear*," or the "Third Reich *Lear*" but the Brian Cox, David Bradley, Ian McKellen, Susie Engel, and Clare Higgins *Lear*. It was actor led and actor inspired and I still believe that that is a very good way with Shakespeare. Belief in casting and the group creation of the world is what matters.

Nunn: Shakespeare says that King Lear is the king of Ancient Britain. On the other hand, Shakespeare includes scenes involving dueling with swords, there are references to a graced palace, to women wearing gorgeous clothes that scarcely keep them warm, and Gloucester refers to wearing spectacles. Shakespeare is making clear that he doesn't mind breaking the rules as far as historical accuracy goes. It's very likely that *King Lear* was performed at the Globe, or indeed at court performances, with the actors wearing a mixture of contemporary Elizabethan/Jacobean clothing, with some additional elements of cloak and robe that would indicate an earlier period.

I think Shakespeare was interested in the idea that a history play should apply acutely and precisely to the age that the *audience* lives in, so he was keen to have it both ways. I've seen Stonehenge-based productions of *King Lear*, and frankly it does seem very odd that Lear should make such a fuss about being out on a heath in a storm when his normal domestic condition appears to be open to the elements.

Shakespeare is presenting the huge contrast between a man who has been encouraged to believe that he is the closest thing to a god in human terms, and the man who comes to perceive he is like a beggar "no more but this." Lear is a conduit of the gods and he's in totally autocratic authority. His smallest whisper is converted into law, and nobody, such as Kent, can question him. So, in this production, I have elected to set the play in a seemingly nineteenth-century environment with resonances of the tsarist order in Russia and/or the Austrian autocracy of Franz Joseph. The intention is to stress that Lear's power is total and dictatorial like a tsar or an emperor, in all matters, political and social, and that it derives from god with whom he communicates. This, I think, allows us to encompass the requirements of the social structure of the play and, what's more, the anachronisms make complete sense. Lear's journey takes him from that autocratic power to somebody who, in the storm, asks himself for the first time, "How do wretches survive in conditions like these, if they cannot keep warm because they have no proper clothing?" And then, wanting to embrace that houseless situation, he meets Tom o'Bedlam (who happens to be a man going through the same crisis, another man who's been used to comfort and is now, in order to survive, turning himself into a crazed beggar), and as he studies the beggar's naked exposure, Lear urgently wants to place himself in that condition, so he can experience being the "forked animal" for himself.

Shakespeare had long been fascinated with the philosophical idea that a king can journey through the guts of a beggar. He has used the notion of king to beggar on a number of previous occasions, but in *Lear* he takes it to the extreme. I think *Richard II* is almost a sketch for *King Lear;* here we have a godlike king who in the end is sobbing, "I need friends and since I am ordinary like you—how can you say I am a king?" Shakespeare takes that king to a small prison cell, and then, alone and the lord of nothing, he grants him extraordinary self-knowledge. But in *King Lear,* the journey of the king is to a yet more extreme destination.

Why did your Lear react so extremely to Cordelia's refusal to play the game of quantifying her love in words (or perhaps of quantifying her love all too literally—if I marry, my father will have 50 percent of my love and my husband the other 50 percent)?

Noble: In a way you have to go back a step from that to ask yourself why Lear loves Cordelia so much more than the other two girls. There are dozens of reasons why, and I think most families could find their own reason why one child is, or appears to be, more beloved than the other. If the character in question is an obsessive like Lear then it starts getting potentially dangerous. His little girl has grown up and defies him, and he can't deal with that at all. He can't deal with retiring, he can't deal with getting old, he can't deal with not being in control anymore. And as a consequence of all these things poor Cordelia gets it in the neck. And he regrets it almost immediately. Within a day he regrets it—probably within hours.

Warner: My Lear was a spoilt Lear, a vain Lear—a man who wants to hear what he wants to hear. His foolish gung-ho confidence is to wrap and disguise his need—a desire for a public show of affection—in a party game. He makes light of something that is weighty and important to him so that nobody suspects his underlying vulnerability. He demands that his daughters play out in public something that is private, and he claims this right because the prizes are high and marvelous. However, he knows who will take which prize because the "game" is rigged—the parcels of land are already named, signed, and sealed by king and court. The whole extravagant business is a

6. Ian McKellen as Lear in Trevor Nunn's 2007 production, in the opening scene with quasi-military "Ruritanian" regalia.

contrivance to feed his vanity, to continue to make him feel that he holds the center even in old age. We are witnessing a grotesque public massage of ego. Lear is a man used to getting what he wants, but he gets badly burnt. He discovers that love is not a commodity, that it must be given freely. It may be that he has lost sight of what love is a long time before the play begins. He's getting the answer he wants in two cases from the very daughters he did not treat well—if their behavior later in the piece is anything to go by—and seems to barely know the character of his favorite—Cordelia—whose reaction is a huge surprise to him. There is a lot we do not know about this mysterious man, but his short-sightedness is placed on the table at the very opening of the play. Here is a man who will need to travel far to begin to gain the gift of personal insight. His friend Gloucester will literally lose his sight: blind men both.

And why didn't your Cordelia, or why *couldn't* she, put her love into words?

Noble: That's a much more difficult question to answer. It's a young person's thing, whereby the spoken truth is more important than making your mum and dad happy. It's the moment of leaving home. The domestic psychological detail is very precise in the play. In Lear's household, Cordelia is at the point of leaving home to go and get married. That's a huge moment in every family, although it's very often not recognized. Some daughters never leave home. They are still at home, in the thrall of their parents, when they're seventy. Cordelia leaves home and Lear can't deal with that. But she knows she has to do it, especially with a father like him.

Warner: Cordelia does not want to play this extravagant and obscene party game. She is young, she is shy, and she is about to be married, perhaps even the public nature of this serious business of land division is difficult for her. Anyhow, extravagant party game or not, it is the wrong moment for her to speak of her love to her father, and she certainly does not want to talk about such matters in public. When her sisters speak she is appalled by their preparedness to speak on cue, and especially so since she knows they are being dishonest. Cordelia wants to hold to her own truth. Horrified by what is hap-

7. The opening scene in Deborah Warner's 1990 production: a party game
goes horribly wrong, with Brian Cox as Lear in wheelchair and paper crown.

pening around her, she wants to stop the game, and that is just what
she does. It goes horribly wrong because she won't play, and she
advertently or inadvertently humiliates her father in public. She is
young and she believes with stern clarity in the virtues of honesty,
truth, and love. She is earnest—some might say overearnest in this
context, and she causes an atomic explosion.

**Lear is both a king and a father. That often seems to be a choice
that directors and actors have to make—are you going to give the
primary emphasis to Lear's journey as a king giving up his crown,
or is the primary emphasis going to be on the family relationships? Or do you actually think that the essence of the play is
that the two are inextricably intertwined?**

Noble: Without question they are entwined. I didn't find that a
choice. It isn't a choice that I recognize.

Warner: The father relationship is the most interesting, he is a father
who happens to be a king; but since all fathers are kings then, yes, all
is intertwined. There is a lot we don't know about him, about his

reign—but we know that he owns the land of his country and chooses to divide that up in such a way that will benefit his retirement most comfortably. He is a king/father heading toward retirement, a dangerous time in all families and in all monarchies.

Nunn: You won't be surprised to hear that your "third way" alternative is the one this production goes for. Shakespeare is frighteningly brilliant at doing "family breakup." He does it superbly—in *Hamlet*, for example. I would say he does it equally shockingly in *The Merchant of Venice*, and in *Macbeth* we watch a marriage coming apart at the seams. There are small insights in *King Lear* into how the king's family has been pushed apart by events and attitudes. Lear is eighty years old. He has three daughters, and there is no Mrs. Lear. The older daughters are married to powerful men and live in their own palaces. The youngest daughter is only just of marriageable age. Hidden behind the play, is there a story that he was a king who had two wives?—the first wife producing two daughters, Goneril and Regan, and then after her death (as we can frequently see in modern complex family histories) there is the child of a second marriage, the late child (as far as that father is concerned) who then dominates the father's affections. There's sufficient evidence in the play to suggest that jealousies and rifts within the family derive from such a backstory.

But I don't think exploration of a family feud is where Shakespeare wants matters to stop. It's not where his focus is. Routinely at the start of rehearsals, I say we have to first uncover the *theme* of a Shakespeare play. If you're a director, you must X-ray the play to find out what its bone structure is and where its vital organs are. A production shouldn't work from the outside, it must proceed from a sense of what the *internal* structure is, and thereby discover how everything contained in the play is meaningful because it is contiguous to that thematic structure.

In the case of *Lear*, it being one of the greatest plays of Shakespeare's maturity, the investigation is not going to be easy and the wellspring is not going to lie very close to the surface. Those who have written about *Lear* as Shakespeare's study of Nature are, to my thinking, somewhere near the mark, in the sense that Shakespeare is certainly inquiring into *human* nature in *Lear*, and he often uses the term "nature" to encompass human behavior and its contradictions. But let's take that definition of a theme just a little bit further. I would say Shakespeare is wanting to look at the human being, both sublime and ridiculous; I think he is asking, "What is the human condition?" Why do humans say to themselves they are close to being angels, aspiring toward those qualities that are spiritual and godlike? And yet, why are they, in much of their action, so close to behaving like animals? Why, as it were anthropologically, do they have animal instincts that the species appears not to be able to get rid of?

I think it's no surprise that in this play Shakespeare doesn't define exactly who the god or gods are. There's a shadowy Apollo or Jupiter, and the sun is sacred, but the largely anonymous gods are referred to, as a sort of necessity for human beings to believe in, so that somehow humans can feel their actions are predestined, or governed by forces above and beyond themselves. Everything is under the control or the will of the gods.

But then, close to the center of the play, there's a young man who says: "Thou, nature, art my goddess: to thy law / My services are bound"—a young man who seems to be saying, "I don't believe in the gods above, it's human nature that I am influenced by." At the end of that first soliloquy, Edmund says, I sense almost in mockery: "Now gods, stand up for bastards." Well, he implies, you "gods" have supposedly stood up for everybody else, it's high time you let bastards have a go. It's an extremely dangerous bit of comedic dramaturgy, but atheistical Edmund, creating mayhem in his world, is placed in sharp contrast to the majority who genuinely beg the gods to intervene, at times almost obsessively. And I think Shakespeare makes it clear that "the gods" don't. Repeatedly they are deaf or callous or nonexistent. They do nothing, even when their intervention would be an affirmation of "the good" in opposition to what is evil; they don't utter, they don't move a muscle. Are the heavens empty?

An actor who has played Lear has said that the real difficulty in playing the part is deciding how much to let rip how soon—if you give too much to the anger in the first half you're too exhausted for the madness in the second half, but if you have too much con-

trol to begin with, the transition into madness can seem too sudden and extreme to be convincing. Do you recognize that difficulty? And as a director, what can you do to help your Lear through it?

Noble: I think that's very true. Most Lears I've talked to find the second half much easier than the first half, because the first half requires such a level of energy and a very skillful control of your resources. The truth is, it's almost unplayable—the pain is so great, the vocal demands so much. I've seen people cop out of it and say I'm going to do it quite quietly, but that's complete crap. They are selling the part and the audience short. It gets actors down a lot actually, because it magnifies your failures. The same is true for directors. It's like Everest, it's an unforgiving mountain, and people die on the way up, or they get badly hurt. It is like singing Wagner, and not everybody can sing Wagner.

Warner: You need all your energy and all your fight to play Lear, just as an opera singer needs theirs for Tristan, Wotan, or Siegfried. You cannot leave it too late. Brian Cox was forty-four when he played it for me. The first scene demands that the actor hit raw and engulfing fury within minutes. Throughout the opening scenes this anger is further released until it lets fly and the play climbs from there. You have to risk exhaustion to play it well. This play is not gentle on its lead actor, but where Shakespeare is brilliant and kind is in letting the evening be shared and there is, of course, the famous break at the start of the second half for a rest in the dressing room. Shakespeare always acts as helpful assistant to the director and he supports the actors by graphing and arcing their evening. Actors must follow him for their physical well-being, but they must follow what he asks for too. Real anger, real madness . . . or, no play.

How did your production deal with the part of the Fool and his disappearance halfway through the action?

Noble: In the first production in 1982 with Michael Gambon and Tony Sher it became quite famous. We did an improvisation in rehearsal, and I said just hold that a fraction longer, and the net

8. "The oldest hath borne most": Robert Stephens (right) as Lear and David Bradley as Gloucester, finding a human bond in their anguish, in Adrian Noble's 1993 production.

result was that King Lear accidentally stabbed the Fool, and he died. I had teachers coming in to say "You have to write in your program that that is not what Shakespeare wrote!" Because it is completely logical. Just before this, there's: "The little dogs and all, Trey, Blanch and Sweetheart, see, they bark at me" and there's "lie here and rest awhile"; "draw the curtains." And so we had the Fool using a cushion and Lear chasing him, and in stabbing the cushion he accidentally stabs the Fool. And then the little feathers became dogs. It was very beautiful and completely logical.

The Fool's function in life is entirely tied up with the king. He's like a soldier's batman. There's no logic for him to exist once the master's dead, or mad.

Warner: My National Theatre Fool (David Bradley) died during the interval of exhaustion and cold. He went to sleep in a wheelbarrow

9. Michael Gambon as Lear and Antony Sher as the Fool, with mask, in Adrian Noble's 1982 production.

somewhere in the dark interior of the hovel and never woke again. A sad and quiet death that went practically unnoticed. In my Kick Theatre production the actress Hilary Townley played both Cordelia and the Fool (a doubling I am sure Shakespeare intended), which solves so many issues so very easily. For example, "my poor fool is hanged" draws effortless and painful meaning from such casting.

One striking feature of Shakespeare's reworking of the old anonymous *Leir* play is his removal of its Christian frame of reference (that was one of the reasons why Tolstoy perversely said he preferred the old play!). The characters are always appealing to the gods but not getting the response they want. And then there is Edmund appealing to "Nature" as his goddess. What was your thinking about religion in the play?

Noble: The first time I did it I quite consciously sought a godless universe. I was very influenced by Brecht and Beckett. I sought a godless universe and a quite vengeful, spiteful universe. I made heavy cuts at the end of the play to highlight that fact.

The second time I imagined a universe that was not godless, but in which the gods sat back and refused to interfere. The choice is as much to do with the director or interpreter as the writing.

Warner: The removal of any uniting Christian frame makes this text all the more available to us now. The characters are struggling away as we are all struggling away, and have ever been struggling away for centuries. From the seventeenth century to the twenty-first, Shakespeare allows us no simple answers, and that is why productions should beware of giving them.

Nunn: Remember, in the old *Leir* play, the king is restored to his throne and Cordelia lives. By changing the ending, Shakespeare deliberately violates a seemingly fundamental rule of drama, namely that plays serve as a moral or cautionary influence on their audience, because they show, regardless of trial and vicissitude, that the good will triumph in the end. In *King Lear* we're surely expecting just that, but Shakespeare won't allow it. I think this is proof positive that Shakespeare's intentions were very different from those of the old play. Shakespeare's investigation of the extremes of human behavior, into the nature of man the species, concludes that life *isn't* like a morality play. When everything in our religious and cultural history requires us to believe that ultimately the gods will intervene on the side of virtue, Shakespeare says emphatically that they don't. It's more than the conclusion that his play is not Christian, it's that he moves to a conclusion that is, at the very least, agnostic.

For me, it is centrally important that there is no sense of divine justice in this tragedy. I'm wondering whether any other writer during the Elizabethan age ever ventured to question whether or not the heavens might be empty? In the early scenes, as I said, Shakespeare's play sets up the fundamental belief in his characters that human actions are overseen by the gods. Lear seems to believe that, like him, the gods are old men, that they are intelligent, and that they're watching, and he clearly sees himself as in privileged contact with the gods. But as the play progresses, Shakespeare shows us more people praying for the intervention of the gods, to no avail. The battle at the climax of the story will determine whether or not the "good" will triumph. Gloucester is urged by Edgar to "Pray that the right may thrive." He does. They don't. Finally, as it's realized that a death sentence is on both Lear and Cordelia, Albany leads all present in a final prayer as soldiers run to the prison—"The gods defend her!" The first word of the next line is "Howl." Cordelia is dead. No intervention. The gods aren't mentioned again.

So yes, I think Edmund is placed before us early on as evidence of a solitary, dangerous, atheistical intelligence. Then as Lear's journey takes him increasingly toward challenging the behavior of the gods, arriving at his epiphany in the "unaccommodated man" speech, his more fundamental questions begin. "What is the *cause* of thunder?" "Is there any *cause* in nature that makes these hard hearts?" His questions now seem to be reaching toward Darwinian rather than divine explanations, and his belief in the gods begins to evaporate.

What about Edgar? He's quite an actor, performing in different voices, isn't he? He's Poor Tom, but then after that, after the cliff fall, he's the man on the beach and after that he's the peasant with the accent who kills Oswald—why does Edgar have all these different languages and voices and play all these different roles? Why doesn't he much sooner just say, "Look, Dad, I'm sorry. You should be sorry, you got the wrong son, I'm the good one. You're blind, this is me . . . " So many opportunities in so many different roles . . . until he finally gets around to telling his father the truth, by which time he's left it so late that all Gloucester can do is die of a heart attack.

Noble: I think he takes upon himself the sins of others, in particular the sins of the father, in order to redeem himself. It's a profoundly religious, spiritual journey that Edgar goes on and a very tough regime that he imposes upon himself. The disguises, flagellation, and infliction of misery are all part of that. Through the course of the play he cleanses himself. He's like a character out of a George Herbert poem.

Nunn: Edgar does say, at a crucial moment of the play, at the moment where he could cease to be the Tom o'Bedlam character at last, "I cannot daub it further," and then in the very next instant, "And yet I must." In this production we've tried to identify something specific about that change of mind. There are men on Gloucester's orders scouring the country on the hunt to capture and kill Edgar if they find him. We have a troop of those soldiers passing at that point, so Edgar's "yet I must" is clearly justified as self-preservation, and by association the preserving of his father.

But there's a deeper explanation that Edgar himself also provides when he takes Gloucester, who is suicidally bent, to an imaginary cliff edge. Just before the death plunge moment, Edgar has an aside to the audience, "Why I do trifle thus with his despair / Is done to cure it." This is fundamental in Edgar's journey. He observes that his father is now only full of resentment and hatred for the world, of believing that there was never anything worth believing in. Edgar, still clinging to his belief in divine justice, cannot allow his misguided, misled father to die a bad death or an unredeemed death. Therefore he makes it his mission to bring his father beyond suicidal thoughts to a different, reconciled set of attitudes. The gods seem to be unwilling to back up that reconciliation and continue to rain down horror, but Edgar's changes of identity are entirely to bring his father to a better spiritual place.

There's something of a fairytale quality to the play, isn't there? Goneril and Regan as the ugly sisters, Cordelia as a Cinderella with an unhappy ending. But, especially since Peter Brook's famous production and film, there's also an approach to the play that emphasizes Lear's unreasonable rage, the chaos caused by his riotous knights, and the sense that his daughters, Goneril especially, aren't villains through and through.

Noble: It's hard to really admire anybody in the play actually. You can like them all a lot, and you can feel for them a lot, but it is hard to admire anybody. You can admire Gloucester, and probably Edgar's morality. As for the sisters, Shakespeare always writes what is needed. It can be very frustrating, especially for actresses, because it often happens with the female parts, that Shakespeare sees no point in showing you the bits of the iceberg under the water. He thinks that is a complete waste of scenes. It doesn't mean that the bit that is revealed does not have a complete world of which it is a part. Exactly the same thing applies to Gertrude and Lady Macbeth, whereby when the function ceases to have a crucial element or a driving force, Shakespeare just stops. Lady Macbeth and Gertrude just stop. Actresses tend to think there must be a missing or lost scene, but there isn't. Like the Fool in the second half of the play, it isn't there because there's no need for it. It doesn't mean you can't make it completely real, but you have to come at it from his time, not like a movie. The actor may have a backstory, but you can only show so much because you don't need anymore.

Nunn: I think it would be wholly wrong for a production to suggest that Goneril and Regan are of evil disposition at the beginning of the play; but there is a degree of ambition in their behavior, and there is a degree of competition between them, and possibly there is that element of hidden resentment of how their much-the-younger sister has become the favorite of their old father.

Traditionally, late-nineteenth-century and early twentieth-century versions of *Lear* did indeed go very strongly for the interpretation that Lear himself was always to be seen as kind and gentle and white-haired and frail. And therefore a delightful old man goaded intolerably by two wicked sisters. When Peter Brook did his production in 1962, there was a sense that an extraordinary revolution had taken place because Brook, absolutely honest to the text, said: "Lear is behaving entirely unjustifiably, now he's behaving appallingly, and now he's behaving absolutely beyond the limit to the point where no father can expect to get away with that." It was a production that tried explicitly to exonerate the sisters. I remember that, at that time, the impact of revealing Lear's behavior as frequently unacceptable hit home very strongly. Now, of course, any production trying to propose that Lear is a close relative of Father Christmas would be laughed off the stage. The Brook view has become the standard view.

However, we do still have to explain how Goneril and Regan get to a condition of alarming ruthlessness in the second half of the play. All I will say is—especially if anybody hasn't seen the play before—watch out for the moment when Lear utters his curse on Goneril, and particularly his curse on Goneril's womb—a curse more bloodcurdling than I hope any lady in the audience will ever hear in her life. We all know that when dreadful things are said in rage, those words can never be unsaid. This is a major turning point of the play and causes Goneril to become vengeful, regardless of consequence.

The blinding of Gloucester is perhaps the most horrific moment in all Shakespeare. How did you stage that and did it have contemporary resonances for you? In Trevor Nunn's 2007 production Regan behaves with sadistic glee that's also a kind of fear—it inevitably conjured up the American soldiers in Abu Ghraib jail in Iraq. Torture in times of war is something that just doesn't go away . . .

Noble: Yes, it had resonances in the sense that it confronts you with the most shocking things that humanity can do to humanity, but I almost never make references to contemporary events, because in my view it's a blind alley. Scenes like that talk directly to the audience and their souls and hearts. You don't need people coming on in flak jackets and dressed as Iraqis.

It is a dangerous scene for a number of reasons. It's dangerous because the blinding is done to an old man, and secondly, it's completely plugged in to this extraordinarily dangerous sexual relationship between Cornwall and Regan. It's plugged in to the scheme of the play in terms of the breakdown of order and the dawn of chaos. It's a wild, very, very unpleasant scene.

Warner: The theater is a very safe place to explore the taboo and the pornographic. That safe place of examination may be the very point of theater. As a theater director, if you have to do a blinding you want to make it as ghoulish as you can. The audience is then left working it through in the safety of the evening, and a live and engaged audience will inevitably draw contemporary parallels. All great plays have the power to do this and the greater the performances the greater that power to prompt connection. This brings us back to what I said about these plays flowing through our imaginations. Few of us experience directly something like the horror of Abu Ghraib, but the theater allows us to imagine such a reality, to process it, and to question it from every angle. The Greek theater was a public debate where the audience tested their response to the barbaric and nudged toward a legal system and the founding of modern democracy. Shakespeare's theater took this debate into the new-found world of the seventeenth century and put up onstage every single human emotion, so that we could have a place to go where we might discuss ourselves. Sometimes one can view Shakespeare's legacy as the complete human emotional encyclopedia. A place to go to study each and every human experience—to map ourselves in the safety of the theater.

Nunn: As you know, this is not a production that is trying to say "Here we are in the Middle East in the twenty-first century." But it is hoping that all the things that are part of our experience now will be brought to bear on a contemporary audience watching and receiving the play.

Shakespeare's play was almost certainly heavily censored when it was first performed. It was probably first performed at court and so it is likely that quite a number of cuts were applied to the text because statements were being made that would not be acceptable to a royal ear, and possibly shouldn't be heard by anybody. There are a host of things that Lear says about human institutions, "justice"—"which is the justice, which is the thief?"; "authority" as in the police or governmental authority—"a dog's obeyed in office"—getting its power from name or uniform, but not by standards of behavior. He talks about "politicians"—"Get thee glass eyes, / And like a scurvy politician seem / To see the things thou dost not." Lear goes through a list of modern and, to our ears, highly recognizable contemporary institutions and says so many of them are corrupt and therefore worthless. But Shakespeare had the perfect reply to the censors. The man saying these terrible things is mad. Who knows, if he had not had that defense, Shakespeare might have done a spell in jail.

Over previous generations the blinding scene has been cut down or merely "suggested," as something taking place in the dark. Such bowdlerization of Shakespeare is based on the judgment that these things are not for civilized people to watch, or hear. In the twentieth century, believing that Shakespeare should be very much like Samuel Beckett (who was so obviously greatly influenced by the play), the blinding scene became increasingly essential to the play.

As we watch, Shakespeare is saying, "Face up to the fact that human beings are capable of unspeakably animal behavior toward each other." These days, as we read of torture, of the callousness of the suicide bomber who blows up children, we ask how any group of people can say they are justified by any cause whatsoever in doing such things to another group of people? But Shakespeare tells us that it is in us. We humans do it. We do it as a species, and we must face the truth that it's in human nature to be inhuman.

Academics get very exercised about the variants between the Quarto and Folio texts of the play—the fact that Lear has different dying words in each version, that a different person inherits the gored state at the end of each version (Albany speaks the final lines in Quarto, Edgar in Folio), and so on. Did you concern yourself with these textual matters or do you feel that the director is free to pick and mix, cut and paste, his or her own version of the play?

Noble: I think the director is free to do what he wants to do, but he must also be answerable for what he does. I've never been very interested in the textual variations. What I did, particularly in the first production, was skin the last three hundred or four hundred lines— I was absolutely brutal with the cuts there. And the impact of it was that, at the very moment of repentance, it was too late. There was no time to save Lear and Cordelia's lives, because the people on stage had been chatting, talking all the time. That was all very much to do with the fact that it was a godless universe. The truth is on both occasions I created a world that seemed to me to be logical from all the different versions. I would then be responsible for that and I would stand by that.

Nunn: I don't think that in 1968 when I first directed the play anybody was yet saying, "The Quarto and the Folio are two quite different plays." I remember at the time consulting John Barton and arriving at a "best of both worlds" conflated text. That text became the basis of the text I used in 1976 with Donald Sinden, but then when I started out this time with Ian McKellen I did read a number of scholars who were telling me that I *should* be making a choice between Quarto and Folio. Alas, I found myself unwilling to lose rich and evocative material from either version, and so I worked with a slightly different conflation, but a conflation nonetheless. For me, the more important change since I first directed the play is not in scholarship, but in the simple fact that I am thirty years older now. Shakespeare's engagement with ultimate questions about mortality, what we construct for ourselves to explain or to accept our mortality, of course speaks more potently to me now. The play, as I have said, is very hard on organized human society and institutions of every kind. There is very little Lear and Gloucester have left to believe in, before they must endure their going hence. Edgar is left to conclude the play, and I think deliberately, it is a conclusion of a man who has nothing really to say. He offers no positive, no beliefs, no journey to a better future. He is by then almost the only character left standing, and in the bleakest of all Shakespeare's endings, he seems to know that all we can determine on is to "endure."

SHAKESPEARE'S CAREER IN THE THEATER

BEGINNINGS

William Shakespeare was an extraordinarily intelligent man who was born and died in an ordinary market town in the English Midlands. He lived an uneventful life in an eventful age. Born in April 1564, he was the eldest son of John Shakespeare, a glove maker who was prominent on the town council until he fell into financial difficulties. Young William was educated at the local grammar in Stratford-upon-Avon, Warwickshire, where he gained a thorough grounding in the Latin language, the art of rhetoric, and classical poetry. He married Ann Hathaway and had three children (Susanna, then the twins Hamnet and Judith) before his twenty-first birthday: an exceptionally young age for the period. We do not know how he supported his family in the mid-1580s.

Like many clever country boys, he moved to the city in order to make his way in the world. Like many creative people, he found a career in the entertainment business. Public playhouses and professional full-time acting companies reliant on the market for their income were born in Shakespeare's childhood. When he arrived in London as a man, sometime in the late 1580s, a new phenomenon was in the making: the actor who is so successful that he becomes a "star." The word did not exist in its modern sense, but the pattern is recognizable: audiences went to the theater not so much to see a particular show as to witness the comedian Richard Tarlton or the dramatic actor Edward Alleyn.

Shakespeare was an actor before he was a writer. It appears not to have been long before he realized that he was never going to grow into a great comedian like Tarlton or a great tragedian like Alleyn. Instead, he found a role within his company as the man who patched up old plays, breathing new life, new dramatic twists, into tired repertory pieces. He paid close attention to the work of the university-educated dramatists who were writing history plays and tragedies for the public stage in a style more ambitious, sweeping, and poetically grand than anything that had been seen before. But he may also have noted that what his friend and rival Ben Jonson would call "Marlowe's mighty line" sometimes faltered in the mode of comedy. Going to university, as Christopher Marlowe did, was all well and good for honing the arts of rhetorical elaboration and classical allusion, but it could lead to a loss of the common touch. To stay close to a large segment of the potential audience for public theater, it was necessary to write for clowns as well as kings and to intersperse the flights of poetry with the humor of the tavern, the privy, and the brothel: Shakespeare was the first to establish himself early in his career as an equal master of tragedy, comedy, and history. He realized that theater could be the medium to make the national past available to a wider audience than the elite who could afford to read large history books: his signature early works include not only the classical tragedy *Titus Andronicus* but also the sequence of English historical plays on the Wars of the Roses.

He also invented a new role for himself, that of in-house company dramatist. Where his peers and predecessors had to sell their plays to the theater managers on a poorly paid piecework basis, Shakespeare took a percentage of the box-office income. The Lord Chamberlain's Men constituted themselves in 1594 as a joint stock company, with the profits being distributed among the core actors who had invested as sharers. Shakespeare acted himself—he appears in the cast lists of some of Ben Jonson's plays as well as the list of actors' names at the beginning of his own collected works—but his principal duty was to write two or three plays a year for the company. By holding shares, he was effectively earning himself a royalty on his work, something no author had ever done before in England. When the Lord Chamberlain's Men collected their fee for performance at court in the Christmas season of 1594, three of them went along to the Treasurer of the Chamber: not just Richard Burbage the tragedian and Will Kempe the clown, but also Shakespeare the scriptwriter. That was something new.

The next four years were the golden period in Shakespeare's

career, though overshadowed by the death of his only son, Hamnet, age eleven, in 1596. In his early thirties and in full command of both his poetic and his theatrical medium, he perfected his art of comedy while also developing his tragic and historical writing in new ways. In 1598, Francis Meres, a Cambridge University graduate with his finger on the pulse of the London literary world, praised Shakespeare for his excellence across the genres:

> As Plautus and Seneca are accounted the best for comedy and tragedy among the Latins, so Shakespeare among the English is the most excellent in both kinds for the stage; for comedy, witness his *Gentlemen of Verona*, his *Errors*, his *Love Labours Lost*, his *Love Labours Won*, his *Midsummer Night Dream* and his *Merchant of Venice:* for tragedy his *Richard the 2*, *Richard the 3*, *Henry the 4*, *King John*, *Titus Andronicus* and his *Romeo and Juliet*.

For Meres, as for the many writers who praised the "honey-flowing vein" of *Venus and Adonis* and *Lucrece*, narrative poems written when the theaters were closed due to plague in 1593–94, Shakespeare was marked above all by his linguistic skill, by the gift of turning elegant poetic phrases.

PLAYHOUSES

Elizabethan playhouses were "thrust" or "one-room" theaters. To understand Shakespeare's original theatrical life, we have to forget about the indoor theater of later times, with its proscenium arch and curtain that would be opened at the beginning and closed at the end of each act. In the proscenium arch theater, stage and auditorium are effectively two separate rooms: the audience looks from one world into another as if through the imaginary "fourth wall" framed by the proscenium. The picture-frame stage, together with the elaborate scenic effects and backdrops beyond it, created the illusion of a self-contained world—especially once nineteenth-century developments in the control of artificial lighting meant that the auditorium could be darkened and the spectators made to focus on the lighted stage. Shakespeare, by contrast, wrote for a bare platform stage with a standing audience gathered around it in a courtyard in full daylight. The audience were always conscious of themselves and their fellow-spectators, and they shared the same "room" as the actors. A sense of immediate presence and the creation of rapport with the audience were all-important. The actor could not afford to imagine he was in a closed world, with silent witnesses dutifully observing him from the darkness.

Shakespeare's theatrical career began at the Rose Theatre in Southwark. The stage was wide and shallow, trapezoid in shape, like a lozenge. This design had a great deal of potential for the theatrical equivalent of cinematic split-screen effects, whereby one group of characters would enter at the door at one end of the tiring-house wall at the back of the stage and another group through the door at the other end, thus creating two rival tableaux. Many of the battle-heavy and faction-filled plays that premiered at the Rose have scenes of just this sort.

At the rear of the Rose stage, there were three capacious exits, each more than ten feet wide. Unfortunately, the very limited excavation of a fragmentary portion of the original Globe site in 1989 revealed nothing about the stage. The first Globe was built in 1599 with similar proportions to those of another theater, the Fortune, albeit that the former was polygonal and looked circular, whereas the latter was rectangular. The building contract for the Fortune survives and allows us to infer that the stage of the Globe was probably substantially wider than it was deep (perhaps forty-three feet wide and twenty-seven feet deep). It may well have been tapered at the front, like that of the Rose.

The capacity of the Globe was said to have been enormous, perhaps in excess of three thousand. It has been conjectured that about eight hundred people may have stood in the yard, with two thousand or more in the three layers of covered galleries. The other "public" playhouses were also of large capacity, whereas the indoor Blackfriars theater that Shakespeare's company began using in 1608—the former refectory of a monastery—had overall internal dimensions of a mere forty-six by sixty feet. It would have made for a much more intimate theatrical experience and had a much smaller capacity, probably of about six hundred people. Since they paid at least six-pence a head, the Blackfriars attracted a more select or "private" audience. The atmosphere would have been closer to that of an indoor performance before the court in the Whitehall Palace or at Richmond. That Shakespeare always wrote for indoor production at court as well as outdoor performance in the public theater should make us cautious about inferring, as some scholars have, that the opportunity provided by the intimacy of the Blackfriars led to a sig-nificant change toward a "chamber" style in his last plays—which, besides, were performed at both the Globe and the Blackfriars. After the occupation of the Blackfriars a five-act structure seems to have become more important to Shakespeare. That was because of artifi-cial lighting: there were musical interludes between the acts, while the candles were trimmed and replaced. Again, though, something similar must have been necessary for indoor court performances throughout his career.

Front of house there were the "gatherers" who collected the money from audience members: a penny to stand in the open-air yard, another penny for a place in the covered galleries, sixpence for the prominent "lord's rooms" to the side of the stage. In the indoor "private" theaters, gallants from the audience who fancied making themselves part of the spectacle sat on stools on the edge of the stage itself. Scholars debate as to how widespread this practice was in the public theaters such as the Globe. Once the audience were in place and the money counted, the gatherers were available to be extras on stage. That is one reason why battles and crowd scenes often come later rather than early in Shakespeare's plays. There was no formal prohibition upon performance by women, and there certainly were women among the gatherers, so it is not beyond the bounds of possi-bility that female crowd members were played by females.

The play began at two o'clock in the afternoon and the theater had to be cleared by five. After the main show, there would be a jig—which consisted not only of dancing, but also of knockabout comedy (it is the origin of the farcical "afterpiece" in the eighteenth-century theater). So the time available for a Shakespeare play was about two and a half hours, somewhere between the "two hours' traffic" men-tioned in the prologue to *Romeo and Juliet* and the "three hours' spectacle" referred to in the preface to the 1647 Folio of Beaumont and Fletcher's plays. The prologue to a play by Thomas Middleton refers to a thousand lines as "one hour's words," so the likelihood is that about two and a half thousand, or a maximum of three thousand lines, made up the performed text. This is indeed the length of most of Shakespeare's comedies, whereas many of his tragedies and histories are much longer, raising the possibility that he wrote full scripts, possibly with eventual publication in mind, in the full knowledge that the stage version would be heavily cut. The short Quarto texts published in his lifetime—they used to be called "Bad" Quartos— provide fascinating evidence as to the kind of cutting that probably took place. So, for instance, the First Quarto of *Hamlet* neatly merges two occasions when Hamlet is overheard, the "Fishmonger" and the "nunnery" scenes.

The social composition of the audience was mixed. The poet Sir John Davies wrote of "A thousand townsmen, gentlemen and whores, / Porters and servingmen" who would "together throng" at the public playhouses. Though moralists associated female play-going with adultery and the sex trade, many perfectly respectable citizens' wives were regular attendees. Some, no doubt, resembled the modern groupie: a story attested in two different sources has one citizen's wife making a postshow assignation with Richard Burbage and ending up in bed with Shakespeare—supposedly eliciting from the latter the quip that William the Conqueror was before Richard III. Defenders of theater liked to say that by witnessing the comeuppance of villains on the stage, audience members would repent of their own wrongdoings, but the reality is that most people went to the theater then, as they do now, for entertainment more than moral edification. Besides, it would be foolish to suppose that audiences behaved in a homogeneous way: a pamphlet of the 1630s tells of how two men went to see *Pericles* and one of them laughed while the other wept. Bishop John Hall complained that people went to church for the same reasons that they went to the theater: "for company, for custom, for recreation . . . to feed his eyes or his ears . . . or perhaps for sleep."

Men-about-town and clever young lawyers went to be seen as much as to see. In the modern popular imagination, shaped not least by *Shakespeare in Love* and the opening sequence of Laurence Olivier's *Henry V* film, the penny-paying groundlings stand in the yard hurling abuse or encouragement and hazelnuts or orange peel at the actors, while the sophisticates in the covered galleries appreciate Shakespeare's soaring poetry. The reality was probably the other way round. A "groundling" was a kind of fish, so the nickname suggests the penny audience standing below the level of the stage and gazing in silent open-mouthed wonder at the spectacle unfolding above them. The more difficult audience members, who kept up a running commentary of clever remarks on the performance and who occasionally got into quarrels with players, were the gallants. Like Hollywood movies in modern times, Elizabethan and Jacobean plays exercised a powerful influence on the fashion and behavior of the young. John Marston mocks the lawyers who would open their lips, perhaps to court a girl, and out would "flow / Naught but pure Juliet and Romeo."

THE ENSEMBLE AT WORK

In the absence of typewriters and photocopying machines, reading aloud would have been the means by which the company got to know a new play. The tradition of the playwright reading his complete script to the assembled company endured for generations. A copy would then have been taken to the Master of the Revels for licensing. The theater book-holder or prompter would then have copied the parts for distribution to the actors. A partbook consisted of the character's lines, with each speech preceded by the last three or four words of the speech before, the so-called "cue." These would have been taken away and studied or "conned." During this period of learning the parts, an actor might have had some one-to-one instruction, perhaps from the dramatist, perhaps from a senior actor who had played the same part before, and, in the case of an apprentice, from his master. A high percentage of Desdemona's lines occur in dialogue with Othello, of Lady Macbeth's with Macbeth, Cleopatra's with Antony, and Volumnia's with Coriolanus. The roles would almost certainly have been taken by the apprentice of the lead actor, usually Burbage, who delivers the majority of the cues. Given that

10. Hypothetical reconstruction of the interior of an Elizabethan playhouse during a performance.

apprentices lodged with their masters, there would have been ample opportunity for personal instruction, which may be what made it possible for young men to play such demanding parts.

After the parts were learned, there may have been no more than a single rehearsal before the first performance. With six different plays to be put on every week, there was no time for more. Actors, then, would go into a show with a very limited sense of the whole. The notion of a collective rehearsal process that is itself a process of discovery for the actors is wholly modern and would have been incomprehensible to Shakespeare and his original ensemble. Given the number of parts an actor had to hold in his memory, the forgetting of lines was probably more frequent than in the modern theater. The book-holder was on hand to prompt.

Backstage personnel included the property man, the tire-man who oversaw the costumes, call boys, attendants, and the musicians, who might play at various times from the main stage, the rooms above, and within the tiring-house. Scriptwriters sometimes made a nuisance of themselves backstage. There was often tension between the acting companies and the freelance playwrights from whom they purchased scripts: it was a smart move on the part of Shakespeare and the Lord Chamberlain's Men to bring the writing process in-house.

Scenery was limited, though sometimes set pieces were brought on (a bank of flowers, a bed, the mouth of hell). The trapdoor from below, the gallery stage above, and the curtained discovery-space at the back allowed for an array of special effects: the rising of ghosts and apparitions, the descent of gods, dialogue between a character at a window and another at ground level, the revelation of a statue or a pair of lovers playing at chess. Ingenious use could be made of props, as with the ass's head in *A Midsummer Night's Dream*. In a theater that does not clutter the stage with the material paraphernalia of everyday life, those objects that are deployed may take on powerful symbolic weight, as when Shylock bears his weighing scales in one hand and knife in the other, thus becoming a parody of the figure of Justice who traditionally bears a sword and a balance. Among the more significant items in the property cupboard of Shakespeare's company, there would have been a throne (the "chair of state"), joint stools, books, bottles, coins, purses, letters (which are brought onstage, read, or referred to on about eighty occasions in the complete works), maps, gloves, a set of stocks (in which Kent is put in *King Lear*), rings, rapiers, daggers, broadswords, staves, pistols, masks and vizards, heads and skulls, torches and tapers and lanterns, which served to signal night scenes on the daylit stage, a buck's head, an ass's head, animal costumes. Live animals also put in appearances, most notably the dog Crab in *The Two Gentlemen of Verona* and possibly a young polar bear in *The Winter's Tale*.

The costumes were the most important visual dimension of the play. Playwrights were paid between £2 and £6 per script, whereas Alleyn was not averse to paying £20 for "a black velvet cloak with sleeves embroidered all with silver and gold." No matter the period of the play, actors always wore contemporary costume. The excitement for the audience came not from any impression of historical accuracy, but from the richness of the attire and perhaps the transgressive thrill of the knowledge that here were commoners like themselves strutting in the costumes of courtiers in effective defiance of the strict sumptuary laws whereby in real life people had to wear the clothes that befitted their social station.

To an even greater degree than props, costumes could carry symbolic importance. Racial characteristics could be suggested: a breastplate and helmet for a Roman soldier, a turban for a Turk, long robes for exotic characters such as Moors, a gabardine for a Jew. The figure of Time, as in *The Winter's Tale*, would be equipped with hourglass, scythe, and wings; Rumour, who speaks the prologue of *2 Henry IV,* wore a costume adorned with a thousand tongues. The wardrobe in the tiring-house of the Globe would have contained much of the same stock as that of rival manager Philip Henslowe at the Rose: green gowns for outlaws and foresters, black for melancholy men such as Jaques and people in mourning such as the Countess in *All's Well That Ends Well* (at the beginning of *Hamlet,* the prince is still in mourning black when everyone else is in festive garb for the wedding of the new king), a gown and hood for a friar (or a feigned friar like the duke in *Measure for Measure*), blue coats and tawny to distinguish the followers of rival factions, a leather apron and ruler for a carpenter (as in the opening scene of *Julius Caesar*—and in *A Midsummer Night's Dream,* where this is the only sign that Peter Quince is a carpenter), a cockle hat with staff and a pair of sandals for a pilgrim or palmer (the disguise assumed by Helen in *All's Well*), bodices and kirtles with farthingales beneath for the boys who are to be dressed as girls. A gender switch such as that of Rosalind or Jessica seems to have taken between fifty and eighty lines of dialogue—Viola does not resume her "maiden weeds" but remains in her boy's costume to the end of *Twelfth Night* because a change would have slowed down the action at just the moment it was speeding to a climax. Henslowe's inventory also included "a robe for to go invisible": Oberon, Puck, and Ariel must have had something similar.

As the costumes appealed to the eyes, so there was music for the ears. Comedies included many songs. Desdemona's willow song, perhaps a late addition to the text, is a rare and thus exceptionally poignant example from tragedy. Trumpets and tuckets sounded for ceremonial entrances, drums denoted an army on the march. Background music could create atmosphere, as at the beginning of

Twelfth Night, during the lovers' dialogue near the end of *The Merchant of Venice*, when the statue seemingly comes to life in *The Winter's Tale*, and for the revival of Pericles and of Lear (in the Quarto text, but not the Folio). The haunting sound of the hautboy suggested a realm beyond the human, as when the god Hercules is imagined deserting Mark Antony. Dances symbolized the harmony of the end of a comedy—though in Shakespeare's world of mingled joy and sorrow, someone is usually left out of the circle.

The most important resource was, of course, the actors themselves. They needed many skills: in the words of one contemporary commentator, "dancing, activity, music, song, elocution, ability of body, memory, skill of weapon, pregnancy of wit." Their bodies were as significant as their voices. Hamlet tells the player to "suit the action to the word, the word to the action": moments of strong emotion, known as "passions," relied on a repertoire of dramatic gestures as well as a modulation of the voice. When Titus Andronicus has had his hand chopped off, he asks, "How can I grace my talk, / Wanting a hand to give it action?" A pen portrait of "The Character of an Excellent Actor" by the dramatist John Webster is almost certainly based on his impression of Shakespeare's leading man, Richard Burbage: "By a full and significant action of body, he charms our attention: sit in a full theatre, and you will think you see so many lines drawn from the circumference of so many ears, whiles the actor is the centre. . . ."

Though Burbage was admired above all others, praise was also heaped upon the apprentice players whose alto voices fitted them for the parts of women. A spectator at Oxford in 1610 records how the audience was reduced to tears by the pathos of Desdemona's death. The puritans who fumed about the biblical prohibition upon cross-dressing and the encouragement to sodomy constituted by the sight of an adult male kissing a teenage boy on stage were a small minority. Little is known, however, about the characteristics of the leading apprentices in Shakespeare's company. It may perhaps be inferred that one was a lot taller than the other, since Shakespeare often wrote for a pair of female friends, one tall and fair, the other short and dark (Helena and Hermia, Rosalind and Celia, Beatrice and Hero).

We know little about Shakespeare's own acting roles—an early allusion indicates that he often took royal parts, and a venerable tradition gives him old Adam in *As You Like It* and the ghost of old King Hamlet. Save for Burbage's lead roles and the generic part of the clown, all such castings are mere speculation. We do not even know for sure whether the original Falstaff was Will Kempe or another actor who specialized in comic roles, Thomas Pope.

Kempe left the company in early 1599. Tradition has it that he fell out with Shakespeare over the matter of excessive improvisation. He was replaced by Robert Armin, who was less of a clown and more of a cerebral wit: this explains the difference between such parts as Lancelet Gobbo and Dogberry, which were written for Kempe, and the more verbally sophisticated Feste and Lear's Fool, which were written for Armin.

One thing that is clear from surviving "plots" or storyboards of plays from the period is that a degree of doubling was necessary. *2 Henry VI* has more than sixty speaking parts, but more than half of the characters only appear in a single scene and most scenes have only six to eight speakers. At a stretch, the play could be performed by thirteen actors. When Thomas Platter saw *Julius Caesar* at the Globe in 1599, he noted that there were about fifteen. Why doesn't Paris go to the Capulet ball in *Romeo and Juliet*? Perhaps because he was doubled with Mercutio, who does. In *The Winter's Tale*, Mamillius might have come back as Perdita and Antigonus been doubled by Camillo, making the partnership with Paulina at the end a very neat touch. Titania and Oberon are often played by the same pair as Hippolyta and Theseus, suggesting a symbolic matching of the rulers of the worlds of night and day, but it is questionable whether there would have been time for the necessary costume changes. As so often, one is left in a realm of tantalizing speculation.

THE KING'S MAN

The new king, James I, who had held the Scottish throne as James VI since he had been an infant, immediately took the Lord Chamberlain's Men under his direct patronage. Henceforth they would be the

King's Men, and for the rest of Shakespeare's career they were favored with far more court performances than any of their rivals. There even seem to have been rumors early in the reign that Shakespeare and Burbage were being considered for knighthoods, an unprecedented honor for mere actors—and one that in the event was not accorded to a member of the profession for nearly three hundred years, when the title was bestowed upon Henry Irving, the leading Shakespearean actor of Queen Victoria's reign.

Shakespeare's productivity rate slowed in the Jacobean years, not because of age or some personal trauma, but because there were frequent outbreaks of plague, causing the theaters to be closed for long periods. The King's Men were forced to spend many months on the road. Between November 1603 and 1608, they were to be found at various towns in the south and Midlands, though Shakespeare probably did not tour with them by this time. He had bought a large house back home in Stratford and was accumulating other property. He may indeed have stopped acting soon after the new king took the throne. With the London theaters closed so much of the time and a large repertoire on the stocks, Shakespeare seems to have focused his energies on writing a few long and complex tragedies that could have been played on demand at court: *Othello, King Lear, Antony and Cleopatra, Coriolanus,* and *Cymbeline* are among his longest and poetically grandest plays. *Macbeth* only survives in a shorter text, which shows signs of adaptation after Shakespeare's death. The bitterly satirical *Timon of Athens,* apparently a collaboration with Thomas Middleton that may have failed on the stage, also belongs to this period. In comedy, too, he wrote longer and morally darker works than in the Elizabethan period, pushing at the very bounds of the form in *Measure for Measure* and *All's Well That Ends Well.*

From 1608 onward, when the King's Men began occupying the indoor Blackfriars playhouse (as a winter house, meaning that they only used the outdoor Globe in summer?), Shakespeare turned to a more romantic style. His company had a great success with a revived and altered version of an old pastoral play called *Mucedorus.* It even featured a bear. The younger dramatist John Fletcher, meanwhile, sometimes working in collaboration with Francis Beaumont, was pioneering a new style of tragicomedy, a mix of romance and royalism laced with intrigue and pastoral excursions. Shakespeare experimented with this idiom in *Cymbeline* and it was presumably with his blessing that Fletcher eventually took over as the King's Men's company dramatist. The two writers apparently collaborated on three plays in the years 1612–14: a lost romance called *Cardenio* (based on the love-madness of a character in Cervantes' *Don Quixote*), *Henry VIII* (originally staged with the title "All Is True"), and *The Two Noble Kinsmen*, a dramatization of Chaucer's "Knight's Tale." These were written after Shakespeare's two final solo-authored plays, *The Winter's Tale*, a self-consciously old-fashioned work dramatizing the pastoral romance of his old enemy Robert Greene, and *The Tempest*, which at one and the same time drew together multiple theatrical traditions, diverse reading, and contemporary interest in the fate of a ship that had been wrecked on the way to the New World.

The collaborations with Fletcher suggest that Shakespeare's career ended with a slow fade rather than the sudden retirement supposed by the nineteenth-century Romantic critics who read Prospero's epilogue to *The Tempest* as Shakespeare's personal farewell to his art. In the last few years of his life Shakespeare certainly spent more of his time in Stratford-upon-Avon, where he became further involved in property dealing and litigation. But his London life also continued. In 1613 he made his first major London property purchase: a freehold house in the Blackfriars district, close to his company's indoor theater. *The Two Noble Kinsmen* may have been written as late as 1614, and Shakespeare was in London on business a little more than a year before he died of an unknown cause at home in Stratford-upon-Avon in 1616, probably on his fifty-second birthday.

About half the sum of his works were published in his lifetime, in texts of variable quality. A few years after his death, his fellow actors began putting together an authorized edition of his complete *Comedies, Histories and Tragedies*. It appeared in 1623, in large "Folio" format. This collection of thirty-six plays gave Shakespeare his immortality. In the words of his fellow dramatist Ben Jonson, who contributed two poems of praise at the start of the Folio, the body of his work made him "a monument without a tomb":

And art alive still while thy book doth live
And we have wits to read and praise to give . . .
He was not of an age, but for all time!

SHAKESPEARE'S WORKS: A CHRONOLOGY

1589–91	*? Arden of Faversham* (possible part authorship)
1589–92	*The Taming of the Shrew*
1589–92	*? Edward the Third* (possible part authorship)
1591	*The Second Part of Henry the Sixth*, originally called *The First Part of the Contention betwixt the Two Famous Houses of York and Lancaster* (element of coauthorship possible)
1591	*The Third Part of Henry the Sixth*, originally called *The True Tragedy of Richard Duke of York* (element of coauthorship probable)
1591–92	*The Two Gentlemen of Verona*
1591–92; perhaps revised 1594	*The Lamentable Tragedy of Titus Andronicus* (probably co-written with, or revising an earlier version by, George Peele)
1592	*The First Part of Henry the Sixth*, probably with Thomas Nashe and others
1592/94	*King Richard the Third*
1593	*Venus and Adonis* (poem)
1593–94	*The Rape of Lucrece* (poem)
1593–1608	*Sonnets* (154 poems, published 1609 with *A Lover's Complaint*, a poem of disputed authorship)
1592–94/ 1600–03	*Sir Thomas More* (a single scene for a play originally by Anthony Munday, with other revisions by Henry Chettle, Thomas Dekker, and Thomas Heywood)
1594	*The Comedy of Errors*
1595	*Love's Labour's Lost*

1595–97	*Love's Labour's Won* (a lost play, unless the original title for another comedy)
1595–96	*A Midsummer Night's Dream*
1595–96	*The Tragedy of Romeo and Juliet*
1595–96	*King Richard the Second*
1595–97	*The Life and Death of King John* (possibly earlier)
1596–97	*The Merchant of Venice*
1596–97	*The First Part of Henry the Fourth*
1597–98	*The Second Part of Henry the Fourth*
1598	*Much Ado About Nothing*
1598–99	*The Passionate Pilgrim* (20 poems, some not by Shakespeare)
1599	*The Life of Henry the Fifth*
1599	"To the Queen" (epilogue for a court performance)
1599	*As You Like It*
1599	*The Tragedy of Julius Caesar*
1600–01	*The Tragedy of Hamlet, Prince of Denmark* (perhaps revising an earlier version)
1600–01	*The Merry Wives of Windsor* (perhaps revising version of 1597–99)
1601	"Let the Bird of Loudest Lay" (poem, known since 1807 as "The Phoenix and Turtle" [turtledove])
1601	*Twelfth Night, or What You Will*
1601–02	*The Tragedy of Troilus and Cressida*
1604	*The Tragedy of Othello, the Moor of Venice*
1604	*Measure for Measure*
1605	*All's Well That Ends Well*
1605	*The Life of Timon of Athens*, with Thomas Middleton
1605–06	*The Tragedy of King Lear*
1605–08	? contribution to *The Four Plays in One* (lost, except for *A Yorkshire Tragedy*, mostly by Thomas Middleton)

1606	*The Tragedy of Macbeth* (surviving text has additional scenes by Thomas Middleton)
1606–07	*The Tragedy of Antony and Cleopatra*
1608	*The Tragedy of Coriolanus*
1608	*Pericles, Prince of Tyre,* with George Wilkins
1610	*The Tragedy of Cymbeline*
1611	*The Winter's Tale*
1611	*The Tempest*
1612–13	*Cardenio,* with John Fletcher (survives only in later adaptation called *Double Falsehood* by Lewis Theobald)
1613	*Henry VIII (All Is True),* with John Fletcher
1613–14	*The Two Noble Kinsmen,* with John Fletcher

THE HISTORY BEHIND THE TRAGEDIES: A CHRONOLOGY

Era/Date	Event	Location	Play
Greek myth	Trojan War	Troy	*Troilus and Cressida*
Greek myth	Theseus King of Athens	Athens	*The Two Noble Kinsmen*
c.tenth–ninth century BC?	Leir King of Britain (legendary)	Britain	*King Lear*
535–510 BC	Tarquin II King of Rome	Rome	*The Rape of Lucrece*
493 BC	Caius Martius captures Corioli	Italy	*Coriolanus*
431–404 BC	Peloponnesian war	Greece	*Timon of Athens*
17 Mar 45 BC	Battle of Munda: Caesar's victory over Pompey's sons	Munda, Spain	*Julius Caesar*
Oct 45 BC	Caesar returns to Rome for triumph	Rome	*Julius Caesar*
15 Mar 44 BC	Assassination of Caesar	Rome	*Julius Caesar*
27 Nov 43 BC	Formation of Second Triumvirate	Rome	*Julius Caesar*
Oct 42 BC	Battle of Philippi	Philippi, Macedonia	*Julius Caesar*
Winter 41–40 BC	Antony visits Cleopatra	Egypt	*Antony and Cleopatra*
Oct 40 BC	Pact of Brundisium; marriage of Antony and Octavia	Italy	*Antony and Cleopatra*
39 BC	Pact of Misenum between Pompey and the triumvirs	Campania, Italy	*Antony and Cleopatra*

39–38 BC	Ventidius defeats the Parthians in a series of engagements	Syria	*Antony and Cleopatra*
34 BC	Cleopatra and her children proclaimed rulers of the eastern Mediterranean	Alexandria	*Antony and Cleopatra*
2 Sep 31 BC	Battle of Actium	On the coast of western Greece	*Antony and Cleopatra*
Aug 30 BC	Death of Antony	Alexandria	*Antony and Cleopatra*
12 Aug 30 BC	Death of Cleopatra	Alexandria	*Antony and Cleopatra*
Early first century AD	Cunobelinus/ Cymbeline rules Britain (and dies before AD 43)	Britain	*Cymbeline*
During the reign of a fictional (late?) Roman emperor		Rome	*Titus Andronicus*
c.ninth–tenth century AD	Existence of legendary Amleth?	Denmark	*Hamlet*
15 Aug 1040	Death of Duncan I of Scotland	Bothnguane, Scotland	*Macbeth*
1053	Malcolm invades Scotland	Scotland	*Macbeth*
15 Aug 1057	Death of Macbeth	Lumphanan, Scotland	*Macbeth*
7 Oct 1571	Naval battle of Lepanto between Christians and Turks	The Mediterranean off the coast of Greece	A context for *Othello*

FURTHER READING
AND VIEWING

CRITICAL APPROACHES

Booth, Stephen, *King Lear, Macbeth, Indefinition and Tragedy* (1983). Not for beginners, but very penetrating.

Bradley, A. C., *Shakespearean Tragedy* (1904). Still worth reading a century after publication.

Cavell, Stanley, "The Avoidance of Love," in *Disowning Knowledge in Seven Plays of Shakespeare* (1987). A skeptical philosopher's reading; still less for beginners, but so full of deep insight that it has claims to be among the best pieces ever written on the play.

Colie, Rosalie L., and F. T. Flahiff, *Some Facets of "King Lear": Essays in Prismatic Criticism* (1974). An unusually strong collection of critical essays.

Danby, J. F., *Shakespeare's Doctrine of Nature* (1949). Contexts for Edmund.

Dollimore, Jonathan, "*King Lear* and Essentialist Humanism," in *Radical Tragedy: Religion, Ideology and Power in the Drama of Shakespeare and His Contemporaries* (1984). Inflected by neo-Marxist cultural politics.

Elton, William R., *King Lear and the Gods* (1966). Useful contextualization in the intellectual history of Shakespeare's time.

Empson, William, "Fool in *Lear*," in *The Structure of Complex Words* (1951). Superb essay on a key word.

Goldberg, S. L., *An Essay on King Lear* (1974). Consistently thoughtful.

Greenblatt, Stephen, "Shakespeare and the Exorcists," in *Shakespeare Negotiations: The Circulation of Social Energy in Renaissance England* (1988). Inventive account of why Shakespeare used an anti-Popish treatise for the mad language of Poor Tom.

Heilman, R. B., *This Great Stage: Image and Structure in King Lear* (1963). Good account of image patterns.

Kermode, Frank, ed., *King Lear: A Casebook* (1969). Fine collection of studies from the nineteenth and early twentieth centuries.

Kott, Jan, *Shakespeare Our Contemporary* (1964). The chapter on *King Lear* as a bleak, absurd drama analogous to Samuel Beckett's *Endgame* has been hugely influential; Peter Brook saw an early version, which did much to shape his 1962 production.

Mack, Maynard, *King Lear in Our Time* (1966). Remains valuable in our time.

Taylor, Gary, and Michael Warren, eds., *The Division of the Kingdoms: Shakespeare's Two Versions of King Lear* (1983). Groundbreaking collection of essays on Quarto and Folio variants.

THE PLAY IN PERFORMANCE

Brooke, Michael, "*King Lear* on Screen," www.screenonline.org.uk/tv/id/566346/index.html. Overview of film versions.

Chambers, Colin, *Other Spaces: New Theatre and the RSC* (1980). Includes fine account of the powerfully intimate Buzz Goodbody production.

Jackson, Russell, and Robert Smallwood, eds, *Players of Shakespeare 2* (1988). Interviews with actors, including Antony Sher on playing the Fool in Adrian Noble's production.

Leggatt, Alexander, *King Lear,* Shakespeare in Performance (1991). Good survey.

Ogden, James, and Arthur H. Scouten, eds, *Lear from Study to Stage: Essays in Criticism* (1997). Contains several illuminating essays.

Rosenberg, Marvin, *The Masks of King Lear* (1972). Many fascinating details of performances down the ages.

AVAILABLE ON DVD

King Lear, directed by Peter Brook (1970, DVD 2005). Bleak interpretation with magisterial performance by Paul Scofield.

King Lear (*Korol Lir*), directed by Grigori Kosintsev (1970, DVD 2007). Powerful Russian version.

King Lear, directed by Jonathan Miller (BBC Television Shakespeare, 1982, DVD 2004). Michael Hordern as Lear in a reworking (with fuller, perhaps overlong text) of an earlier television version by Miller, based ultimately on a stage production at Nottingham.

King Lear, directed by Michael Elliott (Channel 4 Television, 1983, DVD 2007). Laurence Olivier's last Shakespearean performance.

Ran, directed by Akira Kurosawa (1985, DVD 2006). Epic Japanese adaptation in Samurai setting.

A Thousand Acres, directed by Jocelyn Moorhouse (1997, DVD 2006). Jessica Lange, Michelle Pfeiffer, and Jennifer Jason Leigh in a film version of a novel by Jane Smiley that transposes the story to the American Midwest and tells it from the point of view of the three daughters.

King Lear, directed by Richard Eyre (BBC2 Television 1998, DVD 2006). Filming of Eyre's exemplary small-scale National Theatre production.

My Kingdom, directed by Don Boyd (2001, DVD 2005). Richard Harris' last role: the *Lear* plot transposed to the world of a twenty-first-century Liverpool drug baron.

REFERENCES

1. Gamini Salgado, *Eyewitnesses of Shakespeare: First Hand Accounts of Performances 1590–1890* (1975), p. 38.
2. James Boswell, in a diary entry on 12 May 1763, in *Boswell's London Journals: 1762–1763*, ed. Frederick A. Pottle (1950), pp. 256–7.
3. George Steevens, review dated 16–18 February 1773, quoted in *Shakespeare, The Critical Heritage*, ed. Brian Vickers, vol. 5, *1765–1774* (1979), pp. 501–2.
4. Leigh Hunt in an originally unsigned review of *King Lear* in *The Examiner*, No. 21, 22 May 1808, pp. 331–3.
5. *The Times*, review of *King Lear*, 25 April 1820.
6. William Hazlitt, in a *London Magazine* review of June 1820.
7. William Hazlitt, in a *London Magazine* review of May 1820.
8. John Forster, "The Restoration of Shakespeare's Lear to the Stage," *The Examiner*, No. 1566, 4 February 1838, pp. 69–70.
9. "Review of *King Lear*," *The Athenaeum*, No. 1066, 1 April 1848, p. 346.
10. William Winter, "The Art of Edwin Booth: King Lear," in his *Life and Art of Edwin Booth* (1893), pp. 177–85.
11. Henry James, "Tommaso Salvini," *The Atlantic Monthly*, Vol. LI, No. CCCV, March 1883, pp. 377–86.
12. John Gielgud, "Granville Barker Rehearses *King Lear*," in his *Stage Directions* (1963, repr. 1979), pp. 51–5.
13. James Agate, review of *King Lear* in *Brief Chronicles: A Survey of the Plays of Shakespeare and the Elizabethans in Actual Performance* (1943, repr. 1971), pp. 201–3.
14. *The Times*, review of *King Lear*, 21 April 1936.
15. W. A. Darlington, "Old Vic at Home," *New York Times*, 13 October 1946.
16. Alan Brien, "Simulation in the Fields," *The Spectator*, Vol. 203, No. 6843, 21 August 1959, pp. 223–4.
17. Maynard Mack, *King Lear in Our Time* (1966).
18. James Ogden, "Introduction," in *Lear from Study to Stage: Essays in Criticism*, ed. James Ogden and Arthur H. Scouten (1997).
19. *Illustrated London News*, Vol. 241, No. 6433, 17 November 1962.
20. Stephen J. Philips, "Akira Kurosawa's *Ran*," in *Lear from Study to Stage*, p. 102.

21. Benedict Nightingale, *New Statesman*, 3 December 1976.

22. Sheridan Morley, *Daily Express*, 2 July 2004.

23. Tom Piper, *King Lear*, RSC Online Playguide, 2004.

24. Corin Redgrave, *King Lear*, RSC Online Playguide, 2004.

25. Benedict Nightingale, "Some Recent Productions," in *Lear from Study to Stage*, p. 236.

26. John Peter, *Sunday Times*, 31 October 1999.

27. Michael Billington, *Guardian*, 30 October 1999.

28. Colin Chambers, *Other Spaces: New Theatre and the RSC* (1980), p. 71.

29. Nightingale, "Some Recent Productions," p. 232.

30. Irving Wardle, *Independent*, 15 July 1990.

31. David Fielding, designer of the 1990 production, in interview with Lynne Truss, *Independent*, 8 July 1990.

32. John Gross, *Sunday Telegraph*, 15 July 1990.

33. Michael Billington, *Guardian*, 13 July 1990.

34. Note in *King Lear*, RSC program, 1993.

35. Irving, *Independent*, 15 July 1990.

36. Chambers, *Other Spaces*, p. 69.

37. Michael Billington, *Guardian*, 30 June 1982.

38. Billington, *Guardian*, 30 June 1982.

39. David Nathan, *Jewish Chronicle*, 9 July 1982.

40. James Fenton, *Sunday Times*, 4 July 1982.

41. Antony Sher, "The Fool in King Lear," in *Players of Shakespeare 2*, ed. Russell Jackson and Robert Smallwood (1988).

42. Adrian Noble, interview for *King Lear*, RSC Education Pack, 1993.

43. Robert Wilcher, "King Lear," in *Shakespeare in Performance*, ed. Keith Parsons and Pamela Mason (1995), p. 91.

44. Gordon Parsons, *Morning Star*, 5 July 1982.

45. Alexander Leggatt, *King Lear, Shakespeare in Performance* (1991), p. 55.

46. Wilcher, "King Lear," p. 93.

47. Janet Dale, in RSC Education Pack, 1993.

48. Benedict Nightingale, *The Times*, 12 July 1990.

49. Billington, *Guardian*, 13 July 1990.

50. Nightingale, "Some Recent Productions," p. 231.

51. Emily Raymond, *King Lear*, RSC Online Playguide, 2005.

52. Nicholas de Jongh, *Evening Standard*, 21 May 1993.

53. Michael Billington, *Guardian*, 22 May 1993.

54. Nightingale, "Some Recent Productions," p. 239.

55. Paul Taylor, *Independent*, 5 July 2004.

56. Peter J. Smith, in *Cahiers Élisabéthains,* No. 66 (2004).
57. Billington, *Guardian,* 30 June 1982.
58. Charles Marowitz, "Lear Log," *Tulane Drama Review,* Vol. 8, No. 2 (Winter 1963), pp. 103–21.
59. Redgrave, *King Lear.*

ACKNOWLEDGMENTS AND PICTURE CREDITS

Preparation of "*King Lear* in Performance" was assisted by a generous grant from the CAPITAL Centre (Creativity and Performance in Teaching and Learning) of the University of Warwick for research in the RSC archive at the Shakespeare Birthplace Trust. The Arts and Humanities Research Council (AHRC) funded a term's research leave that enabled Jonathan Bate to work on "The Director's Cut."

Picture research by Helen Robson, Jan Sewell, and Kevin Wright. Grateful acknowledgment is made to the Shakespeare Birthplace Trust for assistance with picture research (special thanks to Helen Hargest) and reproduction fees.

Images of RSC productions are supplied by the Shakespeare Centre Library and Archive, Stratford-upon-Avon. This library, maintained by the Shakespeare Birthplace Trust, holds the most important collection of Shakespeare material in the UK, including the Royal Shakespeare Company's official archive. It is open to the public free of charge.

For more information see www.shakespeare.org.uk.

1. Robert Armin © Bardbiz Limited
2. Mr. Macready (1838). Reproduced by permission of the Shakespeare Birthplace Trust
3. Directed by Theodore Komisarjevsky (1936). Reproduced by permission of the Shakespeare Birthplace Trust
4. Directed by John Gielgud and Anthony Quayle (1950). Angus McBean © Royal Shakespeare Company
5. Directed by Peter Brook (1962). Angus McBean © Royal Shakespeare Company
6. Directed by Trevor Nunn (2007). Manuel Harlan © Royal Shakespeare Company

MODERN LIBRARY IS ONLINE AT
WWW.MODERNLIBRARY.COM

MODERN LIBRARY ONLINE IS YOUR GUIDE
TO CLASSIC LITERATURE ON THE WEB

THE MODERN LIBRARY E-NEWSLETTER

Our free e-mail newsletter is sent to subscribers, and features sample chapters, interviews with and essays by our authors, upcoming books, special promotions, announcements, and news. To subscribe to the Modern Library e-newsletter, visit **www.modernlibrary.com**

THE MODERN LIBRARY WEBSITE

Check out the Modern Library website at
www.modernlibrary.com for:

- The Modern Library e-newsletter
- A list of our current and upcoming titles and series
- Reading Group Guides and exclusive author spotlights
- Special features with information on the classics and other paperback series
- Excerpts from new releases and other titles
- A list of our e-books and information on where to buy them
- The Modern Library Editorial Board's 100 Best Novels and 100 Best Nonfiction Books of the Twentieth Century written in the English language
- News and announcements

Questions? E-mail us at **modernlibrary@randomhouse.com**.
For questions about examination or desk copies, please visit
the Random House Academic Resources site at
www.randomhouse.com/academic

With new commentary, as well as definitive
text and cutting-edge notes from the RSC's
William Shakespeare: Complete Works,
the first authoritative, modernized edition of
Shakespeare's First Folio in more than 300 years.

Hamlet

Love's Labour's
Lost

A Midsummer
Night's Dream

Richard III

The Tempest

Also available in hardcover
William Shakespeare: Complete Works

**"Timely, original, and beautifully
conceived . . . a remarkable edition."**
—James Shapiro, professor, Columbia
University, bestselling author of *A Year in the
Life of Shakespeare: 1599*